ODETTE
Mrs. Peter Churchill, G.C., M.B.E.

ODETTE

THE STORY OF A BRITISH AGENT

★

JERRARD TICKELL

CHAPMAN & HALL · LONDON

First published 1949
Second impression October 1949
Third impression March 1950
Fourth impression July 1950
Fifth impression August 1950
Sixth impression November 1950
Seventh impression March 1951
Eighth impression July 1951
Ninth impression January 1952
Tenth impression January 1952
Eleventh impression December 1953
Twelfth impression July 1955
Thirteenth impression September 1956

Printed in Great Britain by Bishop & Sons Ltd., Edinburgh.
Bound by G. & J. Kitcat Ltd., London.
Cat. No. 4133/4

To all Odette's comrades
who failed to return
and
especially to Arnaud

AUTHOR'S PREFACE

What was it that impelled Odette, an elegant and vivacious young Frenchwoman, to undertake one of the most dangerous jobs created by modern war? It was neither boredom nor a form of escape. It was not only a zest for adventure—though Belloc's "holy hunger" surely played its part. It was not crude hatred of the German people but a detestation of the Nazi system and of the mechanized leviathan of the police state. Odette saw more clearly than did most people that the greatest wrong ever done to Germany was unwittingly achieved by Bismarck who intended to unify. "He left behind a nation," wrote Max Weber, "without any political will, accustomed to allow the great statesman at its head to look after its policy for it." This vacuum provided Hitler's opportunity and Europe's tragedy.

Odette went to the war for three main reasons. She was a *Picarde* and the place for the men—and the women—of Picardy has always been in the vanguard of the battle. Duty, therefore, came first. The second reason was more obscure. It was an inarticulate and unrealized revolt against general sloth and indifference to the fact that a great—if politically immature— nation had openly accepted evil as its good. The third reason lay in her profound love of England and of France and in her passionate belief that in their joint survival lay the bright hope of freedom and civilization.

In comparison with the work of some of her comrades Odette's part in the field was necessarily slight. She was captured after six months, at a moment when the last labyrinth she had helped to create was beginning to surge into activity. The "Raoul-Lise" circuit was only one of nearly fifty secret organizations directed from Baker Street and run by British agents in Occupied France. It was rarely possible to make a complete parcel of an operation, so to speak, and to tie up its ends neatly. The tempo was urgent and swift and the characters transitory. Men and women came into her orbit, were briefly vital, slipped away and she never saw them again. This lack of continuity is unavoidably reflected in these pages and, because of it, I have done far less than justice to a great many people,

A*

both to those who worked in Baker Street and to those in the field.

I am deeply indebted to the War Office and particularly to Major Norman Mott who put files at my disposal and who helped with such genial patience. Colonel Maurice Buckmaster, O.B.E.—busiest of men—has always found time to advise and to guide. Major Stephen Stewart, prosecuting counsel, has contributed a brief, Miss Joanna Townsend a reminiscence, Miss Vera Atkins an unflagging interest. My warm thanks are due to M. Jean Cottet of St Jorioz. . My somewhat oblique thanks are also due to those members of the S.S. who involuntarily completed many sinister gaps in the story. To my friend Peter Churchill—my gratitude and affection.

Since this book was published and the film of the same name shown, Odette, and I to a lesser extent, have received many letters from all over the world. May I try to answer some of the more usual questions ? "Colonel Henri" was captured in Holland and imprisoned in France for some time. I believe he is now home in Germany. Fritz Sühren escaped from prison a few days before his trial and was at liberty until 1949, when he was recognized and arrested. He had been working under an assumed name in a brewery not far from Rhine Army Headquarters. He was tried by the French authorities, condemned to death and appealed. I believe that the appeal was dismissed. The creature whose activities are described on pages 268 to 271 was under sentence of death in Fresnes prison when last I visited that grim establishment. The priest whose ministrations were of such comfort to the women of Fresnes, survived the war and returned to Odette's hands the dolls which she had made within those dolorous walls.

Lastly, I come to Odette herself. Subjected to idignity and humiliation, encompassed by squalor and fear, she remained always a Frenchwoman *bien-elevée* and her cell was her drawing-room into which she had, perforce, to admit distasteful persons. For twenty-six months, she abashed her gaolers. She owes her life to-day to the unassailable dignity in which she enclosed herself. Housewife and hostess, Odette is unique and extraordinary in our times.

JERRARD TICKELL

CONTENTS

ILLUSTRATIONS

PART ONE

Falstaff: "Will you tell me, Master Shallow, how to choose a man? Care I for the limb, the thews, the stature, the bulk and big assemblance of a man! Give me the spirit, Master Shallow."

King Henry the Fourth: Part II

CHAPTER I

HAMBURG—1946.

A FEW minutes after ten o'clock in the morning of December
the fifth, 1946, seven women filed into the dock of No. 1
War Crimes Court at Hamburg and sat down and looked about
them with self-conscious curiosity. Though it was bitterly cold
in the freezing rubble of the streets outside, the court-room was
pleasantly warm. There was nothing physically abnormal
about any of these women. Each one of them might have
stepped out of any bread queue in any German city. Rather
more noticeable than the others was Carmen Mory, a thin
grimacing, black-haired woman on whose breast was displayed
the neutral emblem of Switzerland. She adjusted her red-fox
fur, the better to show the disarming white cross. Pretty Vera
Salvequart looked with lazy carnality at the distinguished
visitors and Elizabeth Marschall, sixty-year-old hospital matron,
sat bolt upright as if she were upholstered in granite stays.

The women ranged themselves demurely along two rows,
obsequiously obeying the calm orders of the A.T.S. Provost.

After a brief interval, nine men, closely guarded by the
Royal Corps of Military Police, were admitted to the dock.
Like that of the women, their appearance was undistinguished.
Most of them looked as if they might work in a minor capacity
for the Control Commission, though Dr. Percy Treite would
have been more at home in a Harley Street consulting room.
They carefully hitched up the knees of their trousers and began
a series of animated conversations with their black-gowned
counsel. All the accused, men and women, wore on their
chests a black number on a square of white cardboard. As this
number was sometimes obscured by the level of the dock, they
were invited to raise it and, with deprecating gestures, each of
them tightened the string around his or her neck, unaware of
the macabre symbolism of what they did.

At exactly 10.30, Major-General V. J. E. Westropp, C.B.,

C.B.E., entered the Court and took his seat in the President's chair. He was followed by C. L. Stirling, O.B.E., K.C., Deputy Judge Advocate General of the Forces, a stooping, school-masterish figure in wig, gown and pince-nez. Six other officers, one of them French, one Polish and four British, made up the Court. These officers ranged themselves on either side of the President. Major Peter Forrest, senior interpreter and old hound on this blood-trail, sharpened his pencil. The Ravensbrück Concentration Camp Trial was about to begin.

Mr. Stirling, K.C. arose. He glanced at the accused over his pince-nez, and read the arraignment. It was a simple one.

Pursuant to Regulation 4 of the Regulations for the trial of War Criminals, the persons in the dock were charged jointly with committing a war crime in that they, at Ravensbrück in the years 1939-1945, when members of the staff of Ravensbrück Concentration Camp, in violation of the·laws and usages of war, were concerned in the ill-treatment and killing of Allied nationals interned therein.

Individually, each of the accused pleaded not guilty to the charge.

Major Stephen Stewart led for the prosecution. He was assisted throughout the trial by Captain (now Major) John da Cuhna and by Squadron Officer Vera Atkins, a smooth, utterly impersonal figure in W.A.A.F. uniform. Stewart arranged his papers leisurely, stood up and began to speak.

His tone was conversational, his manner almost apologetic as, one by one, he drew aside each merciful veil that shrouded a story unparalleled in the long, painful history of human suffering.

*

"May it please the Court," said Stewart.

In Mecklenburg, some fifty miles north of Berlin, there is a group of lakes, a pre-war rendezvous for the more elegant persons of that grisly capital. To the shores of these lakes the Berliners would come by car and by caravan on Saturday afternoons, scorch their bodies in the sun, play merry games, indulge in a little *Nakt-Kultur* and eat considerable quantities of Frankfürter sausages; sun-glasses, leap-frog, male hairnets; the *Horst*

Wessel song, weight reduction and a little mild adultery—it was all very *gemütlich*. On Sunday evenings, the same convoy of cars and caravans would return to Berlin, their owners both refreshed and uplifted after their brief communion with nature.

Heil Hitler!

One of these stretches of water is called Fürstenburg. Unlike those of the other lakes, its shores were swampy and dank and gaseous smells were apt to rise from the imprint of an incautious foot. Because of this, it was less popular as a playground for the fastidious week-ender. Its proximity to Berlin, however, rendered it entirely suitable for another purpose where its physical drawbacks were of no account and to this secondary purpose it was put soon after the outbreak of war in 1939.

A high wall was built round a selected area, a number of huts were erected and Ravensbrück Concentration Camp for Women appeared for the first time on the official budget of the S.S. Long experience in the breaking of the human spirit had shown the need for the usual refinements and these were established. There was *"Appel"*. In summer this daily parade was held at half-past five in the morning, in winter at half-past four. In groups of ten and in all weathers the women stood to attention for periods ranging from two to six hours. Clad only in hideously striped sacking and with shaven or bristling heads, they waited on their masters. Those who stumbled or fainted or fell were ordered to the Bunker. This Bunker was a labyrinth of tiny, airless cells, a gaol within a gaol. It was a place of even greater darkness and fear for here the beatings were carried out and nameless things were done to women's bodies.

Though the whole camp was originally designed to contain a maximum of some six thousand, the modest little undertaking expanded as the Nazis occupied one country after another and, after 1943, there were never less than twelve thousand women within its walls. It is on record that on a single day in January, 1945, there was a total strength of forty thousand—if one can use so virile a word as "strength" to describe the feeble creatures who saw the sun rise over the walls of the Camp that morning. By train, by cattle truck, by lorry and on foot, a never-ending queue of women shuffled through its gate during that eternity that lasted five years. A few left again by convoy, bound for those other camps whose names alone are like a

Satanic drum-beat in the minds of civilized men—Belsen, Auschwitz, Lublin, Mauthausen. . . . The vast majority stayed to die.

On May the 1st, 1945, the Red Army overran the Camp
in their drive to the West. Inside its walls, the Russian soldiery
found twelve thousand breathing skeletons, the formation of
whose bones showed that they had once been women with
wombs to bear and breasts to feed. Cynically watching these
still animate objects gasp and scrabble and crawl were the well-
fed persons who now faced the Court.

⋆

The accused listened with a show of polite attention. As
Major Stewart's address was delivered in English, the measured
sound of his voice was merely interesting for its unemotional
quality. Their time would come when witnesses for the prosecution and for the defence were called and every word spoken
in Court would be translated into German.

Slowly, the faces and the hands of the accused began to
assume a terrible significance. We realized with pain and with
shock that we were, all of us, in the presence of a hitherto
unimagined evil. But it was still difficult to believe that the
eyes of Dorothea Binz had exulted in the cruelties inflicted by
her primly folded hands; it was hard to believe that the bald
Dr. Hellinger had wrenched the teeth from the mouths of the
murdered and sent their fragments of gold to support the
reserves of the *Reichsbank;* could the alert Dr. Percy Treite have
wielded his skilful scalpel on the bodies of children and could
his ears have been deaf to their bewildered crying? Carmen
Mory straightened her red-fox fur and studied her nails. It was
difficult to see her in another rôle—striding into a room where
mad women fought together and beating them with a buckled
belt until they died. Margaret Mewes, chief wardress of the
Bunker, gazed at nothing with bovine eyes, Schwarzhuber bent
his head and his lips moved silently as if he were whispering
the prayers of a debauched monk. . . .

⋆

The Court rose. For a few minutes we went outside and

No. 1 WAR CRIMES COURT, HAMBURG, DECEMBER 10TH, 1946

Dorothea Binz
(*executed*)

Elizabeth Marschall
(*executed*)

Vera Salvequart
(*executed*)

Margarete Mewes
(10 *years imprisonment*)

Greta Bösel
(*executed*)

Eugenie von Skene
(10 *years imprisonment*)

saw the sky and breathed cold, clean air. Then Stewart took up the tale again.

*

As a distance of fifty miles is a pleasant drive in a high-powered car from Berlin, the Camp was honoured by occasional visits from no less a person than Heinrich Himmler himself. He arrived unexpectedly one afternoon in the early spring of 1945 and was shown over the Camp by its Commandant, Fritz Sühren. The waters of the lake danced in the sunshine and the sky was clamorous with birds. Standing in the shelter of the Crematorium—for the wind was cool—Himmler delivered judgment on what he had seen.

"The killings," said the arch-priest of the S.S., gently chiding, "the killings are not going fast enough."

"I understand," said the obedient Sühren, "I will attend to the matter immediately, *Herr Reichsführer. Heil Hitler!*"

"*Heil Hitler.*"

Hitherto women had died from under-nourishment, over-work, exposure, lethal injections and obscene surgery. Now the process was to be accelerated. An S.S. corporal—who had brought to a fine art the method of shooting his victims in the nape of the neck—arrived from Berlin and, having demonstrated his prowess, applied for—and was awarded—proficiency pay. He shot some two hundred women. That was better but still not entirely satisfactory. Sühren decided to consult the real experts in mass extermination. Two middle-aged gentlemen—now before the Court—packed their bags in Auschwitz and travelled to Ravensbrück. Having surveyed the terrain and the human material they made a few calculations on the back of an envelope and recommended the immediate installation of that superb creation of the Nazi mind—the gas-chamber.

In haste a gas-chamber was erected near what was ironically known as "The Youth Camp" and there dawned the most fearful day of all. Nearly forty thousand women were ordered to parade bareheaded and with naked feet before the huts. Fear travels fast and those who were forced to take part in this fiendish Folies Bergères were fully conscious of its dread purpose. Desperate women scraped soot and dirt with their nails from the walls of their prison and tried to blacken the roots of their grey hair; they attempted to step out strongly with swollen ankles and feeble feet; they grimaced and smiled the smile of the damned for they knew that the old and the ill were to be killed and that the young and strong might live to work for a little longer. For hour after hour the parade waited for the arrival of the murderers. At last they came and strolled genially along the serried ranks, smoking and chatting. Hundreds of women were handed a pink card and their names were struck off the roll. These cards were free. They were tickets for the gas-chamber.

In five years, said Stewart, over one hundred thousand women had perished. It was, for example, as if a terrible disease had touched every inhabitant of the City of York and the town had died. Only by comparison could one begin to visualize the magnitude of the crime. And who were the dead?

Some of them had been prisoners of war in so far that they were Russian Red Cross nurses, captured on the field of battle. Some were Poles, some Norwegians, some French, some Dutch, some were Belgians. A few were British. Irrespective of guilt, nationality or education, they travelled the same *via dolorosa* to the crematorium.

What was the policy behind the creation and development of Ravensbrück? That too was simple. It was the efficient and the enduring intimidation of men, the fathers, the husbands, and the sons; it was an organized attack on the life, the health and the dignity of womanhood, an attack rendered the more vile because of its cunning. Like the Sword of Damocles, the word "Ravensbrück" was poised over the head of every woman from the Baltic to the Bosphorus. But for the grace of Almighty God and a narrow strip of tumultuous water, the word might have hung in the English sky.

The story of Ravensbrück was told. The time had now come for the Court to hear the living words of women who had known and had survived and had triumphed over this ante-room to hell.

*

On the morning of the 16th December, 1946, Major Stewart announced that he now wished to call Mrs. Odette Sansom as a witness for the prosecution.

In a tense and silent Court, a slim young woman in F.A.N.Y. uniform walked slowly to the witness box and took the oath. Her face, pale in the strong light was small-featured, delicate and oddly child-like. Her eyes were bright. A mass of dark hair swept upwards from her forehead, almost concealing the slanting beret, and fell thick upon her shoulders. On her breast she wore the blue ribbon and silver miniature of the George Cross.

The Court leaned forward to hear the softly spoken answers.

"Is your name Odette Marie Sansom?"

"Yes."

"What is your nationality?"

"British."

"Will you tell the Court, Mrs. Sansom, when during the war you were first taken prisoner by the Germans and under what circumstances?"

"I was taken prisoner in Annecy in France on the 16th of April, 1943. I stayed with the Italians for three weeks and was then handed over to the Germans."

"When you were taken prisoner, were you a member of His Majesty's Forces?"

"Yes."

"What organization did you belong to—or do you belong to?"

"The French Section of the War Office."

CHAPTER II

ODETTE

ON April the 28th, 1912, Madame Yvonne Brailly bore her husband her first child. To the great disappointment of Gaston Brailly, the infant was a girl. She was received into the Catholic Church and was given the names Odette Marie Céline. She was a plump, blonde baby with brown eyes and remained the sole focus of attention in the Brailly household until her brother Louis followed her into the world a year later.

In 1914 a drum beat and Gaston Brailly walked out of his bank in Amiens and into a French barrack room. To become an officer took time and Gaston was impatient to be at the throat of the enemy. He would consider the question of a Commission later. In the meantime there was much to be done by the 52nd Regiment of Infantry. "*Allons-y!*" His military career was administratively a stormy one and his four years of service were spent fighting, being decorated or narrowly escaping courts martial. On more than one occasion when he was on the eve of being commissioned, the hot-blooded Gaston found himself eating the bread and drinking the wine of the sergeant's mess once again for he had a blazing resentment of red tape and a deep, vocal affection for the tough, grumbling *poilu* of the line. He fought with a hard, steadfast courage which earned for him the *Croix-de-Guerre avec palme* and the *Médaille Militaire*. One became weary of seeing his name "mentioned in despatches". After the battle of Verdun, Sergeant Brailly went back to seek two men who were missing from his platoon. He found them wounded and in distress. It was at that moment that a high explosive shell hit the tiny group and, literally in a flash, France had at once lost a brave and honourable soldier, a staunch Picard and a disruptive element from the barrack room.

Widowed almost in the springtime of her marriage, the years that lay ahead were difficult for Madame Brailly. Dark-eyed, slender and fragile, it was strange to realize that she had borne

two children. In the early years Odette was largely influenced
by her grandparents and particularly by her father's mother.
Grand'mère Brailly was a delicate, stout-hearted *Picarde* with
a long tradition of family and duty in her blood. Gaston had
been her only child and his death in the field of battle had filled
her with sorrow and with pride. In the tumult of the times, she
was a rock of strength and it was to her that Odette turned for
guidance and for counsel. Every Sunday afternoon, a small
procession would make its way to the cemetery of La Madeleine
in Amiens and a cluster of flowers was laid on the grave of
Sergeant Brailly. Looking at her grandson and her grand-
daughter, the old lady was conscious of a deep foreboding. For
generations her family had known and had suffered from the
baleful ambition of the Teutons and she knew with certainty
that these children would one day hearken to the same drum
that had called their father to the fight. She saw clearly
through the windy political optimism of the post-war years and
listened grimly to the reiterated assertion that the combat which
had cost her her son was "the war to end wars". She knew that
fair words do not and cannot change the hearts of conscience-
less men.

"The Bosches are still the Bosches," she said. "They will
march again. This is not victory. It is armistice."

She was an old lady and she had lost her only son. This was
a new and more tolerant world. Let her have her say.

*

Odette was a reserved, silent child. She cared very much for
horses and for music. The combination of bloodstock and
Beethoven is an unusual one but each utterly satisfied a subconscious need. To see a horse galloping filled her with delight
for it was swift and beautiful and strong and there was music
in the sound of fleeting hoofs. In another mood, her mind was
soothed and transported by piano and strings. For nearly two
years she was to be deprived of the one and sustained by the
other.

Just before her eighth birthday, Odette went blind. The
whole world that she had known faded into total darkness and
it was only the painful screen of her mind that she could project

the beloved sight of eager horses walking, trotting, tossing their heads in the sunshine, cantering, breaking into a joyous gallop. For a long time, she could not be comforted. And then her ear-drums began to understand fully what they had hitherto merely received and to distil into her consciousness patterns of light. Her melancholy took the rhythm of Chopin waltzes and her finger-tips—already acquiring a sensitiveness which they have never lost—danced to the formal cadences of Mozart. Hers was a darkness illuminated by sound, by music, by the iron wheels of a cart on cobbles, by the wind, by the splashing of water, by the tireless, affectionate voice of her nurse, old Mademoiselle Gautier, reading aloud the sort of story that began: "Once upon a time. . . ."

The nights were full of sounds unheard by those with sight. It was a strange thing to listen to the tiny helter-skelter of the nails of the feet of mice and to hear the mice breathing in the wainscot. It was queer to catch the creak of the branch of an apple tree in the distant orchard and, after the silence that fol-lowed Beethoven, to listen to the cool, subtle sounds of moon-light.

Summer came, and winter and spring again with the shout of sap rising in the trees and the loud bursting of buds. In the long summer days, the wings of birds were like far thunder and, in the autumn, the sound of leaves falling eddied in her ear-drums. She heard snowflakes in grey December and the silent crack of ice after the turn of the year.

Almost reconciled to blindness because of the acute percep-tion that it had brought, Odette was led one day by her mother to a despised old man, a herbalist who lived in a back street and brewed noisome potions. The specialists had failed. How could this old man with the dirty waistcoat succeed? He lifted her lids with his grimy fingers and peered through cracked spectacles, muttering. He asked questions. Finally he gave Madame Brailly a bottle. The child should bathe her eyes with the liquid. The liquid could do no harm. It would do much good. When the child begins to see again, he said, let light be filtered slowly into her eyes. To restore sight suddenly would be dangerous. She would see in a few days. He shrugged impatiently. He was very busy. The consultation was finished. The price? Oh, a few francs.

Within a fortnight, Odette saw things dimly; she saw "men as trees, walking". With infinite care and patience, the veils of darkness were allowed to flutter down and she saw clearly after two years. She went to a wide space in the very early morning and she could see the muscles move again under the satin coats of race-horses as they flung into a gallop and flowed like a living wave over the grass. She was very happy to see and was only sad for a little while that the sound of moonlight had been mysteriously stolen out of her ears.

*

Le malheur n'arrive jamais seul.

In the early spring, Odette caught rheumatic fever and spent most of the summer in bed. At least she could see and it was a consolation to watch, through the open window, the ever-changing pageant of the sky. When the fever fled at last, she was left weak and partially paralyzed. Again the doctors shook their heads. It was, they said vaguely, a question of time and, no doubt, Mother Nature—in her infinite wisdom and in the years to come would achieve what was, alas, past the power of human hands. One must be patient. Patience is poor comfort for a child whose hands were itching and eager to clap and whose feet wanted to run and jump with other children. What has happened once can happen twice—and Madame Brailly went again to the old herbalist in the back street. "I remember the little girl," he said. "This—this is unfair. It is too much to demand of a child."

His only medical credentials lay in his wisdom and in his knowledge of herbs and in the touch of his fingers. Very gently, he charmed blood back into the starved muscles. Soon, when Odette thought of a song, she could feel her legs wanting to move to its rhythm. Then her legs began to ache and to hurt. It was a long time before she could walk but, by the time spring came again, she could race with other children and clap her hands and grip the swift sides of a horse with her knees.

Her brother Louis was sent to the Lycée and Odette to the Convent of Sainte Thérèse. It was to fill her lungs with the stronger air of Normandy and her body with the sweet milk of the Normandy pastures that Madame Brailly decided to take

her daughter to Saint Sens, a big village between Rouen and
Dieppe. There, in 1925, she found a house and settled down.
Louis stayed on in the Lycée at Amiens, always coming to
Saint Sens for the holidays.

In 1926, when Odette was fourteen, mother and daughter
moved again—this time to Boulogne. In the holidays, Odette
and her brother spent long happy hours scrambling bare-
headed—and frequently bare-footed—about the rocks and cliffs
of the coast. Brother and sister were firm friends and together
the Brailly children made innumerable joyous expeditions.
They chased little green scuttling crabs across the salt pools;
in another mood they took formal coffee and cake with their
relations in the sophisticated drawing-rooms of Le Touquet—
and walked demurely away until out of sight when they began
to scamper to the fair-ground and stuff their mouths with
gingerbread, glutinous nougat and rose-coloured shrimps
straight from the sea. High on the cliffs, Odette gathered
poppies, speedwell and toadflax from the stubble of the Normandy corn where the brown hens glean . . . and ran excitedly
down to the circus to ride the gaudily painted hobby-horses,
dragons and cockerels of the roundabout. Seaweed and swing-
boats, sunburn and naphtha flares; jerseys and torn skirts on
weekdays, ribbons and starch on Sundays. . . .

Introibo ad altare Dei. . . .

Black serge, umbrellas clutched in gnarled fingers, Holy
water, the smell of incense, sweat and stone . . . and seagulls
calling and calling insistently from the harbour.

Ad Deum qui laetificat juventutem meam. . . .

On Sundays the English tripper ships came into Boulogne
and spilled their alien cargo down the gangways briefly to
ravage the town. They would soon be coming alongside to the
sound of seagulls, breaking glass and mouth-organs. . . .

"Ite, missa est. . . . "

It was a joy to Odette and to Louis to escape from the tortured plaster, the incense and the candles and to run breathlessly through the fresh sunshine to the *quais* and to watch the
ships come in. It was a spectacle of which they never tired,
and, once the gangways were clear, they would imitate the
speech and the mannerisms of these thirsty invaders. Many
years ago, Odette had once sat on Mr. Hilaire Belloc's knee

and ever since then, she had considered that to have occupied
that distinguished perch constituted an introduction to the
whole Anglo-Saxon race. But it was difficult sometimes to
reconcile Mr. Belloc's genial England with the cricket-boots,
the Albert watch-chains and the cloth caps of the trippers.
British officers had been billeted in her grandmother's house
towards the end of the Great War and, as a child, she had tried
to chatter to these diffident, kindly, preoccupied figures in
khaki. She had not found the English very *sympathique* on the
whole—except of course Mr. Belloc who was mostly French—
and she decided that the uncouth islanders (who, *après tout*,
had burnt Joan of Arc) were a very mixed lot.

When Louis went back to the Lycée, Odette continued her
walks alone. To her surprise, she found an unexpected and
ever-increasing joy in solitude. Her affection for her brother
had in no way diminished and she was puzzled by the fact of
her desire of loneliness. At finishing school, she was considered
to be "a little difficult, *un peu étrange*". Moody, argumentative and
headstrong, she was subject to swift enthusiasms and to brief,
irrational tempers. It is doubtful if the good nuns made allowances for the bewildering chemistry of adolescence that was
surely working in her body and in her mind. Superficially she
was one young girl in a charming class of young girls who
learnt deportment, polite dancing, painting and singing. She
had as much to distinguish her as any girl of her class. She was
slim, with long, slender legs; dark-haired, brown-eyed,
vivacious. Like any young Frenchwoman *bien élevée*, she was an
elegant needlewoman and a subtle cook. She had a surprising
and unfeminine palate for the red wines of Bordeaux and could
place her finger unerringly on a vineyard and on a year. For
the small flowers of the countryside, she had a passion. Yet
beneath the bright ripples of her conversation which ranged—
according to social requirements—from Flaubert to the correct
mixture of garlic, onion and butter for *escargots de Bourgogne*,
there still flowed this bitter, turbulent stream. She was an
utterly loyal friend and a merciless enemy. The nuns shook their
heads and wished that this volatile, petulant young girl could
have been led into their own kindly paths. What the nuns did
not see was the other Odette, the Odette who marched defiantly along the cliffs in the quiet hour before the dawn. They

did not know that she was acutely frightened of something that she neither knew nor understood and that the future yawned before her like the mouth of a tomb. Perhaps that was why Odette would stop and touch the bark of a tree with the tips of her fingers in sudden gratitude to God because it had been here yesterday, it was here to-day and it would be here to-morrow, alive, sturdy, rooted in the friendly earth and caressed by the free winds. The nuns did not see the young girl to whom the shapeless shape of a stone on the shore gave pleasure, the girl who was proud and ashamed and in tears because of nothing. It was no wonder that the Reverend Mother should write:

Odette est une élève très intéressante—intelligente ayant beaucoup de principes. Malheureusement sa santé délicate ne lui permet pas de suivre régulièrement les cours. Il se fait que, ne pouvant pas suivre les autres, elle perd le gout des études et n'y apporte pas l'intérêt que nous désirerions car son caractère est très obstiné.

With this somewhat oblique benediction, Mlle Odette Brailly ordered her first evening frock, began to consider the varying shades of lipstick and put a timorous, high-heeled sandal over the threshold of womanhood.

*

In 1930 Odette first met Roy Sansom, an Englishman and son of an old family friend. They were married a year later in the Church of Saint Pierre and continued to live in Boulogne. A daughter Françoise was born in 1932 and, soon afterwards, the young Mrs. Odette Sansom sailed across the channel to make her home in England. In 1934 a second daughter Lily was born in London, and in 1936 Marianne arrived to join her sisters in a world of ever increasing fear, dishonesty and violence.

CHAPTER III

ENTRE CHIEN ET LOUP

IT was difficult indeed for Odette Sansom, possessed as she was of a strong streak of political reality, to understand the Zoological pantomime of August, 1939, when Ribbentrop flew to Moscow with the Hitler-Stalin Pact in his pocket. The full purpose of Ribbentrop's flight was clear enough. Had not Hitler himself stated in *Mein Kampf* that: "Foreign policy is but a means to an end whose purpose is exclusively the improvement of our own nation. Words are merely the willing servants of the diplomat and can be used to mask real intention." But Stalin's mind also ran along the same lines. "Words," said he, "must have no relation to action—otherwise what sort of a diplomacy is it? Good words are a concealment for bad deeds. Sincere diplomacy is no more possible than dry water or wooden iron."

In the face of such common and avowed cynicism, it seemed strange to Odette that either of these genial theorists should bother to accept each other's signature on anything. Nevertheless ideology went officially into cold storage that day. Russo-German propaganda had long been conducted on the "wolf-motif" and a sort of lycanthropy in reverse had taken place overnight. To-day a hand-picked guard of Bolshevik ex-wolves presented arms to the visiting Fascist ex-wolves; blood-red and black, the Swastika fluttered from the Kremlin walls: ethereal Soviet ballerinas postured and pirouetted before the arch ex-wolf Ribbentrop and hock and vodka seemed to make a smooth cocktail. Molotov wore the Order of Hitler, Ribbentrop the Order of Lenin. To a *mélange* of the Red Flag and the *Horst Wessel* song, the filthy bargain was struck and, by a stroke of the Commissar's pen, Great Britain and America were designated as the new Whipsnades. It is more likely that the German people knew what their master was up to than did the unfortunate and illiterate Russians. Theirs was not to reason why. Theirs was but to do and die. Their reprieve was only to be short-lived.

When Mr. Chamberlain finished speaking on that sunny Sunday morning of September the 3rd, Odette, in company with some forty million other persons in Great Britain, said with a certain relief: "Well, that's that." When the sirens performed their first slow vomit, she herded her children into the cellar and, while waiting for the all-clear, determined to make a gas-proof room in the house. This task occupied her for some days, in the intervals of plundering her children's wardrobe for the evacuees. She presented the local hospital with a dram of rich French blood, she made over a corner in her house as a school-room for some children who had not yet been evacuated. But by far her most noble contribution to the war effort was the sacrifice of her aluminium coffee-pot. She had brought this coffee-pot with her from France and it had been matured over the years. It was painful to think of this redolent receptacle being casually melted down with a thousand plebeian frying-pans and transformed into the tip of a Spitfire's wing. Still, she felt it her duty to give something she would really miss and she walked back from the collecting point in a glow of sad self-righteousness. To give a pint of blood was one thing; to give a vintage coffee pot was another.

Autumn became winter. Flanagan and Allen played to packed houses; battle-dress, caubeen and kilt in Piccadilly, sweat and khaki in the Ealing train . . . . Finland invaded by U.S.S.R. and Helsinki bombed. . . . The *Graf Spee* beat for shelter to Montevideo. . . . *run Rabbit run, Rabbit run run run.* . . . *Graf Spee* scuttled. There was a little desultory skirmishing in the frozen Saar, to be sure, but the impregnable Maginot Line scowled in concrete at the impregnable Siegfried Line. Things happened vaguely at sea but the real war, the land war, was an affair of loud-speakers, lies and smutty postcards—with France still the best night-club in Europe. It would be a good thing when spring came because the black-out was bad for the children's health. It was pleasant to hear from Mr. Chamberlain on April the 5th that Hitler had missed the bus. Four days later, the war began.

Narvik, Namsos, Trondheim . . . frostbite, bandages and

surgical thread. On May the 10th, the machine-guns sniggered into laughter again as all Europe burst into chaos.

*

On May the 13th, the French Section of the War Office first stirred in the corridors of time. Disguised parachutists were dropped in North-east France. From lazy squadrons of German troop-carriers, a flower-garden suddenly blossomed in the sky, a garden whose flowers were swiftly metamorphosed into heavily-armed agricultural labourers, nuns, policemen, priests, insurance agents, motor-cyclists, radio-operators, prostitutes and butchers. Another new technique had been established— noted this time. Holland capitulated, Belgium followed suit. The French armies were rapidly being destroyed or disarmed, and the British Expeditionary Force, their Bren-gun bullets bouncing off German armour, was staggering painfully towards Dunkirk. By May the 29th, the first troops had reached the beaches and, by the night of June the 4th, seagulls floated over silent sands littered with broken equipment. Over three hundred thousand men had been miraculously snatched away to fight another day.

*

Odette Sansom, native of Picardy, British housewife and mother, read the newspapers and listened to the B.B.C. in the dark days that followed. France, torn from within and assailed from without, was falling. The return of the British Expeditionary Force meant, for England, a brief breathing space; it meant that fathers, husbands and sons were home and, even though the full fury of the enemy must soon be flung against this island, its roads and fields were still inviolate. Not so the fields and roads of France, long familiar to her eyes. But cricket scores still appeared in the stop-press columns of the London evening papers. Even though the buoyant accents of the B.B.C. announcer described one calamity after another, they still held in them the slightly shocked cadences of a well-bred woman turning down an immoral suggestion. In describing the 4th of June at Eton, a special correspondent wrote: "*Gaiety would have been out of place and a cheerful gravity reigned in its stead.*" The

B

impact of the ordeal of France on a tired woman varied between an unbearable vividness and an exhausted reality.

German armies had crossed the Somme and were forcing the Marne.

In the intervals between planning meals and shopping, Odette repeated the names of these old battlefields for it was on their bitter ground that her father had fought the same enemy twenty-five years ago.

German Armies were tearing into Brittany to leap the Loire and others to drive scornfully down the now ludicrous Maginot Line to Lyons.

Sick at heart, Odette pressed a frock for her daughter Françoise and answered the door to the grocer.

The French Government had fled to Tours and from Tours to Bordeaux.

Françoise must still be taken to school; Lily must still sail her boat on "the Round Pond" and Marianne continue to throw everything out of her pram as soon as it was picked up. Sometimes the maternal foreground mercifully dimmed the background. . . .

The French Armies, utterly demoralized by the Government's panic, were in headlong retreat.

Where was the Fifty-Second Regiment of Infantry, her father's old comrades-in-arms, who had fought the *Boches* to a standstill from bloody Verdun to the Champagne country? What blight had touched the sons of those gay and tenacious men?

In tens of thousands, refugees choked every road from Paris to the South, machine-gunned by the contemptuous pilots of the Third Reich as they fled on their pitiful transport.

Checking the laundry, mending, dressmaking for her children, answering the telephone, Odette thought of those roads to the South; she knew the dust of them and the poplars that lined them and the little streams they crossed, streams where her fingers had slid into the cool water to try to tickle a trout— with her brother Louis laughing at her and saying that she'd never catch one that way.

Paris fell.

The long columns of the Wehrmacht marched correctly down the Champs Elysées, flowed apart to enclose the Arc de Triomphe, rejoined, marched on. Louder far than the ghostly tread of Moltke's Grenadiers, Hitler's Panzers shamed the ears of the French.

Odette switched off the six o'clock news to put the fretful Marianne to bed. The Variety programme started at 8.15. Eat Fyffes Bananas for Energy and protection! Guinness for Strength! For a carefree holiday, come to the Isle of Man!

The blows over her heart were soon to cease but the bruise was to remain. On June the 17th, the last remnants of the British Expeditionary Force were taken off the French shore to sail dangerously for home. Next day, Winston Churchill's offer to France was published. It was that the two countries no longer be two nations but one Franco-British Union. Every citizen of France should immediately enjoy citizenship of Great Britain, every British subject become a citizen of France. The call fell on ears numbed by cannon fire and, eight days afterwards, the aged Pétain began to grope his way to Vichy.

*

The evacuation of Norway had already been announced. The sombre picture was now very nearly complete. Defeated by a combination of German armour, Soviet fuel and treachery at home, France had surrendered unconditionally and the only uncaged British soldier left on the continent gazed defiantly from the high rock of Gibraltar at the menace of Africa and at the menace of Spain.

*

With characteristic malice, Hitler decreed that the meeting between the German and French plenipotentiaries should take place at what had become a shrine to the people of France. Brimming with revenge, the conquerors waited for the vanquished in the wood at Compiègne where, twenty-five years ago, Marshal Foch had dictated his terms of Armistice. They made a proud cavalcade as they strutted in the sun and it seemed as if no shadow could ever dim their triumph.

In shame and sorrow, the French signatories came, signed and departed for the even greater indignity of Rome. It seemed as if the New Order had come to darken Europe for a thousand years. But the curse of mankind lay about these proud men. Not in a thousand but in five years, Hitler's petrol-soaked body flamed in a Berlin back-garden to the requiem of Russian cannon; Goering cheated the hangman with a phial of cyanide but Ribbentrop and Keitel went the harder way. Von Brauchitsch was eventually to be discredited by friend and by foe and of the other two, Raeder trudges the yard of a German prison while the lunatic Hess gabbles for ever and plays with his fingers.

Wind, rain, sun and victory have cleaned the wood of Compiègne. But on June the 21st, 1940, the humiliation of France and of the French was complete. It was then that an unknown French General raised in London that same Cross of Lorraine that had led Joan of Arc to Orleans five hundred years ago.

*

Avanti popolo!

When Mussolini chose to hasten to the assistance of the victors, Great Britain knew that she must now fight for her very life. A web of airfields was spun southwards from Rome and over Sicily; a first-class battle fleet dominated the Mediterranean whose name, bellowed from the balcony of the *Palazzo Venezia*, had been changed to "*Mare nostrum*". The Italian fleet, by itself, was no match for the Royal Navy—but the Royal Navy had other preoccupations. It had to scour the grey seas round Britain and to keep the Atlantic sea-lanes open.

" Heute . . .

ist . . .

Frankreich . . .

ganz . . .

tot."

Alone, Italy could not hope to cut the life-line to the Far East. But strong warships of France had beat for shelter to Oran and to Alexandria. If these vessels and their crews and their guns should sail against us, our position would be desperate indeed.

In Alexandria all was well. French and British sailors fought side by side and a combined barrage sent the Italian bombers scurrying for home. To the smack and thunder of Ack-Ack, the *Entente Cordiale* was confirmed and cemented in the wardrooms over pink gin and Pernod. In Oran, pride or folly beset the French Commander and one of the most terrible decisions of the war faced the British Cabinet.

Captain Holland, R.N., was sent to Oran to negotiate. The French Commander refused even to see him and his fruitless visit was followed by an ultimatum. This document, fair and reasonable in its demands, provided the wily Dr. Goebbels with devastating ammunition. The action which followed its refusal, described and distorted by every loud-speaker in France, very nearly succeeded in changing a dazed ally into a furious foe. It was to have incalculable consequences on the work of the French Section in the dark years to come. In the long run, thank God, *la logique française* triumphed and, with clear eyes France saw the mountain towering above the clouds.

A battle-squadron under command of Vice-Admiral Somerville stood off Oran and, with profound regret, opened fire on the French ships. In the engagement which followed, a battleship, two destroyers and an aircraft carrier were sunk. The cruiser *Dunkerque*—ill-omened name in British ears—was battered. Admiral Somerville's squadron cleaned its guns and put to sea, secure in the knowledge that the Royal Navy had now only one enemy in the Mediterranean.

*

To Odette Sansom, sitting in the sunshine of Kensington Gardens while Marianne rolled on the grass and Françoise and Lily talked to a stray puppy, the naval strategy behind this melancholy action was a mystery. Only the fact was clear. A British fleet had attacked a French fleet and French sailors, blasted by an ally's guns, had drowned in oil and blood. For all she knew, her friends might have been amongst them. In a world of terror, panic and confusion, it was difficult at first for this young Frenchwoman to see where her loyalty should lie. She had not had very long to peer behind the forbidding façade of the English and during the early, lonely years, she had seen little to admire and much to condemn.

The weeks that followed were hard and unhappy. The English, smarting under the "moral victory" of Dunkirk attributed their humiliation to the French and the French in their turn, muttered against the English, who, they said, had deserted them in their desperate hour.

In the intervals between cooking, sewing, caring for her children and waiting for the sweet disharmony of the "All clear", Odette pondered this bitter question. She told herself that English guns had fired on French ships because it was necessary. Her country's morale had cracked and crumbled. But what was this intangible quality called "morale"? Every politician used the word glibly. It stared at her from posters and jumped out of newspaper headlines. It was, she decided, a sense of spiritual tranquillity that sprang from faith, faith in the rightness of a cause, faith in ultimate victory, faith, above all, in the honesty of one's leaders. Her leaders had failed France and France had fallen. Under a veneer of patriotism, men in high places had sold their country for greed, for power, from cowardice. The ancient virtues of loyalty had been balanced against profit and flung away. Like fungus on a high beam, the corruption had spread and rotted the timbers of the whole house. If the Army was bad, it was because the officers were bad. If the officers were bad, it was because they lacked faith, because they smelled the corruption from above.

When the Spartans were at the pinnacle of their fame and their military glory, they sent a deputation to the oracle at Delphi and demanded with arrogance:

"Can anything harm Sparta?"

"Yes," came the answer. "Luxury."

★

Vapour trails in the autumnal sky; a burning Heinkel on a burning hayrick; the slow whooping of sirens and tiger-humming in the night; the menacing whistle and the crash of bombs;

the carillon of an ambulance tearing through city streets, fringed with fire.

French, German, Belgian, Dutch—it was all one now. The foreigners had let us down again. Why should they or their children be allowed to eat?

One morning Odette took the three children shopping. She left Marianne in her push-car outside a greengrocer's in West Kensington and took Françoise and Lily into the crowded shop. She waited for a long time to be served. The greengrocer was an obsequious, truculent little man whose eyes looked as if they had been hem-stitched with red cotton. Odette asked for two pounds of tomatoes please. The shopman looked at her and then round the shop. A number of women waited patiently, their string-bags in their hands. He blinked and said loudly.

"I got no tomatoes for you, see?"

Odette frowned.

"But you have plenty of tomatoes. There they are."

"I said I got no tomatoes for you nor any more like you, see? Why don't you go back to France where you come from, you and your kids with you? Maybe your Jerry pals 'll give you all the tomatoes you want. I won't, see?"

For a moment Odette did not understand. She glanced around her quickly. Everybody in the shop was staring at her. Then the meaning of his words became suddenly clear to her. She felt herself flush. Lily's hand tightened in hers. In deathly silence, she walked out of the shop. One of the women said to the shopman.

"You should be ashamed of yourself, you should."

Odette didn't hear that. With her head held high, she was hurrying home as fast as she could go, wanting to get into somewhere where she could hide, praying that the hard lump behind her eyes would not dissolve into tears before she could get into the house and run upstairs and shut her bedroom door and hide her face for ever.

*

Three days later, the coalman from Fulham called. He was a friendly person and, as Odette knew from his constant

reminiscence, captain of the darts team in his local pub. He
had not called since the collapse of France. She opened the
door to his ring. In those three days, she had not once been out
of the house. He greeted her cheerfully and took her order.
When the sacks had been emptied into the cellar, he came up
the steps again. He said:

"You're not looking your bright self this morning." He
frowned. "You're a French lady, aren't you?"

"Yes," she said nervously. "I am—I was—French."

"I was in France in the last war," he said. "Alongside of the
French. Is that what's on your mind, lady, that France has
packed up?"

She nodded.

He spat accurately into the garden. He said.

"France isn't down and out, not by a long chalk, you mark
my words, and I *know* the Froggies, me and them having had a
basinful together, as you might say. One of these days France is
going to wake up and give little old 'Itler the surprise of his
bloody life, pardon me. I know the French and they're all
right, lady, so keep smiling."

"I'll try," she said. "Thank you."

Two pounds of tomatoes or half a ton of coal? England stood
alone.

                                   *

But was England alone? Charles de Gaulle, rallying the
forces of Free France, sounded a trumpet call from London.

*"France has lost a battle. But France has not lost a war. . . .
Nothing is lost because this war is a world war. In the free universe,
immense forces have not yet been brought into play. Some day these
forces will crush the enemy. On that day, France must be present at the
victory. She will then regain her liberty and her greatness. That is why
I ask all Frenchmen, wherever they may be, to unite with me in action,
in sacrifice and in hope. Our country is in danger of death. Let us fight to
save it."*

That was the voice of France. On July the 14th, the National
Festival of France, Odette heard the voice of England. Winston
Churchill said:

"*I proclaim my faith that some of us will live to see a Fourteenth of July when a liberated France will once again rejoice in her greatness and in her glory, and once again stand forward as the champion of the freedom and the rights of man. . . . We shall try so to conduct ourselves that every true French heart will beat and glow at the way we carry on the struggle; and that not only France but all the oppressed countries in Europe may feel that each British Victory is a step towards the liberation of the Continent from the foulest thraldom into which it has ever been cast.*"

Odette looked at her three daughters. In their veins ran the strong mixture of French and English blood. She saw clearly, in that transparent moment, where her ultimate duty lay.

B*

CHAPTER IV

THE TIPPINGS

ODETTE stayed on in London with her three daughters until October. By then the fury of the air raids had become so fierce that she decided at last that it was a right and proper thing to take her children to comparative safety, and the little exhausted family of four left the bombardment for Somerset.

*

From Taunton, the main road to Exeter runs through Wellington to the tiny village of Red Ball and it is about here that Somerset becomes Devon. A quarter mile down a narrow lane, Odette found a cottage occupied only by an elderly lady called Mrs. Balsom and here she took rooms. The front windows of the cottage looked out over a valley to a soft line of hills. Inside its walls were oil lamps, lace curtains, china bulldogs and coloured lithographs of little girls in blue sashes playing with be-ribboned kittens. Outside apples ripened in the sun and cows gazed calmly over the garden fence at the children. For the first time for many weeks, the tired family slept soundly through the quiet nights and it was a joy to Odette to watch health and tranquillity flow back into the strained faces of her daughters.

She was a firm friend of her mother-in-law who lived in a guest-house a mile or two along the main road. When the old lady became ill, it was less of a duty than it was a labour of love to Odette to nurse her. They were usually full and busy days and, as old Mrs. Sansom's health declined, they became even busier. The three children had to be woken, washed and dressed. Breakfast had to be prepared, table manners watched, teeth cleaned, clothes washed and mended. Family shopping was done in the village of Culmstock, some three lonely miles away but, after a very brief probationary period, the tradesmen of Culmstock took Odette to their hearts and she and her children became their most welcome visitors. Genial Mr. Strawbridge, who sold everything from baking-powder to lamp-oil and stays to mouse traps would frequently slide a surreptitious bag of liquor-ice-all-sorts into Marianne's push-cart, Mrs. Fisher, the butcher's wife (née Hogan and the one-time Pride of Waterford) never failed to provide a cheerful greeting and as generous a ration as the law would allow. Laden with parcels, Odette would wheel the push-cart back to the cottage, wash the children's faces and dash up the lane to see if Mrs. Marshall's hens— whose eyes were far less bright than those of their owner—had possibly contributed an egg for to-morrow's breakfast. Lunch was cooked in the shared kitchen and the children sent for their rest. There was little rest for Odette, who would walk to the guest-house to sit with her mother-in-law and, if necessary, walk on to the doctor or the chemist in Wellington, returning in time to give the children tea and read to them and put them to bed. Often she would go back to the guest-house and spend an hour or two there, coming back along the dark main road and turning down into the greater darkness of the lane that led to the cottage where her children slept.

A narrow road turns to the left behind the guest-house and makes in the general direction of the distant hills. It passes under the railway bridge and straggles over the uplands to Culmstock. It was at the bridge that Odette used to leave the road and turn to the right alongside the railway line. About a quarter mile along there is a gate that bars a still narrower path that climbs through a deep wood. Beyond the stile at the fringe of the wood, there is a sloping field and then another field. A track, faint in the grass, winds up to a mound called "The Tippings".

Quite by chance in that autumn of 1940, Odette found her way to the Tippings. She was alone that afternoon and she stood for a long time, filling her eyes with what she saw and her ears with the sound of silence. Then she spread a coat on the grass and sat down and gazed until long after twilight had slid down the steeps of the sky and the ancient hills had retreated into darkness and the first faint stars were sure.

She came again in the early morning. She wanted to rest her eyes once more on that sweet expanse of pasture and plough

and to make sure that this first revelation of England was true.
There was mist over the land that morning and the sun rose
and hung like an enormous orange in the sky and swelled and
turned to fire and sent the grey spectres scurrying and smoking
to the hills. Black and definite in the sunrise she saw the Culmstock Beacon, set up more than three and a half centuries ago
by the sturdy ancestors of Mr. Strawbridge, Mrs. Balsom and
Mrs. Marshall, to warn the people of England that the Armada
was beating up from the West. Here was security and continuity. This was eternal. She walked home to her children with
buoyance in her step and tranquillity in her heart.

As the days passed and the wind began to probe the woods
with fingers that were suddenly cool, that mound on the border
of Somerset and Devon became more and more precious to
Odette. Autumn, with its wet blackberries, its bonfires
quenched before the coloured sunsets and its bright array of
stars, was slipping into the second winter of war. Earlier and
earlier in the evenings, she saw the masked, yellow lamp of the
district nurse's bicycle and already after tea, chintz curtains
were drawn across the windows of little, anxious homes, each
one of which had once sheltered a father, a husband, a brother
or a son. Slowly Odette began to acquire the "feel" of England
and to attune her perceptions to the rhythm of life in the country of her marriage. It had been a strange, interrupted
rhythm. Chaucer had been its singer, Shakespeare its
orchestra. Hilaire Belloc had sounded its note in his loud talk
of Agincourt, Inkpen and the Sussex pubs. In the splintering
glass and the mouth-organs of the tripper ships in Boulogne,
its rhythm had become catchy. It had been concealed behind
the stained-glass fanlights of Kensington and consumed by its
awful, intimate gas fires. Now, as the hunter's moon rose and
the nightwinds lightly dusted the furrows with frost, Odette
heard again the faint sounds of England's timeless John Peel.

Herself an alert and volatile person, she had raged against
that innate sense of British superiority that had seemed to her
to serve as a mere excuse for political and intellectual indolence.
Worse still had been the modesty of the English, that quin-
tessence of possibly justifiable conceit. Now, as she watched the
falling stars of autumn tumble past the constant brightness of
Orion's Sword, she asked herself if superiority—and its twin

brother modesty—were not the means of concealing emotion.
Could it be kindliness and not indolence that prompted
the English to make allowances and to belittle their own glory?

*

It was a terrible winter, a winter that caught and gripped and
split strong trees.

Inside the cottage, Lily's warm finger laboriously drew
Hitler's face on the frosted window of the children's bedroom
while Odette lit the candles on a Christmas tree, uprooted in
secret from the wood below the Tippings and carried home in
guilty triumph after dark.

· . . . *It is announced from Cairo that over thirty-six thousand Italian
prisoners have now been counted in the Western Desert. . . .*

Silver string, surprises, chilblains, chocolate and tears.

. . . . *The figures for civilian air raid casualties in the United
Kingdom during November have been announced by the Ministry of
Home Secruity. Four thousand five hundred and eighty-eight persons have
been killed and six thousand two hundred and two have been injured. . . .*

She switched off the wireless to listen breathlessly to
boys' voices, fitful on the freezing wind outside.

> . . . . *the Angel of the Lord came down
> And glory shone all round. . . .*

*

Snowdrops and daffodils and the thin crying of lambs.

From the Tippings, Odette watched spring flow down the
woods. She saw uncertain, indefinite rains visit the fields
casually and she sensed the excitement of the birds as the young,
cool sun chased the cloud shadows across the uplands. When
she first came to England, she had bitterly resented the half-
pitying, half-tolerant distrust of foreigners. But what about
Mr. Strawbridge, Mrs. Marshall, Mrs. Fisher, shopkeepers of
England with centuries of poetry in their blood? She was herself a foreigner and from these people, from the postman, the
roadman and the squire, she had had nothing but kindness.

Watching the skirts of the rain brush Culmstock Beacon, she
was conscious of a strange wish to deserve the sight of what was
mirrored in her eyes and somehow to serve these people who
had given her and her children their friendship in such warm
abundance.

*

Yellow butterflies wavered in the path through the wood as
spring became summer. It was a pleasant thing to snatch even
a few moments and to be on the mound and to gaze into the
infinite spaces of the sky and to listen. Six Devon Red heifers
had been turned into the field below the Tippings and sometimes they came so close that Odette could hear the little
tugging sounds they made as they tore at the sweet grass.
Sometimes she heard a lark singing, weaving its song into the
humming of innumerable insects and, though she searched and
searched the translucent blue, the song always came from an
invisible singer. The noise of the threshing machine in the long
field was as insistent as the sound of the sea, and during the
heat of the afternoon, the old horse stood in his private shade.
The war seemed very far away.
    Libya, Greece, Crete .... They were unrealized sounds
without meaning. Only Red Ball, Culmstock and Wellington
were real. Old Mrs. Sansom's health was causing more and
more anxiety and, more and more often, Odette came to see
her and to sit with her when the children had been put to bed.
Very occasionally, there were family outings as far as Taunton
in the local bus and there were picnics in the wood below the
Tippings. The arrival of Hess in Scotland set the village agog
and the postman, the roadman and the squire all knew a
man who knew a man who knew a man in the War Office who
knew something but his lips were sealed. Hess, however, was
eclipsed by the rumoured birth of a calf with two heads in North
Petherton and even this phenomenon had to take second
place to a recrudescence of lice in the hair of the evacuees.
    On June the 22nd Hitler, ignoring the entreaties of his
generals, invaded Soviet Russia.
    The black chickens of the Kremlin had certainly come home
to roost. In Berlin, Ribbentrop contemptuously tossed the
Order of Lenin into the waste-paper basket, while in Moscow

" . . . For he's bewitched for ever who has seen,
Not with his eyes but with his vision, spring
Flow down the woods and stipple leaves with sun. . . ."

(*The Land*. Victoria Sackville West).

the taciturn Molotov sourly unpicked the stitches of his Nazi decorations. Dr. Goebbels gleefully turned on the heat and the hitherto harmonious ether stormed into a hurricane of vituperation. "Our Russian comrades" of last night's Berlin broadcast became "Bolshevik Scum" this morning, while "Our German comrades", snarled the transmitters of the Polit-Bureau, had reassumed their role of "Fascist Wolves". The torrent of Russian abuse against the "decadent Imperialist pluto-democracies of the West" was halted in mid-air and the Kremlin cooed to the B.B.C. The verbal *volte-face* was complete and the Commissars began to scratch their heads about practical things. To expect the peasantry to fight for a remorseless and abstract ideology was clearly unrealistic so Holy Russia herself was resurrected and her soil glorified. The unfortunate populace gazed awestruck at the flame-throwers of the friends they had so recently been ordered to take to their bosoms. An incident, as ludicrous as it was shameful to both parties, was over at last.

The attack on Russia had a startling effect on public opinion in France. Up to this time, the Germans had held the initiative everywhere. They still held it—but it was extremely unlikely that England would allow them to hold it any longer. Up to now it had not been a question of victory for Britain but rather one of avoiding defeat. Hitler, blinded by military conceit, had himself disregarded the Holy Writ of *Mein Kampf* and opened a war on two fronts. It was folly on the grand scale and Britain's ultimate victory was sure.

Now there were new arrows on unfamiliar newspaper maps and a host of new words for Odette to learn and to try and realize. Brest-Litovsk, Smolensk, the Dnieper, Leningrad. The Red Army was annihilated with monotonous regularity and a hitherto unknown Soviet Commander called Timoshenko was canonized. One day Lily cut her knee on the rusty reaper-and-binder in Mrs. Marshall's yard and the whole bloody panorama of the war instantly shrank to the size of a strip of elastoplast.

*

Autumn was upon her again and a whole year had passed. It seemed quite extraordinary to Odette that she had seen the

flight of four seasons over Culmstock Beacon but so it was. In
the October afternoons, she saw birds perched on the telegraph
wires, their feathers blowing up the wrong way, and the night
sky blazed with stars.

Odette knew that a knowledge of England had come on her
unawares during the cycle of a country year. She had been
perpetually baffled by the shifting intricacies of a social
system where birth, education, intonation, money and variety
of work all combined to produce a situation which, like his own
grammar, was instinctively known to the Englishman but had
been almost impossible to formulate in terms comprehensible
to a foreigner. She sensed that this certainty sprang from continuity of race experience and race absorption. Like the Cen-
turion, she knew "no other life than this, no other life at all".
About the common people of England was generally a tolerance
and a delicacy in dealing—blended with an infuriating compromise—that at once beguiled her and angered her. There
was nothing she could do about it. In spite of the greengrocer of West Kensington, she was bound, hand, foot and
heart.

On October the 21st a German major was shot in Bordeaux.
One hundred French hostages were seized. Fifty of them were
mown down in cold blood. A woman in Culmstock said that it
was a shame, wasn't it? Odette walked the road between Red
Ball and Wellington that night. Though there were English
fields around her with English cattle grazing; though she felt
as if her body were enfolded in the soft arms of the English
hills, every beat of her blood told her that she must soon rise
and go to the fight.

The ice formed early in the ruts of the road that winter. The
children loved to tread on it and see the smooth surface crack
and become a cluster of cold, white flowers. One morning
when they woke up, every twig on every tree was a shining
splinter of frost and there was a white film of ice on the milk.
Even the cows were cold.

Towards the turn of the year, Odette went with Mrs. Sansom
to London and there, in a very few days the old lady died.
When Odette returned to Somerset, she went one late afternoon
to pay her last visit to the Tippings. Sparrows were shivering
in the hedges and there was a muffled silence over the land.

She gazed her fill at the wintry countryside and at the declining sun. She realized at this moment how dear these acres had become to her. She had recently been in the proximity of death and she knew that she too would one day die. With all her heart she wished that her body could in some way be dedicated to these most beloved fields.

CHAPTER V

"THE FIRM"

S.O.E., C. & D., M.O.1.(S.P.), "the Firm", the "Racket", "the org".

These initials—and many other equally anonymous groupings—slid into the alphabetical mêlée of the war effort during the autumn of 1940. The first stood either for "Special Operations Executive", or "Stately 'omes of England", according to taste; the second was more flippant and stood for "Cloaks and daggers" and the third for "Military Operations One (Special Planning)". All of them were called "the Firm" or alternately, "the Racket", all of them led to Baker Street and from Baker Street by devious routes to Europe.

The "French Section", though born of the one prolific S.O.E. mother, was sired by a number of fathers. It was, in every sense, a war-baby, the embryo having been conceived at the seaside resort of Dunkirk. The period of gestation was a restless one, for the mother had other offspring in the incubator. After a difficult and protracted confinement, the child—one of a multiple birth—first saw the light of day in the early spring of 1941. High-explosive bombs were its rattle, it was suckled from a static water tank and for its night-light, it had the flames of London.

Bloody but only partly bowed, the remnants of the British Army were home and the long coasts of Europe were closed. From the cool waters of the Baltic to sunny Biarritz, the Germans flung a steel hoop that clutched every inch of shore. One strong strand reached out to encircle the Channel Islands so that the men of Guernsey, Jersey and little Sark had to turn their eyes away from home and look askance at the vast, handcuffed Continent. Neutral Spain had long been under Axis domination, Lisbon had become a sort of "under the clock at Charing Cross" for polyglot espionage and the Vichy police patrolled the Mediterranean shore from the Pyrenees to the

Italian frontier. Tiny and unafraid, British bugle calls flared
from the lonely Rock of Gibraltar.

There was one way to win the war and one way only.
Britain must go back. Somewhere, somehow, a mighty
British Army would have to land on the European shore,
engage the enemy in mortal combat, liberate the enslaved and,
sustained by the peoples it had freed, blast its way to Berlin.
That was the simple, hopeless task that confronted the Cabinet
in June, 1940. Much had to be achieved first. Mr. Winston
Churchill took the long view and steadily reinforced the armies
in the Middle East. Accepting eventual victory in the desert as
a *fait accompli*, his mind ranged even further into the future and
he called for maps of the coasts of France. While the Chiefs of
Staff considered in broad outline the future invasion of Europe,
England waited for the immediate onslaught of the German
armies.

> *"Small is the land we guard;*
> *Small is the house I left an hour ago*
> *To keep my watch for it and all the rest.*
> *Small, small am I in this prodigious night."*

The squire, the farmer and the poacher stood guard in turn
over their familiar fields while their wives prepared pans of
boiling fat to tip into the faces of the *Wehrmacht*. Signposts came
down and pillboxes went up, each with its store of home-made
Molotov cocktails. Along the East coast, half-trained soldiers
drew their P.14s and marched to the cliff edge and counted
their meagre store of ammunition, four in the mag. and one up
the spout, lend us a pull-through, Lofty, don't fire till you see
the whites of their eyes, chum . . . and thank gawd we gotta
navy.

Meanwhile the planning staff was at work.

A number of bitter lessons had been learned during the last
few weeks. From the doleful history of the Norwegian fiasco,
one fact stood out clearly. It was that an invading army must
look for help and for co-operation from the people of the country
it invades. Furthermore these people must be armed and they
must work to a strategic and co-ordinated plan of sabotage
and attack. The solitary, undisciplined *Franc tireur* could readily

wreck a year's careful planning by the untimely pressure of a trigger. The Germans had imposed a rigid discipline on their traitors, not only in Norway but in Holland, Belgium and France. The system had worked. Europe to-day represented the triumph of the traitor and a new word had been added to the vocabulary of all men. That word was "Quisling". England's appeal would not be to the traitor but to the patriot.

Slowly—and despite some disapproving Ministerial shivers—S.O.E. came into official being. The suggestion that Great Britain should dabble in unorthodox methods of warfare caused many a cultured eyebrow to lift and "the Firm"—rather like a housemaid's baby—was regarded as being inevitable in the circumstances but not quite nice. One was reluctantly forced to recognize its existence but one didn't talk about it—a reservation which admirably suited its members. The Firm itself was violently extrovert. Its object was victory, utter and absolute. To achieve that victory, it was prepared not only to examine and exploit all the more successful innovations of the enemy but also to try out several of its own. *Alarm, despondency, and destruction* were to be its exports and these it proposed to despatch—by special messenger—to every country dominated by the Axis. Each country would have its own "Section" in London. By submarine, by ship and by parachute, men, women and weapons would come from the United Kingdom. At the risk of their lives, these men and women would seek out patriots, arm them and train them; they would plan and undertake sabotage, disabling factories, wrecking power-houses, severing lines of communication. The bomb from the air, no matter how accurately aimed, could be no respecter of nationality. It killed where it struck and its proper target was Germany. S.O.E. proposed to render visits of the R.A.F. unnecessary elsewhere than to the Reich by accurately doing the bomb's work from the ground within the occupied countries. Many lives would thus be saved. More than any of these things, the very fact that British men and women were prepared to come and live amongst them—and, if necessary, to die amongst them—would be for the oppressed, a bright symbol of Great Britain's unalterable purpose. One day the British Armies would land again. In that day, the enemy would find the armed hand of all Europe turned against them and the road back to the Reich sewn with death. That was the broad plan devised in London while exhausted soldiers slept like the dead, the salt and the sand of Dunkirk still on their boots.

For the moment—and for the moment only—the fountain-pen would have to be mightier than the plastic explosive.

As no purely military action was yet possible, it seemed right and proper that the project should be vicariously fathered by a Civilian Ministry and the first, tentative stirrings took place under the roof of the Ministry of Economic Warfare in Berkeley Square. A number of commercial gentlemen went to Lisbon and a very few went to Madrid, Dublin, Stockholm and Berne. Their object was two-fold; it was not only to attune their ears to the voice of Europe but also to find means—either with a cheque-book or a garotte—of denying to the Germans those commodities which they most needed to wage war. Brown-paper parcels of tungsten, gold, radium, wolfram, diamonds, platinum *et hoc genus omne* were bandied about the cafés of Estoril and men whose combined pay and allowances totalled less than a thousand a year, stood on the conductor's platform of Portuguese trams with the wealth of the Aztecs in their waistcoat pockets. A third and more diverting duty was the dissemination of anecdotes which showed up the Führer and his associates in a humorous or equivocal light. But it was a frustrating, bloodless way to fight a war and many an ex-patriate Englishman, sipping his champagne cocktail in the neutral sunshine longed for the ropes, the stabbing knives and the burnt cork of the Commandos.

In preparation for the more active future, certain *data* were being collected at home. Elderly and retired business men who had built or equipped or managed factories in any part of Europe were surprised to receive visits from knowledgeable strangers who sought what appeared to be irrelevant information. Where exactly was the telephone exchange in a certain bacon factory in Copenhagen? The condenser in those silk mills in Lyons, could it be pointed out on this blue print? How and precisely where did the points cross in this stretch of line and the overseer of the locomotive repair shop, what was his character and is it true that his wife was machine-gunned on the road between Paris and Orleans? While a list of people and targets was being compiled at home, a vitally important question was put to the gentlemen in Lisbon, Madrid and Berne. How stood the name of England to-day among the patriots of France?

*

Tout français nait Anglophobe: il peut devenir Anglophile.

It was an ancient proverb of gloom and of hope. But the time of self-deception was over. Only by taking off the rose-tinted spectacles of the phoney war could one begin to see clearly and to find the answer to this most significant question. The French have never been pro-British. As the English have stood for England, so have the French stood for France. Because the history of the two nations is laced with distrust, conquest and bloodshed, it would be the gravest folly lightly to assume an automatic friendship. Though twice briefly united against a common foe, the weight of the Centuries remained and all the profligate five-pound notes of pre-war Montmartre bought little other than contempt. *L'entente cordiale étant morte*, it was better far to accept a fundamental Anglophobia as the prevailing sentiment and seek by words and deeds—and specially by deeds —to win the trust and the loyalty of these dour, suspicious, lion-hearted people.

The *mariage de convenance* between John Bull and Madelon was galloping from a separation to a divorce.

Speaking in Secret Session at the House of Commons, Mr. Winston Churchill said:

"The Almighty, in His infinite wisdom, did not see fit to create Frenchmen in the image of Englishmen. In a State like France, which has experienced so many convulsions—Monarchy, Convention, Directory, Consulate, Empire, Monarchy, Empire and finally Republic—there has grown up a principle founded on the '*droit administratif*' which undoubtedly governs the action of many French officers and officials in times of revolution and change. It is a highly legalistic habit of mind and it arises from a subconscious sense of national self-preservation against the dangers of sheer anarchy. For instance, any officer who obeys the command of his lawful superior, is absolutely immune from subsequent punishment. Much therefore turns in the minds of French officers upon whether there is a direct, unbroken chain of lawful command, and this is held to be more important by many Frenchmen than moral, national or international considerations. From this point of view, many Frenchmen who admire General de Gaulle and envy him in his role nevertheless regard him as a man who has rebelled against the authority of the French State which, in their prostration, they conceive to be vested in the person of the antique defeatist, who, to them, is the illustrious and venerable Marshal Pétain, the hero of Verdun and the sole hope of France. . . ."

On July the 5th, 1940, the antique defeatist had broken off diplomatic relations with Britain. Two days later, French aircraft attacked British shipping in Gibraltar—as a reprisal, mumbled the aged Marshal, for the monstrous and unprovoked action of the Royal Navy at Oran.

Cringing before their German masters, the men of Vichy had begun a campaign of vilification directed against their former allies. A blend of defeatism, fear of punishment, and jealousy led these contemptible turncoats to accuse Britain of having dragged France into the war. During the autumn and winter of 1939, it had been the practice of German aircraft to shower smutty post-cards on the French countryside. These post-cards depicted a British soldier in the act of raping a naked French girl while the bleeding body of a *poilu* hung on barbed wire in the background. They had in those days, acquired a certain collector's value and were somewhat cautiously swopped between the Black Watch and their comrades of the French Infantry. Now the obscene message of the smutty post-card was recalled with many sage head-shakings. How wise the Germans had been, how clear-sighted, how prophetic. They had said that England would fight to the last Frenchman! *Comme c'était vrai!* Remember Waterloo, remember Trafalgar, remember Oran! Think of the martyrdom of Joan of Arc! Remember Marlborough—and consider his villainous, insupportable descendant—Churchill! Poor simple France should have pondered that ancient phrase *perfide Albion* and turned away from the decadent democracies towards the golden glow of the Fascist dawn. With a rheumy eye on the Roman Catholic vote, Pétain further ascribed the downfall of France to the use of contraceptives. "Children are our need, more and more children," wheezed the sterile old gentleman. "Do as I say—not as I do. Emulate the human brood-mares of the Third Reich and create. Only thus can France be strong! Let spawn be your watchword! I am further instructed to warn you that the penalty for listening to the B.B.C. is death."

Heil Hitler! Evviva Mussolini! Vive Pétain!

Meanwhile there were certain things that could be done, albeit from a distance. In a sycophantic, sadistic outburst, Charles de Gaulle was condemned to death *in absentia*—a sentence which no doubt provided a *sauce piquante* to his lunch in London. Those Frenchmen who sought to rally France with the aid of Britain were listed as double traitors. It was all very important and trivial—and was scorned by the great mass of Frenchmen who, even though dazed by defeat, could not fail to notice an astonishing harmony between the ponderous edicts of Vichy and the spontaneous yelpings of Dr. Goebbels.

*

Reports from many different sources were checked and cross-checked. From a wealth of sometimes contradictory evidence, it was possible to draw these main conclusions. The senior officers of the French Navy were—by tradition—generally anti-British. They had been so before Trafalgar. The reinforced Anglophobia may have been due to many reasons. One of them was certainly Oran, yet another was Dakar and a third their natural resentment at having to take orders from British Naval Commanders. In dealing with these gold-leafed gentlemen, the word should be "caution". Opinion in the French Army was fairly evenly divided. Those who had served alongside British troops still had a healthy regard for the patience and tenacity of the men in battledress. "*Ils sont des bouledogues, les Anglais*" they muttered. "Hitler will learn." The junior officers of the French Air Force were pro-British to a man and only longed to join their former comrades in the thunderous sky.

So much for the Services. What about grandpère, grandmère, Jean and Jeanne? The legend that Great Britain had, in some mysterious way, "betrayed" or "exploited" France was carefully fostered. In unoccupied France, British residents had a rough time with the Vichy authorities and doors were slammed in the faces of hungry British soldiers trying to make their way to the South of Spain. Though the behaviour of the Germans was superficially "correct", practically every family had relations or friends in the occupied zone and Nazi reaction to pro-British sympathy was swift and merciless. Hardly recognizable at first, the familiar *odeur de l'invasion* began to curl sourly in the nostrils of the people. And then, slowly, little fitful winds began to blow; they gathered strength and became constant; they lifted the smell and carried it spreading, in one direction—towards the locked waters of the English Channel.

*

A German sentry was posted outside the telephone exchange in Rouen. One evening it fell to the turn of Hans Schneider, a simple, not unkindly man with a wife and two sons in München. Schneider was quite willing to take his turn for it meant that he could be alone for two long hours and think about his wife, Trude, and the bright faces of his sons so far away in Germany. As he stood in the gathering dusk, a little boy of eight or nine —about the age of his own Hansi—came along the street, playing with a ball. It rolled at Schneider's feet. Glancing round to make sure he was not observed by any officious N.C.O., Schneider leaned his rifle against the door of the telephone exchange and bent down and picked up the ball. With a friendly smile, he offered it to the little boy and said in his slow, guttural French: "*Voici, mon petit.*"

The little boy gazed at him with clear, blue eyes. Under that calm scrutiny, Schneider shifted his feet. He said again: "*Voici, mon petit. C'est à vous, ça.*"

Very deliberately, the little boy struck the ball from his hand. It rolled across the street and lay in the gutter. The little boy spat scornfully on the pavement and turned and marched away, thin, erect and proud in the dusk. Schneider watched him go. He walked like Hansi walked. After a long time, Schneider took a deep breath and picked up his rifle and put the muzzle into his mouth and pressed the trigger and blew his brains out.

*

To the desk of a high-ranking German security officer in Paris there came one afternoon a middle-aged French lady, the bearer of a famous name. She asked for permission to travel into the unoccupied zone to visit her son who was desperately ill. The Colonel sat back in his chair and lit a cigarette.

"I will be frank with you, Madame," he said. "It is of importance to me politically and socially that I be received in your house. If you will receive me—even for a glass of wine—and present me to your friends, I will be happy to give you the necessary papers to visit your son." He looked at her meaningly. "Is it a bargain?"

"Certainly. At four o'clock to-morrow?"

"Thank you, Madame. May I say that you are not only charming—but wise?"

"You flatter me, Colonel."

At four o'clock exactly, the Colonel, conscious that he was looking his best, rang the bell of the large house in the Avenue Kléber. The door was opened by a solemn butler who took his peaked cap and gloves and led the way up a magnificent staircase to the drawing-room. He opened the double doors and said:

"The German officer, Madame."

Adjusting a smile, the Colonel walked into the room. Surrounded by furniture draped in dust sheets, Madame awaited him alone. He stopped—and the smile drained out of his face like water out of a basin. He said stiffly.

"I don't think you understand, Madame. My request was that I should be received in your house—'received' in its fullest sense—and that I should meet your friends."

"You have been received, Colonel. You are in my drawing-room. And I have arranged to present my friends." She rose, rang a bell and sat down with composure. After a moment of pregnant silence, the solemn butler entered. He was accompanied by the housekeeper, an elderly woman in black with a bunch of keys at her waist.

"These, Colonel, are my oldest friends. I present my house-

keeper, Madame Legrand, and my butler, Emile." She said
to the butler. "Our guest wishes to take a glass of wine, Emile."
"Certainly, Madame."

The butler left the room and re-entered immediately. He
offered a tray to the German officer. On it were two bottles of
champagne—and one wine-glass.

*

The wind gathered force and began to blow a gale.

A German sergeant was stabbed as he walked back to bar-
racks from a brothel in Châlons-sur-Marne. Ten Frenchmen
were dragged from their homes and publicly machine-gunned.
Their bodies were barely cold before another German soldier
died violently and then, within a day, a well-known collaborator
was found hanging from the branch of a tree, his tongue
obscenely out and the Cross of Lorraine pinned to his breast.
This time, twenty Frenchmen were shot. It availed nothing.
More Germans were killed; more Frenchmen were shot. The
fearful switchback of death gathered momentum. The two
great Gallic links of "family and land" were burst asunder and
young men left home and set out for the Pyrenees, for Spain,
for Gibraltar, for London, for de Gaulle. One of them, a boot-
maker in a Normandy village, survived the winter and the
prisons of Spain and came to London and told a story that
lifted one's heart.

The Germans had come to his village, he said, and set up
a secret short-wave radio station. Somebody talked and as a
result, the day it was finished, the R.A.F. came in the dusk
and rained an inferno of high explosive and incendiary bombs
at the building. While the raid was at its height, Grandmère
Ducros, eighty years old and a cripple, stumbled out of her
cottage and hobbled on a stick into the middle of the village
square. Those who had known her all their lives could see her
clearly in the light of the burning houses and they shouted to
her to come back—for the love of God. She was waving her
stick to the sky in jubilant welcome to the British bombers and,
over the roar of their engines and the crackling of flame, they
could hear the sound of her voice screaming the words of the
Marseillaise. . . .

"*Aux armes, citoyens. . . .*" cried Grandmère Ducros, "*formez vos bataillons. . . .*"

A German sentry shot her where she stood.

The time had obviously come to add the plastic explosive to the fountain-pen.

*

Captain Maurice Buckmaster, Intelligence Officer to 50 Division, left France in June, 1940, by way of Dunkirk. Arrived home, he had a wash, brush-up and shave and started to make his way back to the country he loved. Saint Valéry was his objective. He had finally arrived at Southampton and was about to re-embark when the order came through that no British troops were to return to France—yet. Sadly, Buckmaster rejoined Divisional Headquarters. He spoke German well and French with wit and fluency. He was therefore detailed to interrogate captured *Luftwaffe* pilots, some of whom spoke French well but all of whom spoke German with wit and fluency. They all seemed to regard their incarceration as a purely temporary misfortune, soon to be rectified by the forthcoming and irresistible invasion of the English shore by the victorious armies of the Führer. It was very depressing. He was delighted to be appointed to the position of G.3. (Intelligence) to an interesting and mysterious thing called "Operation Menace", which was concerned with West Africa. With a number of cheerful Royal Marines called "A" Force, he sailed in H.M.S. *Devonshire* in the deceptive direction of Sierra Leone. "Menace" was no longer mysterious and from Freetown he would be nicely placed to accompany General de Gaulle almost at a moment's notice, on the occasion of his forthcoming triumphant entry into Dakar.

H.M.S. *Barham*—"that great hunter"—was to be Divisional H.Q.

French Equatorial Africa had already declared for de Gaulle and, according to reports, Senegal was equally anxious to follow the Cross of Lorraine. As it was also known that a number of German agents had been filtered into Dakar and were hard at work, it was decided to mount an expedition in the utmost secrecy and sail for Africa. A party was held in a Jermyn Street restaurant to celebrate the project and, after a cocktail or two, the excited French officers sat down to dine. When the savoury had been eaten, the senior officer present rapped on the table and the party rose to its feet, raising its glasses.

"*A Dakar!*" cried the host.

"*A Dakar!*" replied the guests in unison, draining their goblets of old brandy.

The waiters were very pleased to see the French gentlemen enjoying themselves and told their friends what a jolly party it had been and where the French gentlemen were going.

Practically nothing had been forgotten. Next morning a French officer in uniform visited a large and crowded London store. He required, he said, a very large French flag, an outsize in *tricolors*. "One big enough to fly over the roofs of Dakar," he explained gaily to the shop assistant. "You know, Dakar in Senegal, West Africa? *Vive de Gaulle!*"

"*Vive de Gaulle*," said the shop assistant, wrapping it up. "Will you take it, sir, or shall I have it sent round to Carlton House Terrace?"

In a blaze of reticence, the expedition put to sea and finally arrived off Dakar where the Axis had leisurely prepared a suitable welcome. After a seventy-two hour exchange of radio exhortations, mines, torpedoes, fifteen-inch shells, bombs and verbal abuse, the invading ships withdrew as General de Gaulle was unwilling to shed the blood of his countrymen. Bitterly, he put about and sailed for Brazzaville where he snatched victory out of defeat. Dakar had been one of those things. . . . He was subsequently followed home by Captain Buckmaster who, having heard a number of shots fired in anger, paced the deck of H.M.S. *Barham* in some disappointment as she lifted her bows to the cooler waters of the Western Approaches.

Buckmaster rejoined 50 Division in Bridgewater in Somerset. On March the 17th, 1941, he travelled to London with his Divisional Commander, who was determined to find him more interesting work. Together they went to the War Office where the General, with all the pertinacity of a vacuum cleaner salesman, knocked on door after door, asking the harassed occupants if they could possibly make use of an alert and intelligent officer who was worthy of higher things. . . . Kindly Saint Patrick whose festival it was, must have smiled on Buckmaster for, towards the end of the afternoon, the importunate pair found a man who knew a man who was urgently seeking a G.S.O.2. to assist in running a thing called the French Section in a mysterious thing called S.O.E. who lived "in the purdah" somewhere near Sherlock Holmes' old house in Baker Street.

After a brief interview in Baker Street, Buckmaster exchanged his six pips for a new pair of crowns and settled down to study what had been happening in France since last he had walked the Boulevards.

By the end of March, 1941, the headquarter staff of the French Section consisted of four persons. Ten hand-picked security-screened dual-nationals were in hard training some-where in Britain and, as soon as their training was complete, these men were to be parachuted into France complete with transmitting sets and explosives. Four of the ten were later considered to be unsuitable for the work and, to their great disappointment, were returned to general service. The six survivors applied themselves with redoubled vigour to the cult of the subversive. They learnt—among more important things —the more subtle uses of weapons and how to place innocent-looking but deadly objects such as explosive match-boxes, fountain-pens and oil-cans where they would do the most damage; they were taught how to pick locks as well as pockets, to forge signatures, derail locomotives, kill men silently. Their primary duty was to instruct the resurgent French in the use of British weapons. They became, *inter alia*, experts in coding, transmitting and receiving morse. They jumped out of aircraft at five hundred feet, buried their parachutes, ran a mile, swam a river, dynamited a bridge, broke for the mountains, slept under a snowy hedge. By May, they were as hard as nails and ready to go.

The first of them—George Noble—took off one dusk before a rising moon. He was to be dropped "blind" somewhere in the vicinity of a large estate belonging to Max H., a staunch friend of Buckmaster's. He was to make his way to the house and pre-sent himself to its owner in his true colours as patriot, commando, saboteur. The risk was frightful. Max H. might be in a con-centration camp or dead. Anything might have happened. But if Max H. were alive and at his home, Buckmaster knew that he could rely on him absolutely.

They drove to a distant airfield in Bedfordshire in the late afternoon. There was a lot of rather nervous hanging about while met. reports were studied. Then the pilot said casually, "O.K. Let's go." George Noble shook hands with Buckmaster, grinned and said, "Well, *au revoir*," and climbed into the aircraft. It fussed to the end of the runway, roared and took off. It circled the airfield and flew eastwards, a dwindling, forlorn speck in a very large and darkening sky. With it went the hopes, the fears and the prayers of the French Section.

Some hours later the aircraft returned. Its pilot reported that his mysterious passenger had jumped cheerfully at the exact spot indicated on the map and this news was relayed to London. Hours of almost intolerable suspense followed. Then, punctually to the minute, George Noble came up by radio on his prearranged wavelength.

"Arrived safely stop met boy friend who sends love stop all well stop ends."

The minute staff went for a badly needed drink. The French Section of the War Office had entered the battle, *cap-à-pie*.

*

England is, above all others, the country of the amateur and the wireless operators, couriers and saboteurs who went to France were therefore amateurs, officers working behind the enemy lines. They had a fine contempt for the professional spy. They were ordinary men and women in so far that they sprang from the ordinary walks of life. The don, the stockbroker, the insurance agent and the shorthand typist practised the anarchist art of industrial destruction side by side. In a single stick of parachutists sailed the monk, the mother, the schoolmaster, the bird-watcher, the doctor, the widow, the anthropologist and the head-waiter. There was no room for the thug, the spiv and the smart-alec and the mesh was a fine one. The selectors went by type and by "feel".

With Falstaff, the selectors looked for spirit rather than muscle in men or women. In a very few cases they were wrong but their instinctive judgment was overwhelmingly right. It was backed by psychiatrists whose opinions were treated with respect. If these mental analysts diagnosed an Œdipus complex, for example, arrangements were made for the agent to be met in France by a motherly soul with whom he could work and who would provide subconscious fulfilment. Other complices catered for—within reason. . . . The job had no special financial reward and volunteers were paid at normal service rates appropriate to their ranks plus the usual emoluments. Field allowance was unexpectedly granted by special Treasury concession. The volunteers came to the firm by a hundred different ways and for many different reasons. Some came from patriotic motives; some were bored with regimental soldiering and sought high adventure; some came for revenge. The best of them came because they saw the struggle as one between light and darkness, freedom and slavery, good and evil.

Most of these ordinary people were extraordinary in some respects. They showed a daring, a patience and a courage that is far beyond praise. They met lonely death by the bullet, the rope or the gas chamber in honourable silence. But while they lived, they showed a strange un-English adaptability to the rhythm of Continental life. It is a truism that the only languages a Briton bothers to speak are oriental. This may be because the vileness of the English climate drives him to the sun, but East of Suez, he is linguistically *chez-lui*. A man whose only possible contribution to European conversation is confined to the pen of the gardener of his aunt, can chatter Swahili, Urdu and Cantonese with disarming fluency. A perfect knowledge of French was an essential qualification for the French Section and it was difficult to find. Later it was realized that a "good sound" knowledge was enough for a few "protected" jobs, provided it was accompanied by a fundamental harmony with French thought. One officer, whose command of French was so rudimentary on his arrival that he had to be hidden for weeks with a dictionary and a battered copy of "*Lettres de mon Moulin*" survived to lead a Maquis team and to win not only their love but the *Croix de Guerre*, the D.S.O. and the *Médaille de la Résistance*.

Poet and wrecker, housewife and pickpocket, architect and nihilist—the members of the French Section were all things to all men. Only to their own consciences were they true— and Odette Sansom was to show herself no less brave than the most courageous of a gallant company.

CHAPTER VI

HOTEL VICTORIA

IN the early spring of 1942, Commander Rodney Slessor, R.N.V.R. went to the microphone and broadcast a talk to the nation He described the recent Combined Operations raid on Bruneval where a radiolocation station had been destroyed and much secret equipment carried back to England. He spoke of the meticulous planning that had preceded the raid and how the men engaged knew the exact topography of the ground long before they dropped from the sky. How could a Commando corporal, who had never been further afield than a Butlin's Holiday Camp, be taught the lie of a foreign land so that he knew every hedge, every incline and every tree? This had been done by photographs and by models. From all sorts of sources, Planning Staff had collected thousands of photographs and fitted them together to make a composite picture of that stretch of coast. After weeks of work, it was found that no picture was available of a few vital yards and it looked as if the whole operation would have to be cancelled. Then an officer in Slessor's own department seemed to remember that his Uncle James had once taken a photograph of his Auntie Mabel there or thereabouts. Was it worth trying? Certainly it was. He was sent some hundreds of miles in a staff car to his home to search for the photograph and, in a faded bundle of those dreary strivings towards immortality called "holiday snaps", he found it. Auntie Mabel reclined in a deck-chair, her feet grotesquely enlarged and her face mercifully concealed by a spotted scarf. But of far greater importance than the somnolent Auntie Mabel, was the background of sand and shingle, captured with unwitting and unwanted clarity by Uncle James. Auntie Mabel was rushed through the night to planning headquarters. No film star in her step-ins, no *débutante* in the *Tatler* and no artist's model in the nude was ever scrutinized with as much eagerness as was the corpulent Auntie Mabel asleep in

C

her deck-chair. By one chance in a million, she had chosen to slumber on the exact spot on the beach of which no other picture existed. Her unconscious contribution to the war effort had been of tremendous importance, for, thanks to her, the mosaic was complete and the proposed Bruneval plan became a top priority operation.

Up and down England, in albums and wallets and hand-bags, must repose thousands of potential Auntie Mabels. In that warm persuasive voice that was a delight to his friends, Slessor invited everybody who had ever been abroad to look over their photographs or postcards and to write to the Admiralty describing them. Photographs should not be sent but des-cribed. The envelope should be marked "Photographs" and sent to "The Admiralty, London, S.W.1."

"I will repeat that," said Slessor. "The envelope should be marked 'Photographs' and sent to 'The Admiralty, London, S.W.1.'"

It is possibly characteristic of Odette that she omitted to put the word "Photographs" on the envelope and that she addressed it carefully to "The War Office, London, W."

*

In her letter, Odette said that she had lived in Boulogne for about four years and that she knew that part of the coast intimately. Her parents were French and she had a few photo-graphs. While realizing, of course, that the information she could give would very likely be already known to the authorities, she would be very pleased if it were thought to be of any value. She was theirs faithfully, Odette Sansom (Mrs.).

Much to her surprise, this vaguely addressed letter not only found its way to the relevant department but produced a reply. Writing from somewhere called "Horse Guards, The War Office," a certain Major Guthrie acknowledged Mrs. Sansom's letter and invited her to call at his office at three o'clock on the following Thursday.

Sober black was obvious *de rigueur* for visits to the War Office and Odette had exactly the right frock, simple, modest and business-like. A wide red belt robbed it of any funereal aspect, and she had, too, a black hat that was the envy of her friends. After a number of enquiries, she found that the "Horse Guards" was the very place where she had once taken the children before the war to show them the motionless, breast-plated troopers, sitting their black chargers in a blaze of scarlet, brass and buckskin. Little had she thought then that she would ever enter those majestic gates "by appointment" to take tea with one of the mysterious demi-gods inside. The magnificent cavalrymen were no longer there alas, and instead she was saluted by a uniformed man in blue who wore a revolver and who asked her to fill up a form stating her name, address and business. On it she wrote briefly that she was expected by Major Guthrie and, with a blend of trepidation and import-ance, followed the messenger upstairs.

Major Guthrie was a man with silver-grey hair and blue eyes. He welcomed Odette and offered her with apology, a cup of luke-warm tea. She searched for a word to describe his manner and found it. He was *paternel*. The conversation was surprisingly easy and ranged from topographical data about the French Coast at first to reminiscence of her girlhood in Amiens and Le Touquet. Odette became aware after a little while that his interest in the extent of her knowledge of the French Coast was in fact perfunctory and she wondered why. The War Office was, of course, well-known for its capricious and inexplicable appointments and she could only suppose that Major Guthrie who—though charming—obviously cared little for things like the town plan of Boulogne, had been light-heartedly pitch-forked into an unfamiliar job. There had been, after all, the famous case of the professor of archaeology who found him-self commanding a Mobile Bath Unit in Madagascar. . . . She found that she was talking a great deal and she saw that he was making notes all the time. He was interested in the most sur-prising things, her address in Somerset, even her paternal grandmother's name. She attempted to bring the conversation back to its original theme by saying firmly that she thought she could make a fairly accurate sketch of the Fish Market in Boulogne. He thanked her politely and said that he thought there must be something of the sort in the files already. She was a little damped. Then he seemed to lose interest in her past in favour of her present.

"Has it occurred to you, Mrs. Sansom, that your knowledge

of France and, of course, of French, might be of use in some job
or other? The War Office might possibly be able to find one
for you."

Odette frowned.

"I'd like to do something. Though I was very happy in
Somerset and I am grateful to every blade of grass there, I
know now that I was—and am—out of things. Almost everybody I know is doing something. But you must remember that
I have three children and they need a lot of looking after."
She paused. "I might be able to give two or three hours a day
and do part-time work. Translations or something."

Major Guthrie considered this suggestion with a slightly
disappointed air.

"Yes," he said, "I quite see. Three children are a considerable responsibility. I expect there are part-time jobs. Let
me send your name along to a chap I know. I can't promise
anything but at least I can act as a sort of post-box. Would you
mind if I did that?"

"No. I'd like you to. I do want to do something. Very much
so."

The more she said it, the more she meant it. She knew that
she could never be completely happy in sitting back during
such times. Being a mother wasn't enough. There was that
debt that she owed to the Somerset fields. . . .

"It was so good of you to come this afternoon, Mrs. Sansom.
Really I am most grateful to you for your help. I'll remember
the . . . er . . . Boulogne Fish Market. And don't worry too
much about not having a war job. After all, three children are
a lot. But I'll send a note to this chap I know."

He saw her to his door. She walked out into teeming
Whitehall and the squealing of starlings. She had an empty
sense of anti-climax. It had been an unusual hour. All that
conversation about the old days, her childhood in France, her
coming to England, the tranquil months in Somerset. Everything seemed strangely unreal and the past, of which she had
spoken so freely, was a shadowy pageant, seen through gauze.
Only the Tippings was real. She hurried home in the dusk.
The children, even the children were out of focus. She went up
to her bedroom and looked at herself in the mirror for a long
time. She was aware of a strange foreboding that she didn't

begin to understand. She shook her head and went downstairs.

The children were very disappointed to learn that the two soldiers on horseback were no longer in the big kennels outside the important building where their mother had actually had tea. But could they now have theirs, please?

With *jam*.

*

On June the 28th, 1942, Odette received another letter from the War Office. It was addressed to "Miss" Odette "Samson", thereby achieving a record of two errors in three words. It came from Room 238, Hotel Victoria, Whitehall and it read:

Dear Madam,

Your name has been passed to me with the suggestion that you possess qualifications and information which may be of value in a phase of the war effort.

If you are available for interview, I should be glad to see you at the above address at 1100 hrs. on Friday, 10th July.

Would you let me know whether you can come or not?

Yours truly,
Selwyn Jepson.
Captain.

*

Hotel Victoria was an enormous building in Northumberland Avenue. Having completed the inevitable form, Odette was taken up to the second floor by a one-armed messenger. The building had been taken over in its entirety by the War Office and khaki abounded in the corridors. The messenger tapped with exaggerated discretion on the door of room 238 and, asking Odette to wait, vanished inside, presumably to consult the occupant as to whether he was officially in or not. Captain Jepson was obviously "at home" for the messenger emerged and, with a conspiratorial wave of his remaining arm, ushered her into a small, bare room. Captain Selwyn Jepson sat alone at a small wooden table in what had once been a single bed-room. Facing the table was a plain wooden chair. There was no other furniture in the room. A dusty wash-basin with tarnished taps was fixed to the wall and there was a communicating door. The general effect of the room was one of utilitarian dreariness.

She took rapid stock of Captain Jepson. He was a neat, dynamic person, dressed, not in uniform as she had expected, but in a grey suit, a soft shirt and a dark blue tie. She noticed that he wore beautiful shoes and that his eyes were remarkably shrewd. He seemed very much out of place in this dusty ex-bedroom. She knew from his letter that he was a Captain. Captain of what? Captains, she thought vaguely, wore uniform and were either in the Army or the Navy but this one didn't look as if he belonged to either. She could only suppose that he was some sort of retired officer who did part-time work for the War Office. That was very likely why he had asked her to call on him, to discuss the part-time work that Major Guthrie had mentioned. He greeted her with a sort of electric absentmindedness, indicated the plain wooden chair and offered a Russian cigarette. She sat down. No, she didn't smoke. He smiled pleasantly and said:

"Well, Mrs. Sansom, what do you feel about this German business?"

His manner made her feel as if he had that moment had the fact of the war drawn to his attention and was feeling a little aggrieved about it. He reminded her a little of a *gourmet* who finds a caterpillar in the salad. She was not quite sure what she was expected to say. He gave her no lead. After a long pause she said lamely that she supposed she felt like everybody else that this was the second time the Germans had been bamboozled into giving way to their latent lust for war and that twice in a lifetime was too much. Suddenly she remembered the recent murder of fifty hostages in Bordeaux. In a moment of clarity, she seemed to hear the stammering of machine-guns and to see the men crumple and stumble and fall.

"I hate them," she said in a strong voice. She stopped. That was silly. One couldn't hate a whole nation. One could only hate the men and the system that had poisoned and perverted a nation. She said: "I mean that I hate Nazis. For the Germans, oddly enough, I have pity." She had put more vigour in her tone than she had meant to show. Englishmen—particularly

the official classes—had a distaste for emotion. But Captain
Jepson was evidently impressed with her answer. He said
carefully:

"I thought you might separate Germans and Nazis. I wonder
why. It was not the Nazis but the Germans who killed your
father."

She blinked. She knew now that Major Guthrie must have
given this man fairly complete information about her. She said
slowly:

"Yes, but they were driven then as they are driven now. I
think the Germans are very obedient and very gullible. Their
tragedy—and Europe's—is that they gladly allow themselves
to be hoodwinked into believing evil to be good. Last October
a German major was shot in Bordeaux. You know that?" He
nodded. "The Nazis took one hundred hostages and shot fifty
of them. You know that too?" Again he nodded. "Well it's
not only because of that that I hate Nazis. It's because theirs is
a humourless creed and a damned creed and because they make
men despoil other people's fields and carry misery and fear
wherever they go. That's why."

He sat at his little table, looking at her sideways. She felt a
little thread of anger that he had provoked her to put into
words thoughts that had hitherto been inarticulate. She was
conscious of a dissatisfaction with herself, a sense of impotence.
It had been strengthened since her interview with Major
Guthrie. She had told herself that war was man's business.
Women certainly put on uniforms and nursed the wounded and
drove lorries. Women even shouted the word "Fire!" when the
Ack-Ack guns had been trained but they were not allowed to
pull the trigger-lanyard. The Geneva Convention, long ago
discarded by the Germans, was quite firm about things like
that. She stirred in her chair.

"I do hate Nazis," she said, and she heard herself saying it
as if there were somebody else sitting on that wooden chair and
speaking. "But it's not much good hating people, just like that.
I'm a woman and I can't do anything about it."

"Yes," he said. "It must be most unsatisfactory for you."
He transferred his gaze to the ceiling. After a moment he said
lazily, casually: "How would you like to go to France and make
things unpleasant for those despoilers of other people's fields?"

There was a long silence. Odette looked at him sharply. His eyes were following a small crack in the ceiling's white-wash with absorbed interest. She lifted one hand and shrugged helplessly. She said:

"Go to France! How can one go to France?" She suddenly found his casual air irritating and divorced from the reality of war. If this man in the beautiful shoes couldn't realize the fact of the fifty dead men of Bordeaux, she could. She said with a film of ice over her words: "You may or may not be aware that the Germans have conquered France and that the Channel boats are no longer running. I understood from Major Guthrie that there was a possibility of part-time work. Could you please tell me about that?"

He transferred his gaze from the ceiling to one of the tarnished taps.

"There are ways of going to France other than by the Golden Arrow, Mrs. Sansom."

She was at once aware that the whole tenor of the conversation had changed. She looked at him with narrowed eyes. She said:

"You mean that the War Office can send people to France—in spite of the Germans?" She knew that that wasn't what she had meant to say. She had meant to get back to the practical question of the part-time job.

"The *War* Office!" Captain Jepson seemed a little shocked. "I said nothing about the *War Office* sending people to France. I said that there are ways of going. The War Office is far too respectable an institution to dabble in that sort of thing. It's true that they let me use this room sometimes"—he looked around it with distaste—"but there the matter more or less ends. More or less. Never mind how these things are arranged, Mrs. Sansom. Accept the fact that a journey to France *could* be arranged and tell me how the idea appeals to you."

"It doesn't appeal to me at all. Let me tell you—unless you know already, which is likely—that I am the mother of three children."

"Yes," he said. "Three daughters. Françoise, Lily and Marianne." He began to talk to her about France. He spoke with knowledge and with affection as of a country for which he cared deeply. He led easily from Baudelaire to the Bistro, from

Pau to Pétain. Did it happen that she remembered the Stavisky affair? "That was in the early thirties and"—he said kindly—"you were only a child then." The Stavisky business was as significant in its own way as the Dreyfus affair. The latter had very nearly split the rock of the French Army and the Stavisky scandal had been symptomatic of widespread State corruption. How came it, he asked her, that France, the fountain of all military genius, could collapse after a few days of battle and then stand by, beaten and bewildered, while the traditional enemy ravaged her cities, her fields and her vineyards? It was fatally easy to over-simplify but surely a new social class had sprung up between the wars, an industrial plutocracy without conscience, nationality or loyalty. Let him put at least one *point de vue*, that it was to this moneyed group, this castrated *cartel*, that France owed her downfall. Long before German Panzers crossed the Maas, this group had been toadying to the enemy, and, softly smiling, had sapped the vigour from the muscles of their countrymen. In war, there can be no political compromise and yet the leaders of France had sought one. The sequence was clear. The odour of corruption had spread from *cartel* to politician, from politician to commander, from commander to staff, from staff to regiment, from regiment to the *poilu*, shivering in the freezing labyrinth of the Maginot Line. It was no wonder that he broke before the Germans because he no longer could believe either in the integrity or the efficiency of his officers. Even his weapons were suspect.

"*Quelle débâcle*," said Captain Jepson, "*Quelle jolie débâcle!*"

Now, though the *collaborateurs* still fawned on Abetz in his ludicrous Parisian *Salon*, the situation in France was a very different one. The French people, gulled into the belief that the soldiers of the Third Reich were steely-eyed Nordic supermen, merely found them on closer inspection, to be a collection of humourless bores. One could forgive them anything but that. The tight-lipped, consciously-scowling, heel-clicking morons who barked "*Heil Hitler*" at each other were as dreary as the furtive little sentimentalists who shuffled along to the brothels and showed the scornful prostitutes photographs of Gretchen and Fritzi at home in Frankfurt. Sitting in their *ersatz* underwear on harlot's beds, they wept for Erika or Erna or Mutti. They wanted so very badly to be loved. The Nazis

c*

were neither terrible nor even interesting. They were bores—
and even though they had the power to summon up a firing
squad and kill Frenchmen—they were still bores.

He smiled. He scribbled something on a piece of paper and
showed it to her.

"You know the *Place Blanche* in Paris, in Montmartre?"

"Of course."

"On the day before the Germans marched in, somebody put
up a huge notice in the *Place Blanche*. This is how it read:

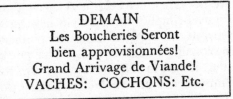

DEMAIN
Les Boucheries Seront
bien approvisionnées!
Grand Arrivage de Viande!
VACHES: COCHONS: Etc.

"It stayed up for weeks. Every street arab in Paris came to
look and to grin and the Germans wondered ponderously what
they were laughing at." His face hardened.

Slowly and surely, the French had acquired a contempt for
their conquerors and, on the heels of this contempt, a determination to cleanse the soil of France of their presence. But
one could not fight steel with flesh; petrol conquered blood;
the jack-knife was a poor weapon against the sub-machine gun.
Resentment was not enough.

"This is where people like you come in, Mrs. Sansom," said
Captain Jepson. "People who know and love France, people
who can move about freely and not be noticed."

In France now, there was an organization of British officers,
men and women, working in the closest collaboration with the
French patriots. It had various names, various alphabetical
formulæ but, for simplicity's sake, it was called "the Firm".
The primary business of the firm was to organize and train a
secret army in France, to supply this army with weapons—
British weapons—and to teach it how to use them—*when the
time came*. Half its work, he said wryly, was to curb the
impetuousness of the French. The Firm had many other activities, with the details of which he would not bother her just now.
It planned and carried out sabotage; it kept a line of communication open with England; it diverted Nazi divisions and

caused headaches to the Gestapo. It was a very enterprising Firm and its members were carefully chosen. Jepson looked at her gravely. Gone was the dilettante. His lightness had vanished and he spoke very seriously.

The job was dangerous, very dangerous. It would be dishonest of him not to tell her that. To use the official phraseology some of the people who went out "failed to return". Of all the dangerous jobs created by modern war, this one was as perilous as any. Would she please realize that?

"You see what I am trying to tell you." He returned at last to the point from which he had started. "My view is that you could be of very great value to us. I do not say that because of your more obvious qualifications but because of the singleness of purpose which I believe you to possess. Twice in your lifetime your country has been invaded and gutted like a fish. I believe that you know the soft spots in the German soul both by reason and by instinct; I believe that you see more clearly than most people that this is not a war of one country's soldiers against another country's soldiers but a war against the powers of darkness. All that I believe."

Odette took a deep breath. She said:

"Captain Jepson, you must know that I am a very simple, ordinary woman. Believe me, I am not very intelligent or well-informed. I do not know about politics or governments or movements. You spoke of Stavisky and Dreyfus. They are names to me, without political significance. I know little of the Germans—only that their acts and their minds have been deliberately made evil and not good in our world. For the rest, my father was a soldier. I am a housewife and as good a mother as I can make myself. Sometimes that's not very good, I'm afraid. Frankly, I don't think I'm the right sort of person to undertake this work."

He smiled. "Possibly not—but I think you are. If you came to us for a period of training, we—you, I and my colleagues—would know for certain. You would have to decide in the first place that you wanted to go through with it but even that would not be final. You could still back out, retire gracefully, *after* training. The Firm only takes volunteers, no matter what the job is. I want you to make a free choice, having worked it out for yourself *and by yourself*. You see, you won't be able to discuss it with anybody. It would be silly to talk to you about what is called 'Security'. But what that word 'security' means is that this business, and every single person concerned in it, is just about as secret as anything can be. For God's sake, and I never take the name of God lightly, keep it so."

"You may rely on me to do that. But . . . but I think the answer will be 'no'."

"I'm not asking you to say 'yes' or 'no' yet. There is no hurry." He looked at her with understanding and without disappointment. "It isn't a matter to decide in a moment. It's a big thing."

"Yes," she said absently. "It's a big thing."

Her eyes sought the single window through which all she could see was an angular iron staircase zig-zagging down a blank wall of sooty brick. It was a queer, squalid little room in which to be faced with such a momentous question. He had said that there was no hurry. No hurry—within reason, of course. . . . The war was at its bitterest. She tried to see the whole fight and to visualize its urgency through what she had read in *The Times* that morning. The headlines came back with difficulty. "*Successful raid against Rommel in the Western Desert. . . .*" But Rommel stood at the gates of Egypt, his Afrika Korps stimulated by victory, and one didn't defeat a triumphant army by raids. "*Russians fighting back on the Don . . . . Timoshenko's left flank pressed back. . . .*" "*Paratroops in Sind, R.A.F. attack in Burma. Pétain issues new decree. . . . .*"

What place had she, the mother of three children, against this bloody backcloth? She said, for no reason at all:

"I don't see how I could possibly hide what I was doing."

Selwyn Jepson's face showed no surprise at this remark. He said casually:

"As far as your children and friends are concerned, you would simply be joining an organization called the F.A.N.Y. Corps, an admirable body of ladies who drive senior officers about, and, in divers ways, make themselves useful. F.A.N.Y. by the way, stands for 'First Aid Nursing Yeomanry' and many are called but few are chosen. In our particular section, even fewer."

"When would you want me to go?" she asked slowly. "Not that I mean to," she added at once.

"Oh not for some time. There would be a longish period of training because, as you can well imagine, there's a lot to learn. You wouldn't go until we—and you—were absolutely sure that you were as fully equipped as you could be, technically, physically and mentally."

She stood up. He saw her out of the ridiculous room and walked beside her along the dark passage to the lift. It was all very bleak and inhuman and . . . and unhelpful. In a way she was glad of that. It would have been far more difficult to say "no" in surroundings other than these. The rickety stale-smelling lift came to a stop and the doors opened. She turned to Selwyn Jepson and held out her hand.

"Thank you for seeing me," she said. "I think—I think I shall say 'no'."

"Well, we'll see. Thank you so much for coming." He gave her a slip of paper and she glanced at it. It was a telephone number, a Welbeck number she noticed with detachment. She put it in her bag. He said:

"You'll ring me up sometime, won't you?"

"Oh yes. I'll do that. Good-bye, Captain Jepson."

"*Au revoir*, Mrs. Sansom," he said with a smile.

*

Selwyn Jepson walked back to Room 238. From the drawer of the wooden table he took a sheet of paper on which had been neatly typed a most surprising number of details about Odette Sansom (Mrs.). On it were given the date and place of her birth, the names of her more recent ancestors, where she had been educated, where she had lived. Everything was there—except possibly her size in gloves and the shade of her lipstick. Jepson could, if necessary, have supplied these with reasonable accuracy. On the top left hand corner of the sheet was scribbled a laconic hieroglyphic. This indicated that the sleuths whose business it was to enquire into the integrity of the individual had satisfied themselves that Mrs. Sansom was in every way, a desirable person.

For a long time Jepson gazed at the angular fire-escape. Then he sat down and wrote carefully at the bottom of the typed sheet.

"Direct-minded and courageous. God help the Nazis if we can get her near enough to them. S.J."

He folded the sheet of paper and put it in his pocket. He looked round Room 238. It was as bare as a cell. He put his hat on his head and went down in the lift and took a bus to the place where the work of the Firm was really done.

*

When she got home, Lily said in her bath:
"What did they want you for, Mummy?"
Looking away into the steam, Odette told Lily the first lie she had ever told her daughter in her life. She said vaguely:
"They actually didn't want me at all. They mixed my name up with somebody else's. Silly of them, wasn't it?"
"Is the War Office always silly?"
"No. Not always."

*

She put them to bed, read them a story, put the light out. They wanted her to sing and so she sang a song that she had known all her life.

> *"Sur le pont d'Avignon*
> *L'on y danse, l'on y danse;*
> *Sur le pont d'Avignon*
> *L'on y danse, tout en rond. . . ."*

There could be no question of leaving them to go to France. Even to contemplate such a thing was sheer madness.

*

From her bedroom window she could see the blue-white shafts of searchlights probing the spring sky. She watched them sweep and cross that night, become tangled in bright geometry, sort themselves out, dust the clouds, flick off, climb the sky once more, slide across the stars. With bitterness and with pain, she remembered the greengrocer of West Kensington and the two pounds of tomatoes. She remembered the coalman from

Fulham. She remembered the sound of the lark over the Tippings and the sound of Devon Red heifers tugging grass. She remembered the sight of wet blackberries and the great galleons of cloud that breasted Culmstock Beacon. It was a good and a wholesome friendship that had been given to her by Mr. Strawbridge, by Mrs. Fisher and by Mrs. Marshall—and it had been given to a foreigner, to one of the people who had let England down. A bag of liquorice-all-sorts or two pounds of tomatoes—which stood for England? Her children slept peacefully in the next room. But she was not the only mother in the world. Other women had children whom they loved. Without realizing what she was doing, she balanced her own Françoise, Lily and Marianne against all the bewildered, homeless children of Europe. There were so many of them, already so many. Yet how many more would there be before this awful thunderstorm of war had passed?

> *"On ne danse plus sur le pont,*
> *Le pont est cassé*
> *Les danseurs s'en vont. . . ."*

*

Sometime before dawn, she woke up breathlessly and with a scurrying heart. She thought for a terrible moment that she wasn't Mrs. Sansom any more but Mademoiselle Brailly. She was utterly alone, she had no children and she was walking blindly along the edge of the Normandy cliffs into a monstrous darkness.

Then her heart quietened and in the silence she found that she knew with certainty what her answer would be. It was a very plain, simple answer and one which she would be proud to give.

The searchlights were still busy about the last of the night sky, spreading the delicate tapestry of war over the unsleeping earth. But they seemed to have changed. It was queer. Then she knew that they, the searchlights, were the same. It was she who had changed. She had become their comrade and she could claim kinship with them now. She and they were part of the war. She said aloud, speaking in the silence of her bedroom, as if she were saying a prayer:

"And with all my strength."

CHAPTER VII

THE SORCERER OF BAKER STREET

Some months had passed since that Feast of Saint Patrick when the then Captain Buckmaster had first found his way to Baker Street. In September, 1941, he was appointed head of the French Section, still retaining his new rank of Major. In six months, the Headquarter staff had more than doubled. Satisfactory liaison had been established with discreet officers in the Air Ministry and the Admiralty and with a number of other interested persons. Though still empirical, the Firm was very much of a going concern as once-fluid policy was slowly canalized to drive the intricate machine. The need was for facts and, to get them, a headquarter staff officer slipped in and out of France, bringing back an exhaustive and detailed report on men and conditions and morale. He was a burly, muscular figure whose voice was a delight to hear and, for this mission and other work, he was awarded the M.B.E., the first of a galaxy of decorations to be given to members of the Firm. For obvious reasons, the official citation was guarded. Later on, he was to take part in the Dieppe landing, to go to North Africa, to squeeze the juice out of Corsica and to launch his genial bulk into the South of France. He survived the war to die casually as the result of a car accident on a German road, a matter of great grief to his host of friends.

There was another member of the "chairborne troops" who had a curious history. French liaison officer to a British regiment, he was captured at Dunkirk and, a sick man, was contemptuously demobilized by the Germans and sent home. Little did they know the quality of the person they dismissed to mind the pigs and tend the vineyard. This man got out of France and into Spain on the grounds that he was going to Brazil via Portugal for his health. He went there, waited on board in Rio de Janeiro harbour for the vessel's turn-round and returned airily to Lisbon—and to London. There he swam into

the S.O.E. net and was trained and sent to France by Lysander
to contact George Noble. The Gestapo picked up his echoes
and snatched. He went to prison. Desperately ill, he was
crudely operated on and, struggling out of the painful mists of
anæsthesia, realized that he was temporarily unguarded. Sick
as he was he stumbled out of hospital and over the fearful steeps
of the Pyrenees to Spain. Somehow he failed to die. Followed
a nightmare in Miranda Prison, herded with cut-throats and
thieves, with release at last and a swift flight to Britain.
He reported back to Baker Street, patient, apologetic, gentle,
still full of guts. He became Operations Officer and,
though he had to live on milk and biscuits, he was at once
an inspiration and an example to every single member of
the Firm.

A *soi-disant* civilian's was the task of pin-pointing targets
for subsequent destruction and of briefing men on their
way to the field as to the most advantageous spot in which
to secrete their plastic explosive. This character was a
Chartered Accountant by profession and he was also responsible for seeing that the agent in the field was liberally
supplied with the appropriate currency. With all the guile
of a snake-charmer, he coaxed hundreds of thousands of
francs from the most infertile sources and arranged for
their profitable distribution elsewhere. A meticulous worker,
he was held in deep respect for the soundness of his judgment
and in affection for the human understanding that illuminated it.

Cool, competent, analytical, Vera Atkin's duties were
multifarious. It was her business to brief agents with up-to-
the-minute regulations governing rationing, travel and work
in France. Data flowed in to her desk from sources official and
unofficial. She was the provider of French tailors' tabs to
English suits, bogus visiting cards for bogus commercial
travellers, suitable photographs of imaginary husbands or
wives. When she wrote a minute, the words were a neat little
row of scalpels and these *billets aigres-doux* were presented with
a smile as remote as it was seraphic.

These people and a number of others ran the Baker Street
office. Most of them had been in the field. All of them smoked
Gauloises for preference and knew their way around le Métro.

Already a number of persons had followed George Noble into France.

Some twenty volunteers were active in the field and others were in hard training. They had gone by various ways. Some— like Noble—had parachuted "blind". Others had jumped into known territory and had been met, not by brass bands and red carpets, but by eager patriots with pocket-torches. Captain Harry Rée was one of them, a man of matchless courage and gaiety. He shot and fought his way out of one Gestapo trap, taking with him two bullets near the lung but leaving behind his teeth marks on a Gestapo man's nose. For this, he was awarded the O.B.E. (Civil Division) as it was not officially considered that his action had been performed in "the face of the enemy". The Gestapo man, fingering his bandaged nose, sourly disagreed with this official view. . . . Harry also won the D.S.O. and the affection of everybody—French and British alike—who came within the radius of his energy and his laughter. Others had been taken to Gibraltar and thence spirited away either by submarine or by *felucca* to paddle ashore in canoes and land in one or other of the little unfrequented bays of the *Côte d'Azur*. In one or two cases, men had flown out in the comparative comfort of a Lysander and come down to step into the moonlight of French fields. Captain "Benny" Cowburn, M.C.—smiling, drawling Yorkshireman—with an effrontery only equalled by his disregard of danger, had gone and brought back an imposing list of oil-installations. He then left again for France to arrange that they should be suitably dealt with when the time came. This Lysander method was used sparingly. Any operation that required an aircraft actually to touch down was both dangerous and difficult and called for the most complicated human planning as well as for the luck of the weather.

The traffic had to be two-way and every officer was issued, so to speak, with a return ticket which—unlike those issued by British Railways—was transferable. The way home was a more serious problem than the way out. The parachute was obviously excluded. On the other hand, the same Lysander that brought people out could bring other people back. The submarine and the *felucca* could usually accept a passenger or two on the return trip to Gibraltar and for the strong, the determined or the

desperate, neutral Spain and a token, terrible term of imprisonment always lay beyond the back-breaking ramparts of the
Pyrenees.

*

Mutual confidence and mutual understanding were absolutely
essential between the Headquarter staff and the men in the
field. Without this sense of partnership, this sense of one-ness,
the whole elaborate fabric must collapse and fall into dust and
ruin. Every man held his comrades' life and liberty at the root
of his tongue. The members of the Firm, therefore, were regarded as being responsible adults and were treated as such.
Every mission was completely voluntary. Its difficulties and its
dangers were admitted in advance and discussed freely. The
maximum of information was given and the minimum sup-
pressed. It was then up to the agent to accept the mission or to
refuse it—and there was no sting in the tail. Wireless messages
from the field would, of necessity, be brief and stilted. Only by
intimate knowledge of the mind of the sender could Buckmaster
—tireless catalyst of the Section—read into those truncated
flimsies the real, human experience of hope, anxiety or jubila-
tion—and breathe into his reply a telepathic message of comradeship. As stated in the prospectus of practically every girls'
school "the system of training is based on the psychological
needs of the individual". Each false identity and each fictitious
"cover story" was devised firstly to deceive the Gestapo but
also subtly to link the lonely agent indissolubly with one whom
he knew to be his staunch friend in London.

The administrative offices of the Firm were still in Baker
Street. But, the better to induce essential freedom of movement,
study and speech, the Firm had acquired a more genial hideout in the immediate vicinity of Portman Square. This was
what is known to house-agents as a "luxury apartment". It
had all the attributes of luxury. The architectural mass which
contained it had an imposing entrance, uniformed porters,
carpets as spongy as those of the Plaza cinema, flowers and subdued lighting. There was a lift with gilded gates. At the door of
"Number Six" stood Park, that confidential Cerberus whose
single head invariably nodded a welcome to his friends and who
never forgot a face.

Certain structural alterations had been made to the interior
of "Number Six"—with the result that visitors could be
segregated from other visitors and one could always be shown
out by the tradesmen's entrance, a narrow staircase that leads
one conveniently near to the 53 bus route. Though the
apartment lacked that *de rigueur* fitting, a tiger-skin rug, the true
glory of "Number Six" lay in its bathroom. . . . Many a
British officer shivering in a field in Provence or Aisne or Nord
or Pas de Calais thought with longing and with nostalgia of
that bathroom, for it housed not only a deep, jet-black bath
with constant h. & c. but also that indelicate symbol of Gallic
civilization—a *bidet* the colour of onyx.

*

In November, the Chiefs of Staff decided that the time for
action had come. The French Section had been in existence for
several months, the B.B.C. *"messages personnels"* system had
begun to work, there had been many mysterious comings and
goings, much money had been spent and surely the moment
had arrived for a sort of French Guy Fawkes Night. Sabotage
should begin on the grand scale and all occupied France should
reverberate forthwith. Unoccupied France, on the other hand,
should be left severely alone. The order was passed to Buckmaster and relayed with some misgivings to the men in the
field. It was work for which they had not been fully trained.
These men were primarily organizers and sabotage was merely
their sideline. Still, if the Chiefs of Staff wanted bangs, bangs
would be produced. The Chiefs of Staff put their ears to the
ground and listened with anticipatory smiles.

Nothing happened. Not a single bang came to disturb the
brooding silence of France. Over and over again, Buckmaster
explained that bangs were on the way but that they took time.
One couldn't simply stroll up to a transformer, put a charge in
it, light the fuse and stroll away. Sabotage had become one of
the Twentieth Century arts. It had progressed a long way
since the first anarchist flung the first home-made bomb at the
first gasworks. Its exponents were no longer hairy, social mis-
fits but scientists, chemists and industrial *cognoscenti*. Gun-
powder, scrap-iron and rusty nails had given way to plastics

" BUCK "

Colonel Maurice Buckmaster, O.B.E.
(*Head of The French Section, The War Office* 1941-1945)

and the innocent-looking matchbox of to-day could wreak more havoc in a split second than all the cannon-balls of the Knights of Malta. If the Chiefs of Staff would only be patient for a little while, the men, who were already hard at work organizing and arming the French patriots, would divert their activities towards the production of the desired bangs.

Buckmaster was made aware of doubtings in high places.

In December, these doubtings were violently dispelled. One after another, those oil installations which had been so accurately pin-pointed by the observant Cowburn, went up in flame and smoke. French locomotives cavorted off the rails like intoxicated plough-horses; French fly-wheels went either berserk or sulky; stolid, pompous bridges became unreliable neurotics, signal gantries launched into Saint Vitus' dance, telephone exchanges developed an inexplicable *delirium tremens*. Heavily-laden barges, sailing placidly on calm canals, shuddered momentarily, sprouted elephantine wings, and took to the air, there to disintegrate in thunder. In Lille, cradle of the Resistance, grimy-faced men looked at each other and at the clock as they heard the punctual rumble of falling masonry. It was obvious that a sorcerer was at work somewhere.

The Chiefs of Staff were very much pleased. The Gestapo on the other hand, raced from one smoking desolation to another, took bloody counsel among themselves, and put up smudged lists of names on windy street corners. These were the names of Frenchmen and patriots, who had that day been shot as *"terroristes"* for *"actes de sabotage contre des installations ferroviaires et autres. . . ."*

In spite of all the Gestapo could do, the cacophony of destruction continued. The mysterious sorcerer went on muttering incantations, not over his out-moded cauldrons, but over his files in Baker Street, London, W.1.

*

While the ears of the Chiefs of Staff were being soothed by the lullaby of distant explosions, field reports from itinerant agents were being studied by the realists of Baker Street. From all of them, one fact screamed aloud. It was that the success or failure of every individual operation depended ultimately on

radio communications. Individual operations were, of themselves, of small importance. They only became important when
linked with the grand strategy and scrutinized in relation to it.
The eager organizer could show as much daring and as much
initiative as he liked. He could disable a tank-track factory,
pulverize a million pounds worth of industrial diamonds or
distort signal-boxes to his heart's content—without swift and
regular contact with London, these anti-social acts availed
little or nothing. They might even be embarrassing to London
for the cheerful wrecker could, of necessity, only know conditions and persons in his own restricted area. His machina-
tions were parochial. He could not be expected to see the complete war-map or the potential effect of his plastic explosive on
neighbouring or distant groups. The light-hearted bomb in Antibes might readily dislocate the plans of the General Staff in
Lisieux. London alone saw the whole picture; London alone
conducted the whole orchestra; London alone had the power
to call up the drums to *crescendo*.

The skilful agent recognized this overriding authority and
the importance of his link with it. His first consideration,
therefore, was the safety and comfort of his radio-operator.
Of two dangerous jobs, that of the radio-operator was infinitely
the more perilous. The organizer, the saboteur *en vacances* or
the courier, having been supplied with cleverly forged documents and a water-tight cover story, *might* be able to lie his way
out of trouble; the wireless operator perpetually carried the
tangible evidence of his guilt in his own hands. A *Michelin* map
might be explained away; a transmitting set, never. The plausible agent might be able to bluff his way into liberty; the wireless operator had always to be ready to blast his way either with
a .38, a hand-grenade or what he referred to colloquially as
"stagger juice".

It is unhappily a fact that, on December the 31st, 1941, the
French Section of the War Office had no radio communication
whatsoever with France. The three operators who were known
to have been recently active, had either gone to ground or been
captured or shot. No one knew. From Calais to Cannes and
from Brest to Bale, there was a silence that could be felt. The
French Section bit its nails as the year turned over and lit
candles to the appropriate Saints. Then chiming more jubilantly

than the anthem of cow-bells in *Haute Savoie*, the morse sounders began monotonously to chatter a welcome to the New Year and, by midnight, the Section was in voluble contact with two groups.

"Happy New Year, London," said Occupied France. "Happy New Year."

CHAPTER VIII

"ICI LONDRES. . . ."

THE lonely agent in the field was at first faced with the almost insuperable problem of communication. As the filaments of his web stretched further and further, rapid contact with distant groups became more and more difficult. For reasons of elementary security, the telephone was barred; trains—though reasonably good—were obviously restricted to certain areas and did not penetrate to the remote villages. As well as this, passengers were subject to interrogation as to their destination if they crossed the demarcation line, and what their business was when they got there. Even if one had the temerity to own a motor-car—a dangerous possession at the best of times —the provision of petrol usually involved another nightmare descent into the Black Market. In the early days, the old-fashioned push-bicycle was the only answer and busy agents developed the calves and the stomach muscles of Olympic champions. But as the circuits expanded, the bicycle became wholly inadequate. News that a parachute operation was "on" could only be expected a few hours before it was actually scheduled to take place for the R.A.F. were subject to the vagaries of the weather. How could one inform the interested group—who might readily have their rendezvous eighty or a hundred weary kilometres away—that English bombers would be overhead at moonrise, scanning the ground eagerly for the signal to drop their dangerous, precious cargoes?

The answer was hidden in the ether.

With diffidence, George Noble made a suggestion. It was that Baker Street might tactfully approach the B.B.C. and ask that immaculate corporation to slip some innocent-sounding sentimental phrase into their normal French transmission on the night chosen for the operation. Most of his groups had receiving sets and were regular listeners. When the interested group heard the particular code phrase which Noble would

agree with them beforehand, they would know that the operation was "on" and make the necessary arrangements. If they
didn't hear it, they would simply go home and listen again the
next night and so on until it did come up. To other groups and
to the world at large, the phrase would merely be the message of
the love-lorn to his love, the son to his mother or even that of
the Boojum to the Snark. As long as one or two patriots in
France realized its belligerent significance, it didn't matter if
twenty million other ears were assailed. Let Berlin, Rome and
Tokio listen to their hearts' content. If the scheme worked, it
meant that he, George Noble, could lock up his detested
bicycle for an hour or two and put his feet on the mantelpiece.
Was it worth trying?

It was.

With some *hauteur*, the European Service of the B.B.C. agreed
to transmit the mysterious message and, when the news
bulletin was over, the announcer gave a deprecating cough and
said coldly:

"*Voici un message personnel. Maurice embrasse sa femme Anna.*"

Although he was blithely unaware of it, George Noble was
like the man who first introduced a pair of breeding rabbits
into Australia.

For some months, the B.B.C. had been transmitting perfectly
genuine greetings from exiled men and women in London to
their friends and relations in Europe. These necessarily brief
messages were considered to be of importance for two reasons.
First of all, they relieved natural human anxiety about loved
ones; secondly they forged an invisible link between London
and the enslaved, uniting them in hope. It was now apparent
that they could also be used as a secret cover for operational
orders.

George Noble's first message had worked like a charm. When
the relevant group heard the news that Maurice had very
properly embraced his wife Anna, they made their way to a
certain field, flashed their pocket-torches to the resonant sky,
collected, distributed and hid the dropped containers and made
their way jubilantly home while the Gestapo yawned and suspected nothing. The whole thing was a *succès fou*. What has
happened once can happen twice and again the B.B.C. played
the rôle of Cupid's deceptive messenger. This time the opera-

tion took place in another part of France and was equally successful. It was clear that the idea could have wider application and, as the weeks went by, the number of *emigrés* who wished to salute their families by proxy, increased unaccountably. Sandwiched between authentic salutations, imaginary Frenchmen greeted imaginary wives, fictitious Norwegians greeted non-existent aunts in Oslo, nebulous Austrians kissed the spectral hands of mythical Mizzis in Old Vienna. The Controller of the European Division of the B.B.C. had agreed to co-operate wholeheartedly and his polyglot announcers supported him to the hilt. From Bush House, a Niagara of unrequited love poured into every corner of Europe, Lysanders alighted and departed, parachutes opened, and the Gestapo began to look at the monitor reports and at each other with narrowed eyes. Now the time had come to control and co-ordinate.

Miss Joanna Townsend was the private secretary of the Balkan Editor of the B.B.C. For some time, she had handled an increasing number of personal messages without much knowledge of their source or import. It was therefore a surprise to her when it was suggested to her that she might care to work for, and be paid by, another organization while formally retaining her *status* as a full-time B.B.C. official. If interested in this proposition—which, by the way, was highly confidential —would she attend an interview in Room 238, Hotel Victoria, Whitehall, S.W.1, where the nature of her new duties would be explained to her?

Like Odette, Miss Townsend wrinkled her nose at the tarnished taps and followed with her eyes the course of the angular fire-escape. By the time the interview was over, she had agreed to become a member of the staff of S.O.E. while preserving the fiction that all her loyalty was concentrated on the British Broadcasting Corporation. She was conducted to Baker Street and the various heads of sections were introduced. There she was given an office and a telephone. Her primary duty was to collect the daily crop of personal messages and to collate them. In the afternoon, she made her way to Bush House and, in her rôle of B.B.C. official, presented the various announcers with their relevant transmissions, listening to every single one as it went out, checking for accuracy and volume.

As the last transmissions were made at two o'clock in the morning, Joanna had had a busy day. . . .

*

As the system spread, it became clear that the observant Gestapo no longer believed in the authenticity of Maurice, Françoise, Pierre, Josette, René, Renée, Roger, Desirée and the rest. Because of this, the "personal message" cover was no longer worth keeping and was light-heartedly thrown away. A note of fantasy was introduced instead and the intellectuals of the Sections began to sharpen their wits and their pencils.

"Ici Londres. . . ."

Every night at 7.30 and at 9.15, there was a brief surge of Beethoven's Fifth Symphony from the European Division of the B.B.C. and a buoyant voice spoke to France from an underground studio in Bush House, London.

First came the news headlines, then the news bulletins. Disaster was not disguised nor was triumph over-glorified. By the very fact of its sincerity and its disdain of subterfuge, the voice of London lifted the people of France high above their parochial despair and showed them another world, a world in which mighty forces were gathering for their liberation and for the liberation of all Europe. Then, the strategic story told, the announcer changed both his tone and his theme. He said, with an oddly impersonal air:

"Voici quelques messages personnels."

Shoulders were shrugged helplessly, hands were spread. Up to this moment, the voice of London had spoken with authority and with clarity. But these *messages personnels* were nonsense. *Ils étaient des bêtises.* It was a waste of time to listen to them. Better to switch off the radio before the Boches kicked the door open.

"Le chat a neuf vies," said the announcer distinctly and, having said it, repeated it at dictation speed. *"Le . . . chat . . . a . . . neuf . . . vies."* There would be a pause: and then slowly:

"Bénédictine est une liqueur douce."
"Bén—é—dict—ine . . . est . . . une . . . li—queur . . . douce."
"La vache saute pardessus la lune."
"La . . . vache . . . saute . . . par—dessus . . . la . . . lune."
"Les diables sont verts."
"Les . . . di—ables . . . sont . . . verts."

In the name of God, why should the English take the trouble to inform a prostrate France that the cat had nine lives and that Benedictine was a sweet liqueur. One had known these things all one's life. Who was this nimble cow which jumped over the moon? The devils were green. What devils? Why green? *C'était de la blague.*

To millions of men and women in Paris or Pau, in Metz or Marseille, these fantasies meant nothing. To the informed, they meant much.

To a group of black-faced coal-miners sitting silently round a receiving set in a back room in Lille, the announcement of the cat's longevity meant much. It meant that a British Lysander was going to touch down on a certain carefully-chosen field sometime between 10 and 2 a.m., disgorging Sten-guns, plastics, food and cigarettes. . . .

The fact that the B.B.C. declared Bénédictine to be a sweet liqueur was a matter of importance to a rich exporter of *foie-gras* in Perigueux. Some days ago, he had been approached by an itinerant peddler of first editions who had calmly stated that he was working for the British Government and wished to borrow no less than one million francs until the end of the war. "My friends tell me that you are not only a patriot but a wealthy patriot, Monsieur. My Government will open an account in a London bank in your name and will lodge to your credit the sterling equivalent of a million francs—at to-day's exchange rate of a hundred and seventy-five to the pound," he had said easily. "You are a business man, Monsieur, and you know that the franc must inevitably fall to four or even five hundred to the pound. It would surely be good business—as well as good patriotism—to have this ostrich egg waiting for you in London when the victory is won." The exporter of *foie-gras* saw clearly that there was a considerable profit to be made by a rich and patriotic man. If Germany were to win the war, his savings would either be confiscated or devalued to the point of extinction. Though he would gladly lend the money to the British Government for nothing, it would still be a pleasant thing to know that a million francs—at a hundred and seventy-five to the pound!—were tucked away, not in his wife's whalebone stays but in London, waiting for the bells of victory to ring. But . . . who was the shabby peddler, who spoke the *argot* of Marseille, to pledge the credit of the British Government?

The shabby man, as if sensing his hesitation, said: "You will agree that it is beyond the power of a travelling hawker of Rabelais to command that the B.B.C. say certain things, Monsieur?"

"Certainly I agree that nobody but a British officer of importance could order the transmissions of the B.B.C."

"Then choose a phrase, any phrase you please. Tell this phrase to me and to nobody else in the world. I will command the B.B.C. to repeat your phrase in their *messages personnels* for three consecutive nights. If you hear it, if you hear London speak to you personally in code, it will be a sign that I am genuine and that the British Government has lodged the money to your credit. Is it a bargain?"

"It is a bargain."

"Good. What phrase would you like?"

"*Bénédictine est une liqueur douce.*"

"The phrase of an epicure, Monsieur! I will return for the money when you have heard the message repeated three times. On behalf of my Government, thank you. I assure you that your money will be put to good use. And now . . . can I interest you in this uncut edition of Baudelaire?"

Now the *foie-gras* exporter switched off the wireless and went upstairs. He extracted his fortune from his wife's pink stays, counted a million in five thousand franc notes and tucked the rest back into the whalebone. Then he helped himself to a glass of Bénédictine. *Vraiment elle était douce!*

A vine-grower in the Burgundy country nodded with satisfaction when he heard that the cow had jumped over the moon. These bovine antics meant that he and his companions would this very night climb the hill above the most gracious vineyard in France, the vineyard of *Nuits Saint Georges*, and wait for British bombers to thunder across the stars and drop moonlit flowers from their bellies, flowers to whose silken petals would be attached guns, cartridges, wireless sets and chocolate. He drank the health of the gallivanting cow in a glass of his own wine. *Tout était au poil.*

Les diables sont verts.

A prominent silk-spinner in Lyons looked silently at his wife and reached for her hand. He turned the wireless off, hid it in the cellar, came upstairs again. Together the elderly couple walked to the church on the corner. There were candles burning steadily before the statue of Our Lady. Side by side, they knelt to pray and to praise God—for the B.B.C. had just told them that their only son Gérard had successfully crossed the Pyrenees, had survived Spain, had reached London and was marching with de Gaulle under the Cross of Lorraine.

*

From fantasy to surrealism was an easy step.

"*La lune est pleine d'éléphants rouges,*" said London solemnly and the Gestapo scratched their heads and wondered what the moonlight would indeed bring. Two hours before the condenser of a factory in Clermont-Ferrand blew up, the B.B.C. had indelicately announced that "*l'unicorn n'est qu'à moitié cocu.*" The descent from the clouds of two laughing agents, a man and a woman, was heralded by a ringing challenge to Pétain: "*Maréchal—nous voilà!*" Messages became more and more numerous, more and more complex. In the dawn of D-Day, over a hundred and fifty separate messages went out from the French Section alone as the airborne divisions of Bush House joined in the mighty assault on Europe.

*

On at least one joyful occasion, the *messages personnels* took a brief holiday from war to broadcast some very important news to an anxious father. In the early hours of May the 5th, 1943, Mrs. Harry Rée gave birth to a child in Beaconsfield. Before he left to parachute into France, her husband had arranged, with a nice sense of timing, that he would listen to the French transmissions from May the 5th until May the 10th. If the newcomer were a boy, the message would be: "*Clément ressemble à son grand-père;*" if a girl—"*Clémentine ressemble à sa grand'mère.*" Though there was no tradition of twins in the Rée household, the Firm considered it wise to make allowances for any contingency and, in the event of Harry being doubly blessed, the message would be: "*Clément et Clémentine ressemblent à leurs grandparents.*" At that point, the Firm's imagination boggled and left the question of the King's Bounty in abeyance.

Harry found himself in a peasant's farm in the Jura on the evening of May the 5th. Surrounded by villagers who were almost as excited as he was himself, he tuned in to London. The Gestapo were jamming hard that night and, during the news bulletin, the receiving set emitted little other than the wailing of amorous cats. Then, suddenly, as if in honour of the new-born, the din was stilled and, clear as a bell, came the announcement. Mrs. Rée and the B.B.C. had both been punctual.

"*Clémentine ressemble à sa grand'mère. . . .*"

The health and prosperity of Miss Rée were noisily drunk in red wine. Then Harry turned gaily back to the war.

CHAPTER IX

"CELINE"

ABOUT a week after Odette Sansom's first interview with Selwyn Jepson, she telephoned to him at the Welbeck number and said briefly that she would like to accept the post they had discussed. He did not seem in any way surprised and suggested that she called at "Number Six". "Number Six" was one of the Firm's *pieds-à-terre*, he said. He gave her the most minute instructions as to where it was and how to get there. She should ask for Major Buckmaster.

In the meantime, she had looked for and found a convent for the children in Brentwood, Essex. It was called St. Helen's and the nuns belonged to the Sisters of Mercy, a French order. The Reverend Mother was a most kindly person and Sister Gerard, a middle-aged Irishwoman who radiated good sense and benevolence took the children to her heart. They would be happy there during the term time and for the holidays Odette made arrangements for them to stay alternately with Mrs. Clay or with Mrs. Geary, an aunt in London. She had simply told them that she was going into the Forces and it might be that she would be sent away, possibly even as far as Scotland. It was the first parting from the children and she came back to London, sitting alone in the corner of the railway carriage and seeing nothing of the fleeting countryside.

Feeling rather as if she should be wearing a veil, some Chanel No. 5, a dark red rose in her hat and carrying a copy of the *War Cry*, Odette found her way to "Number Six". The subdued elegance of the building impressed her. This was certainly a far more suitable setting for dark adventures than had been the strictly functional walls of Room number 238, Hotel Victoria. . . . She stepped out of the gilded lift and, her heels sinking into the corridor carpet, found the unobtrusive door. With his French accent thick on his tongue, the apple-cheeked Park enquired her business. He did not ask her name—an omission which struck her as being a little odd. She said she had an appointment with Major Buckmaster. In that brief moment she was unaware that Park had mentally added her features to his already extensive photographic library. Thereafter he never failed either to recognize her or to make her welcome.

She was shown into a small partitioned room and Major Buckmaster came to see her at once. He was tall and, on that occasion, in uniform. He greeted her with a sort of controlled nervous energy that had hidden in it somewhere a most engaging solicitousness for her comfort. For most of the time, she was conscious of his austere preoccupation with a cause. She decided after a few minutes that his features were cast in a curiously ecclesiastical mould. The painters of the very early Renaissance had portrayed faces such as his, thin, eager, remote. Then, being a Frenchwoman to her finger-tips, she modified the impression for there was a human liveliness in the heel of his eye, usually kept under strict control both in canvas and in pulpit.

He told her about the French Section and the general nature of the work she would very likely be asked to do. He spoke in French from first to last. At the moment, he imagined that she would be a courier but the specific rôle she would play would depend largely on her reports from school. Jepson had told her that she would have to go to school? It wasn't an ordinary school and there was no geometry mistress. It was hidden away in a country house in the New Forest and there she would be taught a number of queer things. One of them, perhaps the most difficult of all, was the art of assuming a new identity, sometimes at a moment's notice, and assuming it so utterly and so completely that every vestige of one's own personality was lost. She might think that was easy—even rather fun in a way, like dressing-up or playing charades. It was, in fact, extraordinarily difficult—as difficult as the spontaneous construction of the perfect cover-story. The perfect cover-story—or fake life-story—must be full of imperfections. That sounded like a paradox but it wasn't. The cover-story started at one's birth— and nobody could be expected to remember every detail of his or her life since he or she had mewled and puked in his or her nurse's arms. Here came the art of imperfection. Those who

D

answered questions too glibly were, *ipso facto*, under suspicion. The Gestapo were shrewd, trained interrogators and should never be underrated.

"In many ways it's a beastly life," said Major Buckmaster frankly. "It will be physically hard. More than that, it will be mentally exhausting, for you will be living a gigantic lie or series of lies, for months on end. And if you slip up and get caught, we can do little to save you."

"To save me from what?"

He looked at her and shrugged.

"Oh from the usual sickening sort of thing; prison, the firing squad, the rope, the crematorium; from whatever happens to amuse the Gestapo. Jepson told you." He said to her earnestly, "Mrs. Sansom, every single person in the Firm is a volunteer. Every job that we ask anyone to do is a voluntary one. I know from your papers that you have three young children. Now that you know more of what it's all about and what it might involve, wouldn't you like to think it over?"

She shook her head.

"No. My mind is made up."

He smiled. Though neither of them knew it, that first conversation with Odette was to prove the foundations of a life-long friendship. He said: "May I tell you a story?" and she said, "Yes please." She thought how easy it would be to work with people such as this. . . .

There was, he said, a certain British officer who had been working as a saboteur in France for many months. His cover-story was that of an itinerant watchmaker who had been conveniently born in New Caledonia. He had merged himself so completely into his new profession that he actually thought in terms of main-springs, winders and balance staffs. One night he was returning by train to his hide-out in Central France after a sabotage operation in the *Nord*. He had not slept for two nights and he was utterly exhausted. He sat in the corner of a crowded carriage as the blacked-out train jolted through the night. After a little while he fell asleep. While he slept, passengers came and went. At one local station, a German sergeant got in and pushed him roughly and sat down beside him. He stirred and mumbled and went on sleeping. The

German sergeant left the train at the next station. Arrived at his destination, the officer woke up with a start and stumbled blearily on to the platform. A scruffy little man in a beret fell in beside him as he left the station. The British officer tried to shake him off but he went on talking about this terrible war and the shortage of food and the cruel raids of the R.A.F. At last the officer stopped at a lonely street corner and said sharply:

"*Mais enfin, Monsieur, que me voulez-vous?*"

The scruffy little man glanced around him and smiled. He said, speaking lazy, flawless English:

"I just thought that I'd let you know that when a fat lout of a German sergeant pushed you, you said in English, 'I'm so sorry'. That's all." He grinned, pulled off his dirty beret and bowed. "*Au revoir*, Monsieur," he said. That was the end of the story.

Buckmaster laughed. "I only tell you that to show how terribly important it is—and how difficult—to be on one's guard all the time, waking and sleeping. That's why the Gestapo choose to interrogate their prisoners under strong electric lights when the unfortunate people are half asleep. Both these men happened by chance to work in this Section so all was well. We brought the watchmaker home and gave him a badly needed rest. He went out again last week."

He was arranging a party to attend the school in the New Forest, *un groupe féminin*. He hoped the party would be ready to leave in a few days. Every pupil, student, undergraduate, should choose a name, a Christian name, and during the period of training, she would be known only by that name. Now what name would Mrs. Sansom like?

Odette thought for a moment. Her real names were Odette Marie Céline. She said cautiously:

"Would 'Céline' do?"

"Certainly. We haven't got a Céline. For purposes of training, you are simply 'Céline' from now on. Now I'm going to introduce one or two people to you and then turn you over to a very nice woman in the F.A.N.Y's. She'll decide whether you measure up to their standards or not and, if you do, she'll tell you about the Corps and how our Section of it functions. *Au revoir, Céline.*"

She said formally: "*Au revoir, mon Commandant.*"
She was to know him better later.

*

During the next days, Odette was faced again with two
matters which she thought she had left behind at school. One
was the wearing of uniform and the other was her entry into a
community.

If she had thought at all about women in khaki, it had been
with the superficial and inarticulate sympathy of one whose
neck had never known a collar and tie and who was free to wear
her hair on her shoulders. Now she had been to call on Lillywhites
and was herself about to become—temporarily at least—one of
these "Mädchen in Uniform". She wondered how she would
react to the severity of khaki and it was with curiosity that she
looked into the long mirror.

She was startled to realize immediately that a change had
taken place—a change not only in her appearance but in her
attitude to what she could only think of as "the idea of service".
It seemed quite absurd that a yard or two of khaki serge, a belt
and a beret could bring about this mental metamorphosis but
so it was. She was still a Frenchwoman by instinct and, as such,
had a rather more acute perception than most Englishwomen
of the psychological significance of clothes. But this, this
spiritual *volte-face*, had nothing to do with silk, satin or serge.
She frowned. In search of an explanation, she took refuge in
what she had been told about the F.A.N.Y. Corps. She was a
member now, a member of a free and voluntary association of
women who, somehow in thirty odd years of existence, had
managed to build up and to burnish all the more decorous
traditions of a crack cavalry regiment. Things had changed
since 1907 when the foundation members had reported for duty
with their own hunters, turned chargers. Nowadays the
F.A.N.Y. Special Forces were issued, not with snaffles but with
Sten guns, and on active service the hunting boot might, on
occasion, be replaced by the high-heeled shoe. But the same
golden thread of adventure shone in the Corps' fabric. It was
difficult at first for Odette to see where and how this essentially
insular institution fitted into the cosmic sisterhood. It had

seemed to her that a great many Englishwomen wore their evening frocks like Harris tweeds and swung their fans like shooting-sticks; those very few F.A.N.Y's she had met wore their uniform hats like tiaras. But it wasn't only that. It was, she thought with humility, because this Corps had accepted her as one of themselves and had given her, a foreigner, the honour of wearing the uniform of their King.

She left the house to go to "Number Six". She took a bus to Oxford Street and began self-consciously to walk, her unfamiliar respirator slung over her shoulder. As she turned towards Portman Square, two British soldiers in battledress saw her coming and nudged each other and saluted her. It may well have been done in derision of women in uniform; it may have been an ordinary, vulgar attempt at a pick-up; it may have been done with respect, hilarity, duty, contempt or sex-consciousness.

Whatever the cause, Odette blushed to the roots of her hair She wished that the greengrocer of West Kensington had happened to have been passing. . . .

*

In Baker Street a file was started and numbered "S.23". Between its blue covers went every document relating to Sansom (Mrs.), O.M.C. and this number —"S.23"—was to be her permanent reference in the French Section. To a senior F.A.N.Y. officer she yielded up her identity card and received in exchange a small blue certificate of membership of the Regimental Association. This was numbered F.10. Having thus become two numbers as well as one person, Odette left for the New Forest.

The school was unobtrusively guarded by alert soldiery, and identification, both of visitors and of students, was meticulously carried out. Once past the cordon, Odette found a charming and modern country house. From the french windows, a lawn sloped down to an ornamental lake and, beyond the lake, there were deep woods. In this pleasant and tranquil place, she was to learn the arts of deception; the observant staff were to learn about Odette.

She woke up the first morning and listened drowsily to the

little sounds of the country, agreeably varied by the distant clatter of cups in the kitchen. She had been warned that the work was hard and long. It certainly didn't seem like it. . . . A bird flew past her window in a rush of wings and she yawned. Hard and long indeed! It was at that moment that her servant Kennedy knocked on the door and, putting a cup of tea on the floor, informed her sardonically that her presence—in shorts and gym shoes—was required on the tennis court at O-eight hundred hours precisely, please, to start in on a little health-giving P.T. "Thanking you, ma'am."

The performance of P.T. by women was an insular practice which Odette had always regarded with a certain Gallic derision. Like sensible shoes, cold baths and stockingette bloomers, she had attributed a taste for this mortification of the flesh by numbers to the latent streak of masochism in expensively educated English womanhood. She had, she thought with resentment, volunteered to become a secret agent, not a female Channel swimmer. She laced up her gym shoes, drank her tea and morosely made her way to the tennis court.

After some minutes, she became sharply aware of the presence of several muscles, of the existence of which she had hitherto been profoundly ignorant. As she bent, stretched and swung to the *staccato* command of a young Apollo in a white sweater, she developed the Channel Swimmer theme and wondered painfully if it was the intention of the French Section that she should do the breast stroke from Dover to *Cap Gris Nez.* . . .

"Now we'll just have a breather and a few questions, Céline."

It was a vast relief to rest her aching muscles. Odette watched the flapping flight of a wood pigeon across the summer sky——

"Céline!"

With a start she realized that it was she who was being addressed. She said quickly.

"I'm so sorry. Yes?"

"Suppose a big S.S. man came for you, what would you do?"

"Er . . . how big?"

"Very big," said the instructor patiently. "Six feet one inch high and broad in proportion."

Odette considered the problem.

"I would run away in the opposite direction," she said frankly. "As fast as I could."

"Suppose he caught up with you?"

"Then," said Odette, "I would pinch him."

"Oh you'd pinch him, would you? Anything else?"

"I'd pull his hair."

"You'd pinch him and pull his hair. Poor chap. My heart bleeds for him. Ladies, it will be my unwelcome and embarrassing duty to teach you other and less refined methods of disabling would-be masculine aggressors. It comes in a later lesson and I very sincerely hope that you will, in due course, take it in the spirit in which it will be dished up. I have never before had to teach such things to ladies and"—he took a deep breath—"I am very glad indeed that my wife is not here or I'd never hear the last of it. Now then, hands on the hips, feet well apart and trunk sideways bend. To the left—one. . . ."

*

"Céline."

"Yes, sir?"

The lecturer pointed to a uniformed figure on the coloured chart.

"What's this chap and what do his badges of rank mean?"

She frowned. "He's a *Feld-Webel* in the *Luftwaffe* and he's wearing the Iron Cross, Second Class."

"Quite correct. Now tell the Course who this one is."

"That one. He is an Ober-Leutnant in the Panzer Grenadiers and I don't know what his medal ribbons mean. I consider his medal ribbons to be of no importance."

"Your opinion is not shared by the Staff, Céline. I must insist that you pay attention to what we *know* to be of importance. The next lecture is immediately after lunch and deals with elementary map-reading. Two o'clock in this room please."

*

"Céline."

"Yes, sir?"

"Would you tell the course, in your own words, the topographical requirements for a Lysander pick-up?"

"Lysander pick-up—that's an easy one. I would look, sir,

for a flat field with a hard surface and no trees or telegraph posts or ditches or things. The field would have to be at least six hundred yards long and four hundred yards wide. I would arrange for the pick-up to take place *au clair de la lune*."

"It is London who would arrange for the pick-up, Céline," said the lecturer drily. "What is the requirement for a Hudson?"

"Ah, a Hudson. The general requirement is the same as for a Lysander but the field would have to be bigger. Sixteen hundred yards long and eight hundred wide would do."

"Right. Now to-night at nine o'clock, we are going out on a scheme which will involve taking a back-bearing. . . ."

⋆

"Céline."

"Yes, sir?"

"What is the morse sign for the letter 'L'?"

In the sleepy afternoon, she could hear the sound of her servant Kennedy whistling "Alice Blue-gown" in the kitchen.

"The letter 'L'. Let me think. Oh yes. I know. Dot—dash dash—dot."

"Wrong. Think, Céline."

"But it *is* that."

"I regret to have to contradict you. You are prone to be too hasty with your answers. This is a question of fact, not of opinion, and I repeat that you are wrong. Please think again and give me the morse sign for the letter 'L'."

She frowned and then her face cleared.

"Of course. 'L' is dot—dash—dot dot."

"Good. But you must think calmly before you answer. The lives of an aircrew depend on accurate signals. Now I propose to deal with the best method of disposing of a parachute other than by cutting it up into panties for your girl friends. I'm sorry. I mean pyjamas for your boy friends."

⋆

The Sten gun in Odette's hands suddenly became a banging jitter-bug, hosed the target with bullets, subsided. The marker called out. "All on. Three bulls. Next please."

The weeks were strenuous. Most of all Odette liked the free outdoor work. Even the purpose of P.T. became clear to her and if supple muscles were considered to be part of the equipment of a secret agent, well, she would do her best. On the lake, she learnt how to handle a canoe deftly and silently; in the dark forests, she could soon find her way unerringly with only the stars to guide her; she became an expert poacher. She could take a chicken out of a hen house at midnight without a sound or a squawk … and trap, kill and cook a rabbit without the formality of removing the skin. The war was gathering in fury and she was impatient to tread the soil and smell the smell of France and get at the throats of the King's enemies. She had burned her boats and because of this, because of the utter finality of her decision, the unavoidable make-believe of the school irritated her sometimes—with the result that she was apt to be terse and even offhand in her answers. The staff, well trained in the art of observing their fellow creatures, watched her with understanding. At the end of a month, a confidential and top-secret report on Céline was sent to the headquarters of the French Section in Baker Street. It was signed by the Commandant of the Area, and it read:

FULL GENERAL COURSE S.23

Céline has enthusiasm and seems to have absorbed the teaching given on the course. She is, however, impulsive and hasty in her judgments and has not quite the clarity of mind which is desirable in subversive activity.

She seems to have little experience of the outside world. She is excitable and temperamental, although she has a certain determination.

A likeable character and gets on well with most people.

Her main asset is her patriotism and keenness to do something for France; her main weakness is a complete unwillingness to admit that she could ever be wrong.

25.8.42.

Major Buckmaster considered this report very carefully. It was, frankly, disappointing. The "clarity of mind" which Odette was reported to lack was a *sine qua non* for the work he had in view for her. "Hasty in her judgments." That, he should think, was true but it was a failing which could be cured as it very likely sprang from over-eagerness. "Little experience

D*

of the outside world." That, too, was a view of her that he shared. In his conversation with her, she had given him an impression of innocence, almost of ingenuousness. She had retained a child-like quality. Looking at her and talking to her, one had inclined to the ridiculous belief that her three daughters must indeed have been found one very early morning under a cabbage leaf. . . . Few modern mothers gave one this impression. Far from it, alas, he thought sadly, and mused for a moment on contraceptives and cabbages. "Her main weakness is a complete unwillingness to admit that she could ever be wrong." Many years had passed since the Reverend Mother had written: "*Son caractère est très obstiné*" but obviously marriage and maternity had done little to soften that hard streak. But was obstinacy always a fault? What did one look for in a Secret Agent? Which was the more desirable, a spirit of compromise—or a stark, unshakable certainty in the rightness of one's cause and one's behaviour? What was "weakness" in one set of circumstances could readily be "strength" in another. Buckmaster lit and smoked a cigarette. He read the report again. There was only one way to decide. He yawned and stretched. He was very tired but he got into a fast car and drove down to the New Forest.

★

"Well, Céline." He sat on the edge of a table, swinging his legs. "I've had your report."

She said guardedly. "I hope it is satisfactory."

"Not altogether. It's . . . er . . . mixed."

"Oh."

There was a very long silence. Buckmaster said gently:

"I am very much exercised about you, Céline. You see, the work I had planned for you to do is so desperately important and so . . . so interlocking that we can only dare to send people who are cool in their judgment and who have a crystal clarity of mind." He tried to visualize the points in her report and to answer them and to dispel the doubtings in his mind. He went on, speaking with difficulty. "The trouble is that if even one person makes a slip through being impulsive or hasty, the repercussions can be frightful for others of whom he or she may not even have heard. Please don't think this a criticism of

you, Céline. It isn't. I believe you to be single-minded, loyal
and tenacious. But, let's face it, there is the question of this
mercurial temperament of yours which comes out every now
and again like a nettle-rash." He took a deep breath. "Céline,
would you be very disappointed if I were to say 'no'?"

He glanced at her. He was startled to see that her face was
set and as white as a sheet of paper. He stood up and said
quickly:

"Céline, please don't think that——"

"Major Buckmaster, I would never let anybody down."

"That I know," he said absently. "It's very difficult." He
looked for a long time at the angle of the wall, trying to set
his own judgment and his own instinct against a few words
typed by somebody else on a sheet of paper. He became conscious of a determination in her that glowed like a steady fire.
She had what Voltaire called "*le diable au corps*". He said to her
slowly:

"You do want to go to France?"

"Yes."

He lifted one hand, let it fall again. She stood there, white-
faced, bright-eyed, taut as piano wire. He suddenly knew that
he would be abundantly right to back his own judgment.

"All right, Céline. You're in."

She said, a little unsteadily, "Thank you"

*

The despondent Major in service dress waited till the roar
of a Whitley outside had subsided. Then he said:

"Good morning, ladies and gentlemen. Welcome to the P.T.C."
He recited solemnly:

> "*The Sun is shining in the sky*
> *Shining with all his might*
> *And that is odd because this is*
> *The Parachute Training School, Ringway, near Manchester.*"

He coughed. "I may add that Manchester is normally noted
for its inclement weather. Now, ladies and gentlemen, the
mental reaction to one's first parachute jump has been likened

to that of a man who decides to commit suicide by jumping off
the top of the Nelson Column—with the strong possibility that
the attempt will miraculously fail. In Ringway, ladies and
gentlemen, the attempt will *positively fail*. You will float through
the air with the greatest of ease, like daring young men—and
women—on the flying trapeze. As you are listed as 'Specials'
you will be here for a shorter time than most people. During
your stay, you will go through a course of physical hardening
by means of P.T."—Odette heaved a deep sigh—"and you will
make four parachute descents in all, two from a delightful
silent balloon known as 'Bessie' and two from an equally delightful but noisy aircraft known as 'Wimpey'. Most people make
seven, two from the balloon and five from the aircraft and the
management ask me to say how sorry they are that you will be
unjustly deprived of the other three. You will enjoy every
moment of it—in retrospect! The programme for to-day is an
easy one. First you go to the Medical Officer who will take
soundings of your hearts. Then we take you to the pictures
and show you some films. You will see composed parachutists
floating about the clouds in slow motion and you will realize
how laughably simple it is . . . er . . . provided there isn't a
cross-wind and you handle your lift-webs correctly. We then
use up some Government petrol by taking you for a joy-ride in
a Whitley. It is possible that some of you have not flown before
and we want you to see for yourselves how welcoming Mother
Earth can be and how she opens her arms to you, yearningly. . . .
After an excellent lunch, you will visit Tatton Park, the 'D.Z.'
or Dropping Zone, where you will witness a number of intrepid
characters launch themselves into space and descend as gracefully as if they were sitting in a row of suspended armchairs.
That is all I can think of for the moment so, as Lord Haw-Haw
says, 'thank you for your attention'."

Working parades were at seven o'clock in the morning and
included twenty minutes of brisk P.T. The days were filled
with lectures and practice on the training apparatus. Odette
tumbled dutifully on coconut matting, swung on rungs and
dropped through holes.

"Feet and knees pressed tightly together, elbows tucked into
sides, head forced down. Take the shock on both legs and be
ready for that Japanese roll. Go!"

The prospect of parachuting was one of those inevitable things to Odette. If the French Section considered it necessary for her to descend on France from the sky, it was clear that she must first find out how to do it in England. Nobody in her right mind relished the idea of trusting frail flesh and fragile bone to a few yards of silk, some lift-webs and a length of string, but there it was. Her recent conversation with Buckmaster has shaken her considerably and she realized how close a thing it had been. Now she redoubled her efforts and, when she allowed herself to think about the actual, physical process of stepping into the sky, it was with a sense of resigned fatalism. Her object was to get to France and fight the Germans. Parachuting was nothing more than a rather frightening episode that had to be faced on her journey there.

She had been at Ringway for some days and was now considered fit to do her first descent from the balloon. It had been a long strenuous morning and the jump was arranged for the early afternoon. Odette looked forward to it with tremulous equanimity but, at the moment she was very tired and she had a slight headache. The instructor glanced at his watch and decided that there was time for one more practice jump from the built-up model Whitley. It was a fall of about eight feet. He said briskly:

"We'll just have one more jump before we break off. Now don't forget to keep those knees together, Céline."

She said:

"May I be excused from this one? I've done several this morning and I particularly want to be fresh for this afternoon."

"Be excused? That's a word we don't welcome at Ringway. You've been doing very well and this is the last jump. Have a crack at it, ma'am. Up the ladder and out—and press the elbows well in. Go."

Odette ran up the ladder and along the fusilage to the hole. She swung her legs over the edge, tucked her head down and jumped. She felt a smashing blow in the face, and as her feet hit the mat, an excruciating spear of pain slid from her right ankle to her knee. She must have hit the side of the hole and she felt sick and dazed. She winced and stood up and tried to put her weight on her right foot. Her ankle crumpled under her in a surge of pain. Leaning giddily on the instructor, she hobbled to the Medical Inspection Room. The young R.A.F. doctor examined her swiftly. Things of this sort were his normal daily routine and he gave an immediate diagnosis.

"Concussion and sprain. You may even have cracked a metatarsal but I don't think so. I'll arrange for an X-ray and, in the meantime, you can give up the idea of jumping for several days." He grinned. "Disappointed?"

"Yes," said Odette. "I suppose so." The walls of the room were behaving oddly, advancing and receding.

"Do you know," said the doctor, "it's an extraordinary thing but I actually believe that you are!"

*

Examination in London showed that the metatarsal was uninjured but the blow in the face had temporarily closed up one eye. She was sent to the Ophthalmic Hospital for treatment for severe ocular lesions. When she was reasonably well again, she reported back to Buckmaster. He welcomed her warmly and with rare tact, omitted to make any reference to her bruised face. He asked her if she was willing to go back to Ringway and complete her parachute training.

She shrugged.

"Certainly, if you think it necessary. I don't *want* to go again because it's uncomfortable and tiring and indeed a bit frightening. But if I am to land in France by parachute, then of course I must return to Ringway."

He was watching her very carefully. He said:

"How would it be if we sent you by submarine?"

She smiled faintly.

"That's like parachuting in reverse. I don't suppose I should like travelling in a little metal box under the sea any better than I would dropping down from the sky clutching a silk umbrella. But again, if that's the way you want me to go, I'm quite prepared to risk the claustrophobia."

He laughed.

"It's all right. Don't worry. We'll try to avoid parachutes and submarines. When can you be ready to leave?"

She touched her face delicately.

"I'd like two or three days rest so that this can heal up. I

"MARECHAL—NOUS VOILA!"

British agents and arms drop to resurgent France

can't think that it would be a good thing for me to go to France looking as if I'd been in a fight already—even a purely domestic one! And, if possible, I'd very much like to see the children again."

"Of course you would. Well, we'll get busy on tying up the ends of your cover-story and getting your identity cards and so forth while you skip off and have a few days leave. Could you be here again on Monday morning? Then we can have a talk and give you your papers and final instructions."

"Yes, I can easily do that." She hesitated and looked away. "I assume that I should say 'good-bye' to the children for good this time?"

"Not for good but at least for a time. You may not see them again for some months."

"I see. I shall tell them that . . . that I've been ordered to Scotland."

"Yes. Do that. And there is one more thing. 'Céline' is dead. That charming, wilful, capricious, obstinate young woman died the day you left Ringway and has been cremated. Her ashes were scattered over Manchester. R.I.P. Oddly enough, another young woman of the same shape, features and colouring but one with a more amenable character, has taken her place. The operational name of this new young woman is 'Lise'. In the field, she will no doubt have a number of aliases but here, in the office, she is 'Lise'—henceforth and for ever more.'

Odette smiled. She said:

"*Bien, mon Commandant. Je m'appelle Lise.*"

"*Et je m'appelle 'Buck'.*"

"*Au revoir, Buck.*"

"*Au revoir, Lise.*"

CHAPTER X

DESTINATION: AUXERRE

"Good-bye, Françoise. Look after Lily."

"Of course. You will write to us, won't you, Mummy?"

"Yes. I'll write. Good-bye, Lily. Look after Marianne."

"I will, Mummy, where are you going to?"

"A place called Scotland. Good-bye, Marianne. You'll look after Françoise and Lily for me, won't you?"

"Yes, Mummy. Where's Scotland?"

"It's a long way away, Marianne. And you'll all be good girls until I come back."

"When *are* you coming back, Mummy?"

"As soon as I can."

"Are you going to the war, Mummy?"

"Yes, I'm going to the war. But I'll try to come back soon."

"Promise, Mummy."

"I promise. I'll come back from the war as soon as I can."

*

Odette reported on Monday morning at "Number Six". Park greeted her with lightning recognition. She talked for a little while to the Operations Officer and then he and she went into Buckmaster's office. He said to her:

"Well, Lise, tell us your life story."

"My real one," she asked, "or the one you've given me?"

"The one we've given you. Try to imagine that we two are Gestapo men and that we've pulled you in for interrogation. Take your time and do it in your own words."

She began carefully.

"My name is Odette Metayer and I am a widow. I was born in Dunkirk on the 28th of April, 1912. Both my parents were French. My father's name was Gustav Bédigis, and he was a bank official, employed at the *Crédit du Nord*, Dunkirk. My mother came from Lille and her maiden name was Yvonne

Lienard. At the beginning of the last war, my father was called up and served with the 52nd Regiment of Infantry. He was killed just about a year before the Armistice at Verdun. My mother then took me to a village near Abbeville and we stayed there for two years. In 1919 we moved to Boulogne-sur-Mer where my mother opened a dressmaking business. When I was nine, I was sent to the Ecole Ste. Thérèse which was a convent. The nuns were *soeurs sécularisées* and I stayed there until I was eighteen."

Odette paused. She realized for the first time what a very skilful story this was. Truth and fiction were blended to a nicety. And then she realized that she must not allow herself mentally to unpick the threads. She must herself believe the story in its entirety and relive it utterly as if it had, in fact, been like this. Suddenly Odette Sansom slid into the skin of Odette Metayer.

She gave Buckmaster a swift, sidelong glance, a glance that was infinitely demure.

"The following year I married Jean Metayer. He was"—she shrugged slightly—"many years older than I was, you understand, but he was a good man and a kind man."

"What did this elderly husband of yours do and where did you live?" said Buckmaster casually.

"He was employed in the Hernu Peron et cie Shipping Agency, *rue du Moulin-à-vapeur* in Boulogne. We lived in an apartment at 73 *Grande Rue*."

"Thank you."

"Two years after I was married, my mother died. I carried on with the dressmaking business for a few months and then I wound it up. I was fortunate to be able to sell my mother's house. In 1936—you will remember, *Messieurs*, that it was a cold winter—my husband died of bronchitis." She gave Buckmaster another flickering glance and touched the corners of her eyes with her handkerchief. "I stayed on for about eighteen months in Boulogne after my husband's death. It was very lonely for me and I was glad when, towards the end of 1937, some very old friends, the family Legrand, persuaded me to live with them. They made *de-luxe* leather goods, handbags and dressing-cases and that sort of thing. In the season they were at Le Touquet and in the winter in Amiens."

"Addresses please."

"In Le Touquet, the shop was called '*Au Scarabée*'. In Amiens, in the Rue Delambre. I forget the number."

"Thank you. What happened then?"

"The war came. I was then in Le Touquet. There were soon a great number of British troops there and I do not know, *Messieurs*, if you have any great acquaintance with British troops, but out of their own country their behaviour is not always very correct. It is less correct than that of the Germans—if a little more gay. You understand me when I remind you that I am a widow—and not yet altogether decrepit. Because of this, because of the presence of these light-hearted and *sportives* English, I considered it desirable to take out an identity card in Le Touquet and this I did. When the Germans advanced into France and the English . . . er . . . left for home, I went to the South with my friends, the same family Legrand, finally settling in St. Raphael."

Buckmaster and his colleague considered this recital for some time in silence. Neither could detect a flaw. At last Buckmaster said:

"I think that's all right, Lise. All the addresses you mention are covered." He opened the S.23 file and took out a sheaf of papers. "Now for practical things. You know how to use a code?" She nodded. "Well this is your code with your own private keyword. You can use this either for radio messages or for letters and the keyword is absolutely your own. It should not be divulged to anyone on God's earth, not even to your radio operator. Learn it thoroughly here on the spot and then return it to me and we'll take care of it. This is your identity card. You should sign your name 'Odette Metayer' here under '*Signature du Titulaire*' and under '*Empreinte digitale*' press two index fingerprints in purple. The top of your fingers should point towards the date of issue and round the stamp. We can even supply the purple ink—and a towel to wipe your fingers on." He laughed. "It's all part of the French Section service, Madame."

Odette looked at her identity card with curiosity. It had been easy enough to tell her cover-story with conviction. But the sight of the actual document gave her something of a shock. There, set out coldly and officially, were the biological details of her masquerade. It was like reading one's own obituary—without the knowledge of peace to come.

CARTE D'IDENTITE No. 1273

Nom:	Metayer.
Prénoms:	Odette
Profession:	Sans.
Nationalité:	Française.
Né le	28 Avril, 1912.
à	Dunkerque.
Département:	Nord.
Domicile:	23, rue St. Jean,
	le Touquet.

SIGNALEMENT

Taille: 1m. 68cm.   *Nez.* { *Dos:* rect Base—Normal
Cheveux: Chatains   { *Dimension:* Moyen.
Barbe: —
Signes Particuliers: *Forme générale du visage:* Ovale.
                                      Teint: Clair.
                                      Signature du Titulaire
                                      Odette Metayer.

Her photograph stared at her from the printed card. It was not a good photograph and her face had the cardboard, hang-dog expression peculiar to such portraits. Her finger-prints were like fine purple etchings. She shivered. She said: "Buck, I don't like it."

"People who are sensitive rarely do," he said. "It isn't odd. I can quite see why. Now here's your ration card. You happened to be in Cannes at the end of December, 1941, and you exchanged your ration card on the 24th. You were then living at the Hotel Pension des Alpes, 15 rue Dizier. Coupons for September have been cut out."

REPUBLIQUE FRANCAISE
RAVITAILLEMENT GENERAL

CARTE INDIVIDUEL D'ALIMENTATION

Département:	Alpes Maritimes.
Commune:	Cannes.
Nom:	Metayer.
Prénoms:	Odette.
Profession:	Sans.
Sexe:	féminin.
Age:	—
Né le:	28 Avril, 1912.
à:	Dunkerque.
Adresse:	15 rue Dizier.
Delivrée:	le 24.12.41.
Signature:	
	Cachet de la Mairie.
No.:	8957.

It was a relief to know that the Phœnix that had arisen from the ashes of Odette Sansom had, at least, a human appetite.

"Now, Lise, I'm going to give you a typewritten copy of your final instructions." He glanced at his watch. "It's a long document and I'll give it to you after lunch. I want you to read it and to study it here in the office and then, like your code conventions, I want you to return it to me. Your identity, and ration cards you can take away with you. Don't be like M.I.5 and leave them outside 'The 400' in a taxi! Your journey to France, by the way, is being arranged and we may have news at any moment. I've got one or two other things to check with you—and to give you. By the way, all these departures are given code names—for R.A.F. and Admin. purposes—and yours happens to have been called 'Operation *CLOTHIER*'. That needn't worry you at the moment." He paused and gave her a long, understanding look. He said slowly:

"There is one matter, Madame Metayer, which you omitted to mention in telling us the story of your life. Have you any children?"

She looked at him for a long time without replying. Then
she said in a low, deliberate voice:

"No, Monsieur. I have no children."

*

Odette left Number Six and walked to the lift. She was
surprised to see that it was stationary at her floor and that the
gate was open. A man was standing inside it, a civilian. For
no reason at all, she had the impression that he was waiting for
her. He murmured an apology, shut the gate and the lift sank
to the ground floor. He followed her out of the building. She
turned left towards Selfridges. At the corner of Oxford Street,
he was still behind her. She walked on, frowning slightly. At
the edge of the pavement, an itinerant photographer squeezed
a bulb and pushed a printed card into her hand, saying something about sending a postal order and six copies, postcard
size. Odette turned into Selfridges, went up in the lift to the
fourth floor, came down again to the basement, walked up the
stairs and made her way out to Orchard Street. She glanced
around. The man from the lift was nowhere to be seen but
he *had* been fairly close when the photograph was taken. He
could very easily have signalled to the photographer on the
kerb. . . .

She went back to the building which housed Number Six and
climbed the back staircase. Park let her in through the kitchen.
She told Buckmaster what had happened. She said at last. "I
don't really suppose there's anything in it at all."

"Possibly not. Have you the card the photographer gave
you?"

"Yes, here it is."

"Fine. We'll see that somebody checks on him. Where are
you living?"

"In Kensington. With my Aunt, Mrs. Geary."

"I think you'd better leave your aunt." He mentioned the
name of a certain hotel in the South-west Three area and asked
her if she knew it. She did. He said, "You'd better go there.
I'll ring them up and tell them you're coming. It's a very
peculiar sort of hotel because you won't be asked to give your name
or sign the visitors' book and, better still, you won't be given

a bill when you leave. Everything's on the house. Just another little bit of the French Section service. There may be nothing at all in what's just happened but you can't be too sure. The curse of it is that we'll never know. The M.I. chaps are human oysters. In the meantime, don't worry. *Au revoir*, Lise."

"*Au revoir*, Buck."

★

Odette read her orders that afternoon.

S.23

16.9.42.

Operation:	"Clothier"
Name in the Field:	"Lise".
Destination:	Auxerre.

FINAL INSTRUCTIONS:

You will leave this country by plane for Gibraltar. You will then be taken by *felucca* to a point on the East of the *Golfe du Lion*, where you will be received by certain members of our organization who will assist you to contact "Raoul". Raoul will give you the latest details as to prevailing conditions and will eventually advise you as to how best to cross the demarcation line to reach Auxerre, which is to be your H.Q.

He will also give you an address at Auxerre and will advise friends there that you are coming, so that they will be prepared to receive you and, since you do not know Auxerre, to help you in establishing yourself.

Before going to Auxerre, you propose to visit friends of yours at St. Raphael (M. Louis Legrand, "Au Scarabée", 2 rue Amiral Baux). In principle, we agree that you should do this but you must first consult the members of our organization who receive you and be advised by them whether to visit M. Legrand or not. If you do contact the family Legrand at St. Raphael and find them, as you believe, to be completely reliable, we will use their address as a post-box for you. In this case, you are to ask the members of our organization to advise us of this. They will use their own means.

When you leave for Auxerre, the only contact you will have

with the organization which received you on the Coast will be normally through a post-box. But in case you get into difficulties and have to make a getaway, you will go back to them.

GENERAL BRIEFING

You have been given details as to your own methods of using passwords and post-boxes and the necessity of observing the rules of security at all times has been impressed upon you. You have also been taught our system of camouflaging addresses and our grid system of map references.

You will have the following means of communicating with us:

1. Through the Legrand post-box at St. Raphael if this proves satisfactory.

2. In the case of reports and general information, these will either be passed to us by our friends in Auxerre via the organization in the South or our friends in Auxerre will give you instructions as to how you may yourself pass reports direct to the organization in the South for onward transmission to us.

3. W.T. (Wireless Telegraphy) communication. When you are well-established in Auxerre, you will leave a competent person in charge there and go to Paris to contact certain people in whom you have confidence (Mme. V., 55 rue R., Paris 17e.). You will ask them to receive a message for you and, if they agree and are trustworthy, you will give them a means of communicating with you in Auxerre. We will then send a courier to this Paris address as from the 15th of December, 1942 and he will leave an envelope for you marked "Mlle. Odette". This message will give you instructions to enable you to contact a W.T. operator in Paris and send direct communications to us. If the courier to Mme. V. finds he is not understood, he will try the same procedure with the patron of a restaurant at 11 bis rue de la Mare, Paris 20e. If he is not understood there either, he will conclude that you have not yet reached Paris. and he will, after waiting exactly one week and then one more week, re-contact both addresses—if all goes smoothly, you should have established your Paris contact by December 15th.

BROAD LINES OF MISSION

Your mission is to establish yourself in Auxerre and to find a flat to which we can send members of our organization who are passing that way or which we can use in any other way which we may consider expedient. You should also recruit a limited number of sound people of either sex to help in your work of forming a small circuit in Auxerre, which it will be possible for us to use in the following ways:

1. In order to supply information regarding local conditions to any new arrivals in the field, and, if necessary, to lodge them.

2. In order to assist anyone, new arrival or otherwise, who may be in difficulties.

3. For purely operational ends, if ever necessity arises. The passwords for the new circuit you will establish will be:

"Connaissez-vous un bon coiffeur par ici?"

Answer: *"Ca dépend de ce que vous voulez dire par 'bon'."*

You have been instructed regarding the way in which these passwords will be used.

While in the field, you will be responsible to and under the direct orders of London H.Q.

Our final advice to you is that you should not rush at this job, as we hope that the Auxerre circuit will be thoroughly reliable and we prefer that you should take longer in establishing yourself and assuring General Security rather than in obtaining quick results which might jeopardize your organization and therefore deprive it of that character of security which will be its main advantage to us.

FINANCE

You will take Frs. 50.000 with you and you will be instructed as to the method of obtaining further sums in France.

*

Odette re-read these instructions from beginning to end, memorizing the various points as she had been trained to do. When the whole picture was clear in her mind, she had a further conversation with Buckmaster.

She was, she said, quite ready to "recruit a limited number of people of either sex", to help her in her work. But there was one point. She was a woman. Whereas it was true that women in France—"as elsewhere," she said with a half smile—were the real fountains of power, it was not considered politic to let men think they were. Because of this, because of the resentment which would certainly be engendered among men, and specially among Frenchmen, if she, a woman, were to give direct orders, she felt very strongly that a man should be the titular head of the circuit.

"Let me find a reliable man," she said, "someone who is honest, trustworthy and simple—I use the word 'simple' in its best sense—and let him give the actual orders. I alone will maintain contact with London and work through him. I'm sure that's wiser."

Buckmaster smiled.

"I can't quite see you as a Twentieth Century female edition of *Père Joseph* but if you think it's better to be a sort of *éminence grise*, I'm quite agreeable. You'll soon get the feel of the local form." He glanced at her left hand. "You've been to Cartier?"

"Yes. They had to file off my old wedding ring. This new one is engraved inside '*A Odette: Paris*, 1930', and mates up with my cover-story." She laughed. "It's the only thing it does mate up with! I must say you are pretty thorough—even to the extent of making me carry round a lie on my wedding ring finger."

"If I were a cynic," said Buckmaster drily, "I would say that the third finger of humanity's left hand should be christened 'Ananias'. Have your clothes been checked?"

"Yes. Every stitch I have on is either French or has a French dressmaker's tab. After all I chose them with the help of a girl who only came out of France a few months ago—via the Pyrenees. I picked a dark grey coat and skirt specially—so as not to show the dirt in prison."

"Do you think you're going to prison, Lise?" he asked seriously.

"I don't know. But it's as well to be prepared."

"Yes, I suppose it is. Now comes the faintly embarrassing moment when I give you your various . . . er . . . weapons. One of these pills will incapacitate your enemy for twenty-four hours by giving him or her a violent stomach ache and its attendant disorders. If you want to feign illness yourself, take one. It won't be comfortable but it'll fool any doctor. All clear?"

"Yes."

"Now these, on the other hand, have the reverse effect. They are stimulants and should only be taken when you're damned tired and have to make a special effort. They are guaranteed to keep you going, mentally and physically, and they work. Don't get them mixed with the tummy-ache ones."

"I won't."

"If you slip one of these little chaps into anyone's coffee, it will knock him out completely for six hours—with no after effects. That's tummy-ache, stimulant and sleep dope. There's only one more, Lise." He held up a little brown sphere, about the size of a pea. "Here it is, your 'L' or 'lethal' tablet. If you get into the sort of jam where there's absolutely no way out, swallow this and you'll be out of the jam permanently—in six seconds. I'm told it's not painful."

She took it with detachment and put it in her bag.

"That's not a very pretty going-away present, I'm afraid, so we've decided to give you another. Here you are, Lise, with love from the French Section."

He gave her a little packet. Wrapped in tissue paper was a most lovely silver compact. She was delighted with it. She said at last:

"When do I go?"

"To-morrow. You are to report to the R.T.O. at Paddington to-morrow morning at half-past ten, dressed, I need hardly say, as a civilian. There you will be met by someone from here, someone whom you know. You are Miss Bédigis, a Civil Servant, and your luggage will be exempt from examination. The escorting officer will take you to an airport, have a final check and kiss you lightly on both cheeks. After that, you may go and you may not. That depends on wind, weather and the R.A.F. In case you do go, lots of luck. If you don't, see you soon. Now is there anything you're not clear about?"

"No. Everything's quite clear. There is one thing I'm going to ask you to do for me."

"Gladly. What is it?"

"My children think I'm going to Scotland and they'll expect to hear from me. Because of that, I've written a whole bundle of letters to them, leaving out any date. If I drop the bundle in here on my way to Paddington, could you post them for me at the rate of one a week until they're all used up?"

"I could and I will of course. Anything else?"

"No. That's all. I'll get back to the hotel now and pack."
She held out her hand. "Good-bye, Buck and thank you."

He said, with that cheerful gleam in the unecclesiastical heel
of his eye, "I can't ask you to send me a postcard saying
'Arrived safely. X marks my bedroom window', but we'll know
all right when you do arrive. *Au revoir*, Lise."

"*Au revoir*, Buck."

CHAPTER XI

ILL BLOWS THE WIND. . . .

Radio message in code, transmitted to RAOUL. To be taken on his schedule at 0500 hrs. G.M.T., 17.9.42.

LISE WILL ARRIVE APPROX. TWENTY-SEVEN REPEAT TWENTY-SEVEN STOP B.B.C. MESSAGE PERSONNEL LES CLOCHERS DE MON PAYS STOP SHE WILL GO TO VILLA DIANA AND ASK FOR BARON DE CARTERET STOP ENDS.

*

The familiar London scene, unrealized and unloved, became infinitely dear to Odette as she travelled that autumn morning to Paddington. It was with a sense of unreality that she saw, through the taxi window, the hitherto unperceived sight of plaster, brick, window and chimney. Her taxi shuddered to a stop and waited while a sedate policeman shepherded a crocodile of school-children across the road. To-morrow the same policeman would hold up the traffic and the same little girls would scuttle from pavement to pavement, on their way to prayers, geometry, geography, French. . . .

J'ai . . . I have	*Nous avons* . . . We have
Tu as . . Thou hast	*Vous avez* . . . You have
Il a . . . He has	*Ils ont* . . . They have

To-morrow the bus conductors would still shout, "Hurry along there, please", in the crowded tubes the porters would intone, "Mind your backs, *if* you please". There were gaps among the houses where the bombs had struck, like missing teeth in a smiling mouth. But the sun shone genially. The shop-keepers of London—fishmongers, butchers and greengrocers—were about their business. Edgware Road was agog. Red, amber, green; stop, wait, go. The barrow boys were doing a roaring trade. Sixpence a bunch lovely violets. . . . Don't forget the kiddies. . . . All London—cheerful during the lull in the bombardment—was rooted in human continuity. It seemed the wildest fantasy that she, Odette Sansom, housewife and mother, was driving through busy streets, with a French identity card, a lethal tablet and fifty thousand francs in her handbag, *en route*, God knew how or when, for an unknown town in Occupied France.

For a reason which she knew but which she could not formulate in words, she stopped the taxi and ran across the pavement and bought a bunch of violets. "Good luck, Miss," said the man. "Good luck."

Royal Oak. . . . Ealing Broadway. . . . Maidenhead. . . . Reading. . . . The grime and the brick of London had turned into little back-gardens with washing blowing in the wind and the back-gardens had become fields with cattle grazing. Swindon was a cloud of blown steam, blotting the sun, Bath a huddle of honey-coloured stone. Bristol. . . .

"We get out here, Lise."

The road to the airport was dappled with sunshine. The Whitley bomber trundled across the tarmac, its propellers swinging lazily.

"Good-bye, Lise. Best of luck."

"Good-bye. Tell Buck not to forget to post my letters to the children."

"I will. Good-bye."

The Whitley taxied to the far end of the airfield, steadied. One after another, each engine surged into eager *crescendo*, died away to a greedy mumbling. The aircraft bumped on to the runway, swung in a half circle, stopped. Odette felt the web belt round her waist and sniffed her violets and tried to peer through the windows. Another aircraft was coming in, skimming fast along the concrete. It seemed as if it were coming straight for the Whitley—and then there was a sudden jolt and a smashing sound. The Whitley slewed to the left and the floor lifted steeply. Like a flash, the pilot cut both engines off and there was a confused shouting. Odette stood up on the sloping floor. Somebody opened the door and she jumped down on to the grass. A rather frightened-looking R.A.F. sergeant said, "You all right, Miss?" and she said, "Yes, I'm all right. What happened?" "That kite just touched your starboard wing, that's all. Might have been a bloody sight worse, Miss, pardon me, but your crate's had it. This way, please. . . ."

*

"Welcome back to London, Lise," said Buckmaster sententiously. "It is better to travel hopefully than to arrive. You'd better go back to your hotel for a day or two while we lay something else on."

*

Radio message in code, transmitted to RAOUL. To be taken on his schedule at 0500 hrs. G.M.T., 19.9.42.

FOR RAOUL:
LISE REPEAT LISE WILL MISS FELUCCA DUE SLIGHT ACCIDENT PLANE STOP ENDS.

*

MOST SECRET.
OPERATION: Clothier.
Amendment for Final Instructions for "Lise".
You will leave this country by Lysander aircraft on a date between 27th of September and 30th of September, 1942. You will be landed at a point already chosen:
5 Kms. N.N.E. of MACON.
3¾ Kms. W.S.W. of MANZIAT.
You will then proceed immediately to:
VILLA DIANA
Route de Fréjus
CANNES
where you will be expected. You will ask for "Baron de Carteret", and then ask to be put into contact with RAOUL, to whom you will give
(a) a message in code
(b) Negative of a microphoto
(c) A small document.
RAOUL will make arrangements for your stay in Cannes whence, after a few days rest and acclimatization, you will proceed to Auxerre and take up the mission given to you in your

General Instructions. Apart from the Frs. 50,000 which you are now carrying, RAOUL has been instructed to give you another Frs. 50,000 and will also help you in getting your October coupons for your ration card.

*

Radio message in code transmitted to RAOUL. To be taken on his schedule at 0500 hrs. G.M.T. Sunday, 27th of September.

FOR RAOUL:

ARE TRYING TO SEND LISE BY LYSANDER IN MACON AREA SUNDAY NIGHT STOP SHE WILL BRING MESSAGE IN JULIEN'S CODE STOP AFTER FEW DAYS REST SEND HER ON TO AUXERRE STOP B.B.C. MESSAGE PERSONNEL WILL BE MIEUX VAUT TARD QUE JAMAIS STOP ENDS.

*

As the Lysander was warming up on its English airfield, London heard that the Gestapo had swooped on the reception committee. Three of Odette's future hosts were already dead, the others awaited interrogation and the firing squad.

Radio message in code transmitted to RAOUL. To be taken on his schedule at 0500 hrs. G.M.T. Monday, 28th of September.

FOR RAOUL:

LISE NOT COMING LYSANDER OWING LAST MINUTE DIFFICULTIES OF RECEPTION COMMITTEE STOP WILL ATTEMPT SEND HER ALTERNATIVE ROUTE AS SOON AS POSSIBLE STOP ENDS.

*

"It's better to travel hopefully than to arrive," said Buckmaster. "Nice to see you in London again."

"You said that last time, Buck."

"Sorry, Lise. So I did. The chaps who were going to meet you have had it. How nice your violets are. Come and have lunch."

*

MOST SECRET.

OPERATION: Clothier.

Second amendment to Final Instructions for "Lise". You

will report to R.T.O's office Paddington at 10 o'clock 5th of
October, prior to catching 10.30 train for Plymouth (North
Road) for Mountbatten Airport. You will proceed by seaplane
to Gibraltar and thence by *felucca* as previously arranged.
This cancels first amendment to your final instructions.

★

In the afternoon a wind blew up from the west and veered
towards the north and carried full, wet-bellied clouds before it.
The Catalina floating in the bay, jibbed and pulled at her
moorings as the waves seethed past and her metal hull rose and
fell, smacking the steep seas. Then the rain came and streamed
over the harbour and beat against the windows in drenching
gusts. The pilot and the navigator smoked incessant, damp
cigarettes and waited for the Met. men to give their final
decision. For hour after hour, Odette sat patiently, drinking
innumerable cups of tea. In her hand, she held a bunch of
violets. It had become a sort of symbol to her, to carry these
scented St. Christophers from English fields. There was a
strange inevitability about her failure to go to France and it
was in no way a surprise to her when an R.A.F. officer came
into the room and announced that the weather had finally
closed in. Gib. was off.

Odette stifled a yawn. "What do we do now?"

"Back to London," said the conducting officer cheerfully.
"Better luck next time, Lise."

★

MOST SECRET. S.23.
OPERATION: Clothier.

Third amendment to Final Instructions for "Lise". You will
report to the R.T.O. at Paddington at 10 a.m. on 10th of
October, travelling under the name of "Odette BEDIGIS", a
Civil Servant, for which necessary documents are attached
You will proceed to REDRUTH in Cornwall where transport
has been arranged to convey you to a hotel and subsequently to
the airport. You will proceed by bomber to Gibraltar and
thence by *felucca* as previously arranged. This cancels first and
second amendments to your final instructions.

"I am beginning to know the way from South Kensington to Paddington rather well," said Odette with a sigh. "Well, I've got an awful feeling that I'll be seeing you all again in a day or two."

*

It was raining in Redruth and there was a high wind. Odette was taken to her hotel and went to her room immediately after dinner. It had been arranged that she should be called at 1 a.m. to take off at 2 and she was advised to get what sleep she could. It was a bare, cheerless little room but it was a pleasant thing to lie in bed and listen to the sound of the wind. Her invariable bunch of violets stood in a tooth-glass by her bed and her suitcase was all ready and packed. She slept dreamlessly and woke up to be given a cup of scalding tea. The weather was no better and she wondered if the aircraft would indeed take off in this wind and rain. She turned down her bed and folded the towel. She looked round the room and shivered. It was a horribly bleak and unfriendly place to say "good-bye" to England in—but then, she thought with a wry smile, she had already said so many unsuccessful good-byes.

She walked out of the hotel into a flurry of rain, drove to the airport with the windscreen wipers clearing segments of the windscreen, reported to the control room. Oh yes, they were definitely going. Would Miss Bédigis mind waiting for a little while? There was a petrol stoppage in the Whitley's starboard engine and the mechanics were working on it while the aircraft's cargo was being stowed. Might be about half-an-hour. Odette waited yawning until well after 3 when a car came to collect her and her fellow passengers and take them to the end of the runway where the Whitley waited.

She climbed aboard. The fuselage was packed high with cargo, there were no seats and very little room. The pilot apologized for what he said was going to be a damned uncomfortable ride. Odette sat on the metal floor, her legs stretched out, leaning against a wooden crate. It was very cold and there was no light. She arranged herself as comfortably as she could and glanced at the bunch of violets in her hand. The metal door slammed and the engines woke up one by one to roar and subside. Then both engines thundered in unison and the

E

Whitley bumped along the runway, gathering speed. It seemed a very long time before they were airborne but they finally left the ground with a lurch. Odette smiled wanly at the woman facing her and closed her eyes. She became aware immediately and with certainty that all was not well. The aircraft was rising and sinking steeply as the pilot tried to gain altitude and there was intermittent shuddering. Her fingers curled tightly round the violets and, almost instinctively, she braced her muscles for the shock—and, in a split second, it came. There was a crash like thunder and the Whitley swooped downwards. A wooden crate slid drunkenly into her lap as the cargo shifted and tumbled and the next second, with a paralyzing jolt, the aircraft hit the earth and surged forward a few yards, and stopped and leaned quickly on one side. Odette stood up shakily. In the darkness someone tried to force the door open but it was jammed fast. She saw the reflection of a light slide along the windows and then the door was wrenched open and a voice shouted. "Get out everyone quickly. She may go on fire." Odette climbed over the littered cargo and jumped down on to the grass in the headlights of an ambulance. It was raining in sheets. She stumbled away from the wreckage and suddenly stopped dead. Not ten yards from the twisted propellers, and a hundred feet below the cliff's edge, the cheated sea was tumultuous in a stormy dawn.

Her bedroom in the hotel was as she had left it three hours before. She put her violets back into the tooth-glass and mechanically unfolded the towel and pulled the top sheet and blankets back over her bed. Though she was physically exhausted her mind was wide-awake and alert. She undressed and got into bed and narrowed her eyes as she looked into the half-light. She knew that she had been within an ace of mutilation and of death. She was very grateful to be alive and there was in her mind, a strange buoyancy. She was going to France, and God, who had taken such good care of her up to now, would surely go on looking after her.

CHAPTER XII

FAIR STANDS THE WIND FOR FRANCE. . . .

"Do you still want to go to France, Lise?"

"Very much so. More than ever, in fact."

She gave Buckmaster a brief, slanting smile. "But if one may make a suggestion in a very small voice, couldn't I go by sea? I seem to have rather a blighting effect on aircraft."

"You *are* going by sea. This country can't afford to write off any more bombers on your behalf. This time we're sending you in a troopship from Gourock to Gibraltar and if you happen to strike a mine or get torpedoed on the way, I haven't the slightest doubt that you'll be discovered in mid-ocean sitting on a hen-coop, clutching a bunch of violets in one hand and paddling indefatigably in the direction of France with the other. I need hardly add that you will be looking as if you had just left the *rue de la Paix* and you will, of course, be wearing silk stockings. . . ."

★

Sunshine and eighteen sorts of sherry; monkeys and mandolins.

A khaki flood poured and spilled down the precipitous streets of Gibraltar and, after the British black-out had settled, Tangier was a necklace of light over the pulsing straits. Beyond the suicidal airstrip where the Defiants landed in danger and dust, the windows of *la Linea* watched unceasingly. "Onward Christian Soldiers" piously wheezed the organ of the garrison church of Gibraltar; *Lili Marlene* gibed the guitars of *la Linea* as the German agents took an hour off from their vigil to relax at the brothels and bull-fights of neutral Spain.

Odette had already spent a restless, incarcerated three days in her Gibraltar hideout when a visitor was announced by her Spanish maid.

"There is an officer to see you, Ma'am. He appears to be

foreign gentleman, he is in naval uniform and he says that his name is 'Jan'."

"Good. I am expecting him. Please show him in."

Jan entered the room. He was young—about twenty-six or seven—slim and very fair. The movements of his body and of his hands were nervously swift. He was tawny and lithe, like a tiger. He bowed with formal feline grace, glanced at her and suddenly frowned.

"Lise?"

"Yes. I am Lise."

"I am Commander of the *felucca Dewucca* and I am ordered to take you to France." He looked at her scowling. He said abruptly. "I must now refuse to carry out this operation."

"Oh! Why?"

"You are a woman. I will not take a woman, a young woman such as you, to this . . . this business. A man—yes. A woman—no. The matter is finished. May I have a drink please?"

"Sherry or whisky?"

"Whisky, please."

"Of course." Odette poured him out some whisky, added a little water. He raised his glass and, after an almost imperceptible glance at her left hand, said: "Your health, Madame. You will possibly permit me to invite you for some dancing when I return to Gibraltar?"

"When you return to Gibraltar," said Odette steadily, "you will already have landed me in France. It is an order of the War Office."

He grinned. "The War Office is very far away, Madame."

His glass was empty. She said: "Have another drink," and he said "Of course. Gladly." She gave him some more whisky and she said:

"It may or may not interest you to know that this is my fifth attempt to go to France. A few days ago, I crashed in a bomber. Now that I have managed to come as far as Gibraltar, I certainly propose to go on. Nothing will stop me. If I have to swim there I shall still go."

"Madame would look most beautiful in a bathing dress."

"I demand that you take me to France."

"All one. I will not take you. I am Polish and I will not take a lady like you in my small and dirty boat. The conditions are bad, very bad. It is no good. All over. When I return, I will invite you for dancing. To travel to France is no good for you but only foolish. I refuse to take you and I spit in the face of the War Office. Finished."

*

It was in the dusk of a late October evening that the *felucca Dewucca* cast off and slid unobtrusively past the sleek submarines, her motor gently throbbing.

Before the war she had been a sardine fisher out of Barcelona and somehow she had made her way to Gibraltar to take up a new and more dangerous trade. She was about forty feet from stem to stern, narrow in the beam and she carried one dirty sail. The galley was a mere hutch on deck and housed a malodorous paraffin stove. More indicative of her unlawful occasions was the depth charge lashed aft and ready to slip at a moment's notice, the armoury of Tommy-guns below and the rainbow collection of the maritime flags of all nations in the locker. She was as unromantic a craft as ever carried a packed cargo of anonymous human beings whose sole aim and purpose was the liberation of a continent.

Her Commander, dressed in flannels, a once-white sweater and a filthy sheepskin, scowled as he swung her bows towards the Mediterranean. Jan had good reason to scowl for, squatting on deck with her back to the galley, Odette Sansom smiled complacently as the lights of Tangier blinked into darkness and the *Dewucca* felt with her keel the first surge of Mussolini's inland sea.

*

The third day out, the wind blew up and the colour of the sea changed from blue to slate grey, tipped with white. Most of the other passengers lay miserably on the swinging deck and longed to die while Odette, stung by a challenge of Jan's stood in the galley and grimly washed up a month's accumulation of dirty plates and saucepans in cold sea water. When the storm was passed, he remarked casually that he didn't suppose that in her life her fingers had ever held a broom. She said nothing but she took a bucket and a swab and went over the deck inch by inch until her back ached and the very grain of the wood showed clean. He laughed at her. He was a fine seaman and a fine commander and Odette, swift to get the "feel" of a man, sensed the real quality that lay under his resentment, his bitterness and his violence. He had lost everything in Poland, his parents, his family, his home. Month after month he sailed his crazy craft to and from the French coast, landing men and stores, taking men back to carry on the fight in freedom. His prayer was that he might one day be stopped at sea by a German naval vessel. He had, after all, a depth charge, a few Tommy-guns and a .38 revolver. With these, he was quite prepared to take on the German High-seas Fleet. He had nothing to live for. The Germans had seen to that. He only wanted to see to a few Germans before he died. He drank a lot of whisky and played bad bridge.

He said to Odette one day, smiling:

"Did they give you a big pistol to take to France?"

"I haven't got one. I could have one if I liked but"—she shrugged—"it's cumbersome and noisy."

"You prefer the more subtle, more quiet, more feminine methods of killing, perhaps."

She looked for a long time at the silky sea. She said:

"Have you a pistol, Jan?"

"Yes. One day I hope to meet the *Scharnhorst* and I will sink her with my pistol."

"Give it to me."

She took the pistol in her hand, broke it. It was fully loaded. She said: "If you throw up an empty bottle and I hit it, what will you give me?"

He laughed. "You hit a bottle! You are foolish. As well, this pistol makes a very big bang." He clapped his hands. "Louder than that! Not a bang for small girls. When we return, I will invite you for dancing in Gibraltar."

"What will you give me?" she said again.

"If you hit a bottle, I will give you anything you ask. I will even dance the Tango with you—in Gibraltar. I have some chocolate."

"I don't want chocolate. Will you give me what I ask?"

"Yes, Lise. I will give you what you ask."

"Good. Throw a bottle up."

He took an empty bottle and flung it in a wide semi-circle into the sea. As it touched the water, Odette fired. The bottle flew into a thousand splinters. He said quietly:

"My God."

She handed him back the pistol. She said: "You have a bottle of whisky on board. I want that."

"It is my last bottle, Lise."

She shrugged in silence. He said at last: "I will get it for you."

He gave it to her, watching her like a cat. She said, "Thank you. You like this a lot, don't you?"

"No. Not a lot. I like it, that's all."

"When you drink whisky, you are rude, Jan. You are too good a Commander to drink whisky at sea. We are all of us on our way to the war. It is no good for you." Deliberately she threw the bottle into the sea. It bobbed up and down derisively in their wake. He said after a long time, trying to keep his voice steady: "I knew it was a foolishness to take you to France, Lise. I am for the first time sorry for the people I hate most in the world, for the Germans. After them, you come."

It was very cold that night, and, as usual, Odette slept on deck, huddled under the lee of the galley. She always woke up at dawn and stamped about the deck to restore her circulation. This morning she slept on soundly until long after the sun was about the sea. She was warm and comfortable for, sometime during the night, Jan had spread his sheepskin coat over her. She wished she had a bottle of whisky to give him but she had a little brandy in her flask and she gave him that instead.

*

The next evening, the long grumbling of the engines stopped at last and the sail was hoisted. Fanned by a light breeze, the *felucca* slid very quietly inshore as darkness fell. They anchored, talking in low voices. Odette stood alone in the bows, peering in the darkness towards France. She was utterly calm and detached. She noticed trivial things with an absorbed interest, the grain of the deck, the lap of the sea, the angle of the mast bisecting a host of stars. She had thought that this would be a supreme moment in her life but instead her heart beat without hurry and every movement was cool and deliberate. She was called in a whisper, said a formal good-bye and thank you to Jan, climbed into the dinghy, took her suitcase. Two men came with her. She hardly noticed who they were. As the dinghy moved away, she saw the motionless *felucca* like a black shadow on the luminous sea. Her fingers trailed in the water and, after a little while, she dried them in her handkerchief. When the dinghy grounded, she stepped ashore on a narrow strip of beach under high rocks. One of the men passed her suitcase and she thanked him quietly. She was without emotion of any kind. Somehow she managed to climb the rocks and stood at last on a slope of ground and looked about her.

The silence was profound and the night as soft as *crêpe-de-chine*. A million stars burned in the dark-blue bowl of the sky. She looked over the long levels of the sea and breathed deeply. Into her nostrils came slowly the unforgettable, forgotten smell of France. It was a smell of mimosa and thyme, of pine trees. and seaweed, of concrete, garlic, lipstick and sweat. She closed her eyes. For a long time she stood still, while all France slid into her heart and sang in her bloodstream. Then, suddenly, she knelt down and touched the earth with her fingers as tenderly as if she were touching the face of a living person whom she loved.

PART TWO

it is evident that Hitler
  master of a starving, agonized and
  surging Europe;
will have his dangers as well as we.

The Rt. Honourable Winston S. Churchill, O.M., C.H., M.P.

(Extract from notes of a speech in secret session to the House of Commons.
20th of June, 1940.)

E*

CHAPTER XIII

"RAOUL"

ON the 28th of August, 1942, Captain Peter Morland Churchill, *alias* Monsieur Pierre Chauvet, *alias* Monsieur Pierre Chambrun, known in the field as "Raoul", had arrived in France for the third time since the outbreak of hostilities. On the first occasion, he had paddled ashore at Miramar from the outer casing of P.36, a British submarine. After some adventurous weeks, he had made his way back to the United Kingdom by way of Perpignan, the Pyrenees, Madrid and Gibraltar. For his second visit, he had used similar means of transport, merely changing his submarine from P.36 to P.42 and landing in the Bay of Antibes, returning to Gibraltar by the same hospitable craft. Now he had risen from the sea's bed to the middle airs and had descended on France by parachute in the light of a harvest moon. It was not a particularly felicitous landing. He had jumped "blind" from a Halifax bomber, flown by a crew of cheerful if erratic Poles and, after pirouetting down the night sky with twisted cords, had hit the earth with a resounding jolt on a pathway between a vineyard and an olive grove. Hardly had the sound of the Halifax died away before it was replaced by the shrill venom of attacking mosquitoes and that sound, too, was soon merged into the chirruping of a million crickets. He was undoubtedly in France. Having made sure that his bones were merely bruised and not broken, Raoul disposed of his parachute in the tangled undergrowth and limped painfully over the moonlit vineyards in the general direction of Montpellier. He arrived there as the cocks were carolling the dawn, had breakfast of *ersatz* coffee and black cigarettes and made his way to the station. There was a reasonably good train to Cannes in the early afternoon. He spent the morning leisurely reading the Nazi-inspired newspapers and watching the life of the town.

"Raoul"—old Malvernian, Bachelor of Arts (Cantab.), ice-hockey Blue, Commando and free-lance journalist—arrived in Cannes in the evening. There was little to distinguish him from the crowd which surged towards the exit of the station. Perhaps his shoulders were broader than most and his carriage more upright; but his skin held in it all the warmth of the Mediterranean and his brown eyes, benignly alert through their horn-rimmed windows, seemed to gaze incuriously on a long-familiar scene. There happened that evening to be a snap check on the identity cards of all travellers. After scrutiny, his was returned to him without comment. Smiling gently at the thought that he had dined in London with Major Buckmaster less than twenty-four hours ago, Raoul made his way to a villa where he was awaited. He and a companion left the villa later for dinner and after a grotesquely expensive meal of chicken, wine and grapes in a Black Market restaurant, the two men had a long discussion.

Raoul's companion, a British officer, had been acting as a sort of temporary caretaker following the arrest of his real predecessor, another British officer known as "Olive". "Olive" —he had taken easily to this common Marseillaise pseudonym— had had the misfortune to run foul of the Vichy police and was now languishing in Nice prison. It was Raoul's earnest wish to get him out and back to England at the earliest possible moment but the planning of such an operation would require much thought. In the meantime, there was much to be learned about local politics and personalities.

Both were labyrinthine.

Before his capture, "Olive" and his British radio-operator "Julien" had been in contact with two distinct groups of people, both of whose activities were separately directed against the common enemy. The first of these might be called the "Southern Group".

The Southern Group was a purely French organization of patriots with cells all over the South of France, in Marseille, Grasse, Aix-en-Provence, Arles, Toulouse, even in little la Bocca whose *bouillabaisse* used to be so delicious before the Vichy police reprieved the Mediterranean octopuses by forbidding fishing. This Southern Group was run by an ardent if slightly temperamental patriot called Renard with whose volatile personality Raoul was in the future to come unhappily into conflict. This Group was in touch with London *via* "Julien", the radio-operator who, as a result, was grossly over-worked and exhausted. Though messages given to him by Renard for coding and transmission to Baker Street were apt to be voluminous, discursive and even irrelevant, they frequently contained veins of pure gold and had to be sifted with meticulous care. Their unexpurgated transmission was hazardous in the extreme for, between Marseille and Nice alone, the Gestapo ran no less than eleven swift radio-detecting cars whose mechanical eardrums listened night and day.

The second group was composed of autonomous sabotage units, Frenchmen instructed by and under the command of British officers. These units were in Cannes, Marseille, Arles, Toulouse and Lyon—and had positively no connection with the Southern Group. They were regularly taught the use of weapons and the arts of industrial and railway wrecking by British officers—gentlemen out of uniform. These autonomous units had been formed and directed by "Olive" and would be deeply suspicious of any newcomer. To establish liaison and to retie the severed threads would take much time and patience. Raoul would *ipso facto* be regarded as a potential Gestapo stool-pigeon. That, briefly, was the essential situation with regard to the Groups—whose secrecy-consciousness, by the way, simply did not exist. But Raoul's worries would not stop there. Far from it.

The Groups should be his allies and his friends. He had three main types of enemy, the Gestapo, the Vichy police and the local cops, the *flics* who blew whistles, regulated the traffic and swung their capes with an air. The Gestapo as far as one knew, had their agents everywhere along the unoccupied coast. They wore no uniform and did not advertise their presence. The Vichy police were ubiquitous and worked, by and large, in close collaboration with the Gestapo. The function of the local bobby was primarily to cope with petty offences but his parochial activities could have international repercussions. Suppose, for example, that Raoul were blithely to ride his bicycle up a one-way street. He would be stopped by an outraged *flic* and his papers would be demanded. Unless everything was absolutely watertight, he would automatically be turned over to the Vichy police as a possible "enemy of the State", and he would eventu-

ally find himself handcuffed to a patriotic murderer, abortion-
ist, ponce or pickpocket *en route* to the French Concentration
Camp at Drancy. To this lamentable thieves' kitchen came
frequent delegations of inquisitive Gestapo who would scrutin-
ize each *interné* and his papers through an ideological and
belligerent microscope and casually whisk him off to Germany
and to extinction. It would be galling, said Raoul's companion
with the traditional under-statement of his race, to have to face
the hangman at Dachau for riding a bicycle up a one-way
street in Cannes, but that was roughly the form.

"Have a little *Marc*," he said genially.

Raoul's work, like most of the work of the Firm, would still
be empirical and he must be prepared to adapt himself daily to
a kaleidoscopic set of conditions. Improvisation was the keyword. Broadly speaking, Raoul should not only direct but
restrain the exuberance of the British sabotage groups; he
should be the liaison officer between the Southern Group and
London and—a far more difficult task—impose patience on
these loquacious, impetuous patriots. In addition, he should
organize *felucca* arrivals and departures; the receipt of men and
stores would be his business, as would be the secret distribution
of explosives, Bren-guns, radio sets, cigarettes and food. Landing grounds were important. He must explore, find, measure
and pin-point suitable fields for parachute operations; con-
stitute himself a one-man Watch Committee on the emotional
eccentricities of his subordinates, tactfully separating politically
allergic lovers, canalizing human desire into security-screened
double-beds. He would act as financier and money-lender to
both groups, his monthly salaries bill alone amounting to over
a million accountable francs. He should also operate on the
Black Market without conscience or qualm, making a *cache* of
as much contraband petrol, dehydrated soup, sugar and other
rare commodities as he could find. Local politics and jealousies
should be avoided like the plague and he should always have a
bolt-hole and false papers ready for patriots or compatriots on
the run. In certain respects, the job was comparable to that of
His Britannic Majesty's Vice-Consul; in others to that of the
traffic manager of a lunatic branch of Messrs. Thomas Cook;
in yet others, it was like that of a Levantine horse-coper. To
run it successfully required the patience of Griselda, the

cynicism of Louis XI, the effrontery of Voltaire and the guile of Mazarin. It also required the quality of elusiveness for it was the practice of the Gestapo suddenly to order an arbitrary round-up of all able-bodied citizens in any street of any town and transport the catch overnight, men, women and children, to a Forced-labour Camp in the locked depths of the Third Reich. That hadn't happened in Cannes *yet* but it might at any moment.

The temporary caretaker—naturally elated at the knowledge of his imminent return to England, home and beauty—drained his glass of *Marc* and wished Raoul the best of luck.

Raoul looked thoughtfully round the restaurant. A confirmed Damon Runyon addict, he had suggested to Buckmaster that the authenticity of his reports should always be established by his humble use of the idiom of the Master. With no effort at all he mentally metamorphosed his companion into the person of Good Time Charley and the discreet walls of *Chez Robert* into Chesty Charles' little Sharkskin Grill on Biscayne Boulevard in the city of Miami, Florida and spoke as follows:

"Well," says Raoul, "it is a privilege and a pleasure to hear of these goings-on." He swallowed several mouthfuls of imaginary cold bortsch, pig's knuckles and sauerkraut. "As you are well aware, I am never a person who weighs in the sacks against anybody's method of carrying on a scramble but all I can honestly say about this proposition is that I hope and trust my ever-loving Mama never gets to hear of all these unscrupulous fidaddles or she will be more than somewhat amazed, in fact she will be practically surprised. . . ."

*

Cannes itself was the hub of the surrealist circuit and the fountain of all these unscrupulous fidaddles. For a worthy description of this *"ville des fleurs et des sports élégants,"* let its own *Syndicat d'initiative* speak:

"Cannes . . .
Fairest jewel of the Mediterranean diadem. Clasped in a setting of the sun's pure gold; lain in a casket of celestial blue; where is there a sight more lovely to look upon? Now like an opal tinged by the rainbow; now golden with mimosa; now crimson with the April rose, or pink and

white with blossoms of the May. And now, at sun-set, like a blushing maid, her many-coloured mantle is cast aside to don Diana's silver robe of night. Colours only seen upon a dove's breast or in the dust of a butterfly's wing, flash in that unforgettable panorama of the *Côte d'Azur*, to be seen from Cap d'Antibes, and Cannes is the pearl of them all. Mistress of all the world but bride of none, the gods have made thee wondrous fair...."

Cannes. . . .

Two days after Raoul's arrival, the temporary caretaker left by *felucca* for Gibraltar. Meanwhile Raoul had been somewhat cautiously introduced to Renard and had acquired an ancient bicycle costing thirty pounds. Using yet another false name, he had become the tenant of a discreet one-roomed flat in a side-street off the Croisette. The next thing was to engage a secretary, someone of proved discretion who knew the local form. Here he had a stroke of luck. The previous tenant of his flat was a lady called Suzanne C. who was the proprietor of a *Salon de Beauté* in the rue du Canada. Suzanne was known to be an ardent Anglophile and she was not only willing but eager to do everything in her power for Raoul. To her place of business in the rue du Canada, a tepid temple of subdued lighting, cream silk coverlets and Louis XV chairs, came the jaded *mondaines* of Cannes, to be lulled, pommelled, soothed, creamed, uncreamed, plastered, unplastered, slapped, scented —and over-charged. Suzanne suffered from the occupational disease of cynicism but her devotion to France was absolute. It satisfied her sense of humour and her deep patriotism to massage the facial muscles of a Black Marketeer's overfed wife in the Salon while Raoul and his companions were planning alarm and despondency for the Germans in the next room.

Suzanne had no lack of customers. Cannes, being in the unoccupied zone, had naturally attracted to her sunlit sands a lot that was worst in France and some that was best. The invasion had started with the German attack at Sedan and had reached full flower with the fall of Paris. In dusty Delage and de Soto, *Monsieur, Madame et les enfants*, had come twittering and twitching from the north to storm the hotels of the south. A suite overlooking the sea? One could pay. One had had terrible experiences which one wanted to forget. The war was a

CANNES

" Ville des fleurs et des sports élégants. . . ."

great foolishness and, please, one did not wish to mention it. Winston Churchill was an imbecile who, because he refused to accept the fact of defeat, was bringing ruin on all France. Here in Cannes one could find that tranquillity to which one's diamonds and debentures surely entitled one. Here one could bronze one's dimpled buttocks in peace and fry one's torso; one could merrily toss a coloured ball about and dip one's scarlet toe-nail in the sapphire sea; here one could not only eat, drink, gamble and rumba—but repair last night's rumba ravages under the skilful fingers of Mlle. Suzanne in her caressing little boudoir in the rue du Canada.

> "*The Mediterranean sighs*
> *Because it is so calm*
> *On an evening such as this*
> *The rustling of a palm*
> *Seems almost ominous*
> *Whispering of Nemesis. . . ."*

Away from the sleek hotels, the cut-glass scent-bottles and the shaven armpits of the Croisette, life for the people of Cannes was hard and hungry. There was no milk at all. "National" soap—obtainable with difficulty—was useless. Potatoes cost five shillings a pound, an egg three shillings, a lemon half a crown. For those who could afford to pay, there was, of course, the Black Market. Coffee could be bought at three pounds ten a half kilo, butter at six pounds. A chicken cost from four pounds ten to five pounds according to weight. Fish, lavish in the forbidden sea, was a mere two pounds a kilo and the virtue of one's daughter was the price of a packet of cigarettes.

It was not in the Croisette but in the hungry back-streets that Raoul found his friends and his allies.

*

"Julien", the British radio-operator, shared a flat with a croupier from the Casino, a sardonic but benevolent figure who suavely extracted money from the plutocrats by night and who worked for the British by day. Julien was very young—in his early twenties—and an accurate, fast operator. He met Raoul every day at a different hour and in a different place. Watching him, Raoul could see the first signs of strain. Though Julien himself would have denied it indignantly, he needed a rest and Raoul decided reluctantly that he should be smuggled home as soon as he could be replaced. Good radio-operators were rare and it would be hard to find his equal. Second in command to Raoul was Baptiste, a man who, by his solitary daring, had made Paris too hot to hold him. He gloried in the fact that there was a price on his head. He was loyal and brave but he had never in his life had any training in the need for security. Because of this and because he lived in the voluble Mediterranean sunshine, he was apt to let enthusiasm outrun discretion. It was only fair to him and to those with whom he worked that he should be properly trained and equipped. Raoul suggested that he be sent to England to learn his self-chosen, dangerous trade and Baptiste agreed at once. He was prepared to do anything the better to confound his enemies. He was taken to Gibraltar by *felucca* and then flown to England. After a course in the arts of sabotage and the value of security at all times, he was once more infiltrated to France and worked with distinction in the north. The Gestapo got wind of him and he was arrested. Silent under interrogation, Baptiste honourably entered the ultimate silence of death.

*

Every morning of that golden September, the sun arose in glory and spilled through the slats of Raoul's bedroom. Lying awake in the quietness of the dawn, he would try to sort out the inevitable jumble of the hours that lay before. What he had done yesterday would be almost similar to what he had to do to-day. Blinking in the early sunshine, he read yesterday's scribbled diary.

10.00 *hrs. Meet R. at T. du C.*

He had breakfasted off acorn coffee and made his way to the Théâtre du Casino where Renard, surrounded by his satellites, was painting scenery for a new show. The satellites wandered about waiting for orders and news. Amongst them was a Commissioner of Police, a film star, a senior military officer, head waiter, a croupier and half a dozen heterogeneous young men who hadn't shaved and who were game for anything. There was a radio station by the Antibes Road. To stage a mock attack on it would be excellent practice for his men. It would, one day, be a legitimate target; secondly, it was an architectural eye-sore. What did Raoul think? Gently, Raoul had dissuaded him. The radio station was too heavily guarded and, for the moment, it was politically desirable that all sabotage—immediate or future—should be restricted to the occupied zone. Renard agreed with regret. He said that he had been giving much thought to the possibility of a way of getting Raoul's predecessor "Olive" out of prison. Raoul and he discussed it with the Commissioner of Police. "Olive" was shortly to be moved from Nice prison to Lyon. One could of course arrange to divert the prison van on its way to the station and blow it up. But that, he agreed sadly, would very likely mean that "Olive" would be blown up as well. He would think up something else. *"Patience, mon vieux,"* he said to Raoul, "we will get him out yet." He agreed in the meantime to smuggle a Black Market loaf into "Olive's" cell. Raoul collected a report from the Grasse courier and went out into the sunshine.

11.15 *hrs. Baron de C. Villa Diana.*

He rode his bicycle towards la Bocca, wheeled it up the drive of the Villa Diana, had a long talk to Baron de Carteret. All funds were kept in a secret wall-safe in the villa and the British officer at Toulouse was running short of cash. Raoul took half a million francs and an apéritif and mounted his bicycle.

12.10 *hrs. "A".*

Anton, the Toulouse courier, was unexpectedly punctual. He was sitting outside a café, gazing morosely at the sunny street. Raoul sat down at the same table, ordered another apéritif and opened the *Paris Soir*. The two men ignored each other. Raoul read for five or six minutes, yawned, drained his glass and stood up. Leaving the folded newspaper on the table, he made his way leisurely back to his bicycle and wavered off towards the Croisette. After a moment, Anton idly picked up

the paper and glanced at the headlines. Then he folded the
paper carefully and put it in his pocket. It was a unique copy of
the *Paris Soir* for, tucked between the sports news and a glowing
account of Rommel's success in Africa, was half a million francs.

14.00 *hrs.* *Capt. "B" at A.*

At half past two, Raoul got wearily off his bicycle outside a
café in Antibes and greeted a tall man with a limp who was
waiting for him. This was Captain Bedaux of the *Corps franc*,
the French equivalent of the Commandos. Together the two
men walked to a baker's shop in a side street and, having
passed the time of day with the baker, went down to the cellar.
Here was stored the latest consignment of Bren-guns, each of
them with instructions printed in French. While the Bren-guns
were counted and checked, Raoul and Bedaux discussed a date
and place for the next lecture on tactics of guerrilla warfare. He,
Raoul, would let the lecturer know. The job completed, he
cycled back to Cannes.

16.05 *hrs.* *"J" at C.*

Julien was ten minutes late for his appointment and Raoul
was beginning to feel a little anxious by the time he cycled up.
He apologized profusely. He had had a puncture but he had
mended it. Sitting on a bench overlooking the sea, he gave
Raoul the latest radio instructions from London and Raoul
handed a brief report for coding and transmission. Was everything all right? Yes, said Julien, everything was grand. He
had heard of a new house whose owner was prepared to let him
use the attic for transmitting. It sounded all right. Would
Raoul look at it? Raoul scribbled the address on the back of an
envelope and promised to visit the house that night. They
arranged to meet to-morrow at 11 o'clock in a café near les
Allées. In the meantime, all was well. They spoke in the
Italian vernacular.
"*Ciaou Julien.*"
"*Ciaou Raoul.*"

17.00 *hrs.* *"G".*

At five o'clock, Raoul met "Gervais", a British Commando and training officer. Raoul said that he had seen Captain Bedaux that afternoon and this date and place for a lecture had been arranged. Was that convenient? It was. Good. Now what were Gervais' worries? Well, he had one or two but they weren't urgent. He needed a new suit and new shoes. Could Raoul mention that in his next message to Baker Street? The Firm had complete measurements and could have it made— *à la mode de Paris!*—in London and it could either be dropped by parachute or landed by *felucca*. As to shoes, he would like brown ones, with triangular brass eye-holes—*à la mode du Côte d'Azur!* Raoul slid easily into his rôle of tailoring representative and agreed to include the demand in to-morrow's radio message. Anything else? Yes. Gervais had been introduced this morning to Mlle. "L", a woman of about forty, an artist and a person of vivacity and charm. Marie had been to England before the war where she appeared to have lived in Brown's Hotel, dined in the Connaught and generally hobnobbed with the great. She was now anxious to contribute in any way she could to the war effort. Would Raoul care to use his own means of checking up on her and, if satisfactory, get into touch? She had a large apartment which could be useful for storing food and explosives. That was everything. The two men agreed on their next meeting place and parted.

18.15 *hrs. Villa "M".*

Casually, Raoul called at the villa whose address had been given to him by Julien. He introduced himself as a free-lance journalist, preparing a series of articles on the architecture of the *Côte d'Azur*. Might he see over the house? But of course. He spent half an hour with its voluble owner and decided sadly that it would be unwise to use the house for transmitting. Monsieur was far too loquacious. If he was prepared to unburden his soul to a strange self-styled journalist after a few minutes conversation, God knows what he would do if he had a real, live radio-operator in the attic. Raoul sighed and made a graceful adieu.

19.30 *hrs. Chez Robert.*

Six nights out of seven, Raoul dined *chez Robert*. It was quiet
and discreet and, above all, the chef was an artist who really
understood the subtle significance of garlic. He dined alone,
reading with interest a detailed analysis of the benefits of the
"New Order" as outlined by the editor of *Figaro* and then
ordered a glass of *Marc*. The waiter brought it and because the
restaurant was nearly empty, stayed for a talk. He liked Raoul
because he was quiet, because he caused no fuss and because his
tip was always regular and good without being either mean or
extravagant like the tips given by *la canaille* who lived in the big
hotels. They chatted together for a few minutes and then
François remarked genially:

"I do not know your politics but . . . but . . . Monsieur
Chauvet but. . . ." he shrugged.

"But what, François?"

"Monsieur Chauvet," he said, "the whole coast is teeming
with spies!"

"*Tiens, tiens*," said Raoul putting down his newspaper. "Tell
me more, my friend."

"It is true. Here in Cannes are dwelling British officers who
are organizing resistance against the Boche. They come, they
go—all the time. They work with impertinence under the very
noses of the Gestapo and Vichy police. They are British
officers from England and are the personal friends and relations
of Winston Churchill. They are everywhere. I have a friend
who is in contact with them. The chief of them is a well-known
Englishman, many times a millionaire."

"Oh. What's his name?"

"His real name," said François, "one does not know. But in
Cannes, in Antibes, in Marseille and in Arles, he is spoken of as
'Raoul'."

Raoul thoughtfully played with a tooth-pick. Somebody was
obviously due for the sack.

22.00 *hrs.* "*S*".

Back in his one-roomed flat off the Croisette, Raoul carefully
read the radio messages from London given him by Julien and,
having memorized their contents, burned them. He lit a rare

cigarette. Buck had certainly given him a job! Pondering how best to attack it, he heard a gentle tapping at the door and opened it. His secretary Suzanne came in and sat down. He asked her for her news. She smiled. She said: "I'm afraid that it will be unwelcome to you, Raoul, for I think that you are very tired. It's from Renaudi." He nodded. Renaudi was managing director of a large button factory outside the town, a dapper, alert man who worked as hard at making buttons as he did at resisting the Germans. He said: "What does Renaudi want?" She shrugged. "I don't know. But he sent a courier to me this afternoon to ask that you meet him to-night at his place at 11 o'clock. His wife is back from Paris and it may be that she has brought news."

Raoul stifled a yawn and glanced at his watch. He said to Suzanne. "Good. I can get there in ten minutes on my bicycle. Now listen very carefully to this. I've had a radio message from London which sets us quite a pretty problem. Somewhere in France, there is a man named Charles Roubier. The only address I have is that of his brother, 10 Place de la République, Clermont-Ferrand. His age is about forty, he has reddish hair, his wife has run away with an insurance broker from Dijon and he has a son of ten years old who lives with him. Charles Roubier is an aircraft engineer with a technical process which only he knows."

"Well?"

"If he is alive and traceable from that address, we have to find him. Having found him, we have to induce him to go to England and arrange his passage. If necessary, we make him drunk and put him on board a *felucca*. My Government wants Charles badly and my orders are to produce him." He smiled. "That's something for you to ponder during the night watches. Just tell me the whereabouts of Monsieur Roubier, aircraft engineer, and I'll do the rest. Now I must start off for Renaudi. Is everything all right?"

"Oh yes. Business at the Salon is brisk. To-day I massaged the neck of the wife of a well-known *collaborateur* for over twenty minutes. Figure to yourself! It was with the greatest difficulty that I restrained an impulse to strangle her. It would have been so easy and so very pleasant for me. *Au revoir*, Raoul."

"Au revoir, Suzanne."

23.55 *hrs. Bed.*

*

All that had happened yesterday. Much the same sort of thing would happen to-day.

Lying on his bed, smoking in the early sunshine, Raoul memorized the salient points for inclusion in the Runyonesque report he would write to-night and send by courier. The couriers were very good and, up to now, every single one of his written reports had got through. Some had gone *via* Switzerland, some *via* Spain, some *via felucca* to Gibraltar. He held up the page of scribbled notes, struck a sulphur match and lit one corner, crumpling the ashes to dust. It was going to be another perfect day. Outside, he could hear the little sounds of life beginning to stir in the streets. He yawned and turned on a cold bath. While it filled, he lathered his face and began to shave. He had just reached the curve of the chin when there was a loud knock on the door. Could it be the police? He stood quite still, the razor in his hand. Again there was a knock. Raoul glanced round the bed-sitting room. There was nothing to incriminate him, absolutely nothing. He wiped the soap off his face and impassively opened the door. His second-in-command, the voluble Baptiste, grinned at him and stepped into the room. He waved a hand at a dark, scowling figure in a dirty mackintosh who followed him in.

"This," said Baptiste with a chuckle, "is Arnaud!"

*

Arnaud, alias Lieutenant A. Rabinovich, alias Guy Lebouton, alias Gérard L., *soi-disant* botanical and entomological student, had been parachuted "blind" into France a fortnight ago. He had dropped some twenty-six kilometres north of Grenoble with instructions to make his way to Paris and work as radio-operator to a Paris circuit. Somehow his Grenoble contacts had gone astray and, for the past fourteen days, he had been lying up in a back street. Only yesterday had Baptiste found him and brought him overnight to Cannes—*en route* for Paris.

Before they had finished their coffee, Raoul had come to a momentous decision. His present radio-operator Julien was exhausted and had well earned a rest at home. Here, in the person of Arnaud, was a literally heaven-sent replacement. He would send Julien home by the next *felucca* and keep Arnaud until such time as London sent out a permanent man. He said:

"How would you like to stay here and work for me for a bit?"

"I don't care a damn who I work for," said Arnaud ungraciously, "as long as I can get on with the job."

"Fine," said Raoul, "you stay."

Although neither of them knew it, the second member of a most faithful trio had arrived.

CHAPTER XIV

LISE—S.23

A<small>T</small> ten twenty-five in the morning of the 2nd of November, 1942, a sorry little band of persons filed through the sophisticated portals of the *Salon de Beauté, rue du Canada*, Cannes and looked about them with all the disdainful resentment of women who are conscious that they are looking their worst. Eight hungry days at sea in a dirty *felucca* followed by a banging railway journey through the night had done little to improve either their appearance or their tempers. There were two men and three women. The men were red-eyed and unshaven and—Raoul thought with an inward giggle—the women looked exactly like those tiresome, indefatigable wives who insist on accompanying their husbands from the jungle of Lancashire to the Cup Final at Wembley.

They had been conducted to Cannes from the lonely point near Cassis where they had landed and had been met by the reliable Marsac. Marsac—then head of the Marseille section of Renard's Southern Group—was soon to play a bigger rôle in the Resistance. He was a tall, meagre man of immense energy and devotion. Though he always looked ill, there was no mission which he was unwilling to accept and—gladly sacrificing a night's sleep—he had immediately volunteered to meet the new arrivals and to bring them to Raoul.

Odette looked around the Salon. She sniffed and came to the point at once. She said, with an edge in her voice:

"I am Lise. My instructions were to report to Baron de Carteret at the Villa Diana who should conduct me to Raoul. In spite of that, I have been brought directly here. I should like to know why the orders of London are disregarded."

Raoul managed to look properly contrite. He said soothingly:

"Shall we go into that a little later? In the meantime, welcome to Cannes." He had been to some trouble to get that morning some *pains d'épice* made of raisin-juice, honey and sugar and these, with a bottle of red wine, were waiting. Odette took one, drawing an acid comparison between the austerity of life in England with that which seemed to obtain in the South of France. Raoul explained gently that these particular delicacies had been obtained by using forged bread coupons and that they in no way represented the normal standard of the bakers' shops. Somewhat mollified, Odette consented to eat another while waiting her turn for a hot bath.

Lunch had also been arranged. It was in a restaurant other than *Chez Robert* and was followed by a discussion in the *rue du Canada*. Of the five arrivals, Raoul sent the two men off to the Villa Diana and suggested that the three women should stay for the moment with Suzanne. Odette pointed out that her mission was to go to Auxerre to start a circuit of resistance. It was not to hang around Cannes eating expensive meals and watching the wives of *collaborateurs* lead elaborately clipped poodles along the pavements of the Croisette. Raoul said patiently that he was already aware of her mission but that Auxerre lay in the Occupied Zone. Journeys across the demarcation line were complicated and difficult. What he suggested was that Lise and the others should take it easy for that afternoon—their separate bedrooms were ready for them—and to-morrow, when they had had a very much needed rest he would go into the matter of sending them on to their various destinations. He had a busy afternoon before him and he hoped they would be comfortable.

"I, personally, am not at all tired," said Odette.

He looked at her with a smile. "No, I don't suppose you are. But, all the same, won't you lie down for a little while?"

She shrugged. "If you insist—yes. Possibly you could lend me a book to read?"

"Certainly," he said gravely, "or better still, would you care to read the local newspaper? See the war through German spectacles. I will wake you all up about six and we'll have an apéritif and then dine."

"There will be no need for you to wake *me* up," said Odette. "No need at all."

"Fine," said Raoul.

He showed them all their rooms, handing Odette the morning edition of *Figaro*. Then he went out on his bicycle to meet

Arnaud and to hand him a message for coding and transmission to London. He stated briefly that the latest *felucca* consignment had arrived safely and was awaiting onward transmission. Arnaud said:

"Oh. What are they like?"

Raoul said carefully. "Very tired. One of them—Lise—
disapproves of the whole set-up. She is like an angry gazelle."

"Oh is she. She'll soon learn." He spread his hands. "Raoul,
I still can't get a bloody thing from London."

"How long is it now?"

"Three weeks. Every night for three weeks I've been sending
out my call sign and I can't get an answer. Do you think Baker
Street has been bombed—or are they merely eating plover's
eggs dipped in diamond dust as usual?"

"Arnaud, you are a fool."

He spat on the sunny pavement. He said savagely:

"You know what I think of Baker Street?"

"Yes," said Raoul. "I know. You have told me several
times. It is silly and unjust. I'm certain they are both receiving
and transmitting and that the fault is a technical one. What
time should they be coming up?"

"Nineteen hundred hours G.M.T."

"Well cross your fingers and try again to-night."

"All right. In the meantime, God damn and blast their souls
to hell. *Salut. A bientôt* Raoul."

"*A bientôt*, Arnaud."

Raoul mounted his bicycle. He thought, as he rode along,
how complicated life was and how one must always make allowances for people.

He saw Gervais, Renard and a twisted little man from Grasse.
At a quarter past five, he returned to the *rue du Canada*. Over
the flat brooded a vast silence. He tip-toed from door to door,
opening each very quietly, glancing into the room, closing the
door without a sound. In the last room, he saw on the floor, a
crumpled copy of *Figaro*. He smiled. Lying as still as a statue,
seeming not even to breathe, Odette slept profoundly.

★

Soon after seven, Raoul reassembled the new arrivals in the

main room of the *Salon de Beauté*. Feeling rather like the man
from Cook's, he wished them good evening. An afternoon's
rest coupled with a few minutes at Suzanne's dressing table
had made a considerable difference in their appearance and
they now looked more like human beings than the merry wives
of Wembley. He suggested a restaurant where they should
dine and was describing how to get there when the door was
kicked violently open and Arnaud strode into the room. He
wore a dirty mackintosh and his trouser ends were caught up
in bicycle-clips. He slapped a glass table with a resounding
crash and grinned triumphantly.

"Raoul, I've got through! By God, I have. Six messages
from London—and all decoded. *Quel succès!*"

"*Epatant, mon vieux*," Raoul turned to the silent and astonished half circle. "May I ask you to excuse me for a few
minutes while I cope with this. We've been having rather more
than slight radio trouble for three weeks and now all's well.
Let me have them Arnaud."

"Sure. Here they are."

Arnaud dived inside his dirty mackintosh, pulled out his
wallet, opened it. He pulled out a sheaf of old tram tickets and
used a word rarely heard outside the *Vieux port* at Marseille.
Odette—a Frenchwoman—looked out of the window in a
marked manner. Still muttering, Arnaud began feverishly to
search his pockets. At last, he said desperately:

"Christ! I've lost the bastards."

"I see." Raoul lit a cigarette. He said with detachment,
"Lise, I wonder if you and the others would mind waiting in
the other room for a few minutes. Thank you so much." He
shut the door behind them. "Arnaud, for God's sake don't say
things like that before strange women."

"Sorry, Raoul. My God, I'm sorry. But listen. I really have
lost the bastards."

Raoul sighed. He said, "Are you sure?"

"Of course I'm bloody well sure. I had them ten minutes ago."

"We'll go over your pockets one by one. Let's empty out
your wallet first."

"Sure."

Arnaud emptied the contents of his wallet on to the glass-
topped table. The messages were not there. He threw the empty

case on to the cream silk coverlet. It was followed by an oily spanner, a pair of pliers, a coil of wire, two chewed inches of garlic sausage, a hunk of bread, a .45 revolver and a filthy handkerchief. Arnaud said savagely:

"Go on. Say it." He scowled. "I tell you what I think I've done."

"What?"

"Burned them. You know I had three or four of yours to code and send out. Well, when I had sent them out, I began to receive. Then I meant to burn the stuff I'd sent out but . . . but I'm afraid I may have burned what came in."

"In that case, where are the messages you didn't burn?"

"I shoved those under the lid of my set."

"It's just possible that they may be the ones we want. Where did all this happen?"

"Up at the farm."

"Good. We'll go up there together and have a look around."

He went into the other room, explained shortly that he had to go out on an urgent job. Would they all go to the same restaurant where they had had lunch? He would join them later if he could.

Cycling up the hill towards the farm, Raoul laid a silent if affectionate curse on the impulsive Arnaud. Knowing that the extraction of a good wireless operator out of London was like drawing a tooth, he had taken care to send Julien on his way *before* asking for permission to keep Arnaud. After all, he said guilelessly, he had to have somebody and Arnaud was not only on the spot, but fitted like an eyelid. Might formal permission now be given for him to stay? There had followed a slightly acrimonious exchange of messages between Raoul and Buckmaster ending in Baker Street's benevolent surrender. Arnaud could stay. Wise in his generation, Buckmaster was always ready to help the men in the field, to stretch the elastic, and Raoul knew it. A loyal, violent man with no sense of humour, Arnaud's mouth was full of strange oaths. Headstrong, untidy and brave, he was to become one of the best radio-operators in France.

They arrived at the farm, opened the radio set. Crumpled under the lid were the decoded messages from London. Raoul said, laughing:

"Arnaud, admit that you are a fool."

"Me? Certainly not. I told you I'd get through, didn't I? Well, what the hell. . . ."

*

Odette dined, walked back to the *rue du Canada*, went early to bed. It was strange to lie awake and to gaze through the black framework of the window at the bright pattern of stars that glimmered in the sky and to know that she was seeing them from France. To-day her feet had trod the soil of France and now, in the stillness, the very air she breathed was the air of France. And yet treading that same soil and breathing that same air were the enemies of France and the enemies of the England she had come to love. It occurred to her at first that Mademoiselle Odette Brailly had come home, not casually but dangerously, to fight the enemies of her country and to help to cleanse its soil. Then she knew that she was human no longer. It was a strange thing to lie and to breathe and to look out into the soft, starlit night and to know that she wasn't Mademoiselle Brailly any more or even Mrs. Sansom. She was S.23; she was Lise; she was a secret agent of the British Government and her life was forfeit. She didn't want to change places with anyone in the world. She went to sleep in proud and happy solitude.

*

She woke up early and went out for a walk before breakfast. It was a perfect day with a little light wind and the palms were moving. The streets were still deserted. By the time she returned to the *rue du Canada*, the others were up and about and some Black Market coffee was bubbling on the stove. Soon after nine o'clock Raoul appeared. Odette was eager to continue her journey to Auxerre and she told him so.

"Yes," he said. "That I understand. But, as I told you yesterday, it's not easy to arrange a thing like that overnight. The man who is fixing your papers is a chap called Renard and he won't be available until this afternoon. In any case, the office suggested your spending a few days here for rest and what they call acclimatization."

"How long do you think it will take before I can go?"

"Three or four days I should think."

"Well as I have no wish to hang around doing nothing, can you give me some work to do here? Anything. I don't mind what it is. Surely the best way I can acclimatize myself is to get down to some real work."

He looked at her coolly. He said at last:

"If you want some work, I can find it for you. Do you know Marseille?"

"No. But that doesn't matter. I could find my way about."

"Good. Now listen carefully. This morning, one of the men who came in your *felucca* is going to Marseille. As you have probably noticed, his French is good without being perfect. Also you may or may not know that it is safer to travel *à deux* than alone. The police are more likely to interrogate a solitary passenger than a man and a woman obviously travelling together. How would you like to take him to Marseille and hand him over to his contact? Marseille, I may mention is teeming with Gestapo, German soldiers and Vichy police, and it's one of the towns where they're quite likely to do a sudden round-up for German Forced Labour Camps."

"I will go gladly."

"Good. While you're there, you can also pick up a suitcase of mine and hand over two hundred thousand francs to one of my chaps. You know how to use passwords?"

"Of course."

"Excellent. Here are you instructions."

*

With some two hundred thousand francs concealed about her person, Odette travelled by train to Marseille. One of her companions was to go on to Toulouse—that part of the journey he could easily do by himself—the other was to stay in Marseille. The journey was uneventful and the train punctual. She descended from the carriage with composure—and stopped dead. Standing on the platform was a man in grey-green uniform and a peaked cap. She looked at him with sudden, startled curiosity.

This was a German.

Travelling from Cannes, she had almost forgotten the war in the familiar sights, sound and smell of a French railway carriage. Now it came back to her like a painful hiccough. This was a German; this was a living Boche. This man—or somebody like him—had ordered the execution of the fifty hostages of Bordeaux; a picture of this man—or of somebody like him—had hung on the wall of the training school in the New Forest. Her instructed eye swiftly recognized the collar flashes. He was a Hauptmann, a Captain of Infantry and he wore the General Service and Poland medals. Having satisfactorily classified him, her curiosity focused on the man himself and she tried to see the human being inside the uniform. His age was about forty; he was sallow, sulky and slightly pot-bellied. He looked as if he might well suffer from duodenal ulcers. Her lips curled. This was no Nordic Superman; the Blond Beasts of Nietzsche had little to do with this dreary little conqueror whose stomach was more likely to rumble with indigestion than with the songs of the Valkyrie. Suddenly conscious of her gaze, he glanced at her. He saw a slim, elegant Frenchwoman. On her delicate features was a clear look of interest in him—an interest which he completely mistook. He straightened his tunic, smirked and half saluted. As he turned and raised his arm, Odette saw the butt of a Lueger automatic jutting out of a leather holster at his belt. There, and there alone, reposed his power and his glory, slumbering inside an oiled cartridge-clip. He muttered in execrable French:

"*Bon-jour, Mademoiselle.*"

Odette walked out of the station as if she were passing an over-ripe dustbin.

Her companions and she lunched together in a small restaurant near the station, surrendering the accurate number of bread coupons given her by Raoul. So far so good. Now to find the meeting place. It was a small garage, some half-mile away. As they walked there, Odette saw more and more German soldiers and confirmed her first impression, that they were a homesick, dyspeptic lot. From such as these, a person of wit and mental alertness had little to fear. She was, for a little while, in danger of over-confidence—and had the grace to realize it. The Gestapo were of another fibre . . . and caution should be the watchword, now and always. She found

F

the garage, walked boldly inside. An unshaven man was washing a car and to him she addressed herself.

"*Connaissez-vous un bon marchand de fleurs par-ici, Monsieur?*"

"*Ca dépend de ce que vous voulez dire par 'bon', Madame.*"

He straightened up and wiped his hands on his overalls and grinned. "Madame is expected," he said. "Would you be amiable enough to follow me to the office?"

The whole thing had been easy, almost too easy. Caution, caution, caution, she told herself as she walked out along into the sunny street carrying Raoul's suitcase. The next thing was to find Raoul's Marseille contact, hand over the two hundred thousand francs and catch the train back to Cannes. The hour of curfew which varied according to the behaviour of the town, was to-night at ten o'clock. She would have ample time to complete her mission before that. Almost gaily, she decided to walk the whole way to the hotel where the contact lived. This was a man, a British officer, who went under the name of Paul Vidal and whose cover was that of a parfumeur. She found the hotel in a dirty square, walked inside. She said to the reception clerk:

"Good afternoon. I have an appointment with Monsieur Vidal."

"I'm sorry, Madame. Monsieur Vidal is out."

"Oh!" she coughed. "I wonder if you can tell me at what time he will be in?"

"That I do not know, Madame. He usually returns at about six o'clock."

"Very well," she said with a casualness she was far from feeling. "I will return after six. Would you be kind enough to inform him that Madame Metayer called and will call again this evening? Thank you."

"*A votre service, Madame.*"

Now this was a complication. The best thing to do was to go to the station and find out the times of the trains to Cannes. Raoul had said easily that he would expect her when he saw her and that she should, if necessary, spend the night in Marseille. Well, if necessary, she would indeed do that. Why not? It would surely be easy to find a hotel. Arrived at the station, she consulted the notice board. A train left at 7.10 p.m. Excellent. She would see Monsieur at six, deliver the cash and

be in Cannes by eleven. The time was now 2.25. Happy
thought. She would go to the pictures.

This was less easy than she had imagined for the first cinema
she arrived at had a large notice in German over its portico
and a small crowd of German soldiers in the vestibule. As she
walked to the box office, one of them said something loudly
in German and they all laughed. Odette ignored them and
put down a fifty franc note at the grill. The woman said
sharply:

"This cinema is for German forces only. Can you not read
the notice outside?"

"I am sorry." Swiftly she picked up her money and walked
out. She went out into the street furious with herself. She
had done a thing that was unpardonable, a thing that was
directly contrary to all the rules she had been taught at school
in England. She had made herself conspicuous and, by doing
so, had laid herself open to questioning. One should always be
unobtrusive and suit one's actions, one's behaviour and one's
appearance to that of the norm. She glanced around. She was,
thank God, not being followed.

She found another cinema and, after examining it carefully,
joined the short queue of French housewives waiting to go
inside. She sat down on a rickety chair in the strong electric
light. At a quarter to three, the show began. The first item
was a crackling newsreel. It came at first as a slight shock to
see that it was shown with the lights full on, and then she
remembered another thing she had been told at school—that
in the early days when these German newsreels had been shown
in darkness, they had been the signal for catcalls, boos and even
revolver shots from the anonymous gloom. To-day there was
an armed policeman standing at the end of her row, sourly
scanning the faces of the audience for signs of disapproval.
Odette composed her features into the correct expression of
rapt admiration. Welcomed by a few flatulent chords of Wag-
ner, the figure of the Führer strode on to the screen. Already
he seemed to strut with an unco-ordinated jerk of the incipient
paranoiac. He distributed a few medals to adoring, weeping
widows and faded out—to be replaced by a squadron of Panzers advancing towards the audience in thunder. Bombers
swooped and roared, heavy guns shuddered and boomed,

soldiers marched singing to victory somewhere or other and little Nordics threw flowers under the wheels of flame-throwers; elderly sunburned Teutons with hairy chests laughed as they tossed sheaves of corn to sunburned Rheinmädels with big breasts and balloon buttocks and the week's dose of culture ended with a massed male chorus singing "*Wir fahren gegen England*". As no untoward incident had occurred, the police withdrew and the lights were switched off. Odette settled down to enjoy again that old but brilliant French film "*Poil de Carotte*". She had seen it before—in London. In its pastoral beauty and its poignant sequences, she was soon able to forget the bellicose din that had gone on before.

A few minutes after six, she made her way back to the hotel where "Monsieur Vidal" lived. Again she enquired for him. Alas, he had not yet returned. Would Madame care to wait? Monsieur would be in at any moment. She sat down in the hall and glanced at her watch. At a quarter to seven, a tall man in a dark suit and a *beret*, strolled in. The reception clerk approached him swiftly and murmured in an undertone. The tall man glanced at Odette lifted his eyebrows and shrugged slightly. She stood up.

"*Monsieur Vidal?*"

"*Oui, Madame*," he said politely.

She said, pronouncing each word with care:

"*Je vous apporte des nouvelles de Monsieur Ternier, Monsieur Ternier de Lyon.*"

"Ah." He looked at her with a sidelong glance and asked, equally carefully: "*C'est de Monsieur 'Jean' Ternier que vous parlez, Madame?*"

"*Oui, Monsieur. Précisément.*"

They smiled at each other. *Bonafides* had now been established on either side. He said conversationally: "Perhaps Madame would care to join me in an apéritif? I have to meet a friend in a few minutes."

"Gladly, Monsieur."

They walked together to a café on the corner and sat down at one of the tables fringing the street. She said: "I have brought you some money from Raoul," and put a folded newspaper on the table. He picked it up, put it casually in his pocket. He said quietly: "Thank you. Who are you?"

"I am Lise. I came out with the *felucca* that arrived yesterday. Marsac met us."

He said, speaking very softly:

"How's Buck?"

"Buck's fine."

He went on speaking in an undertone. "The man who is
meeting me here is Bernard, one of the regular couriers. He is a
serious one—and a poet, as well. It would be a good thing if
you could wait and see him so that you would recognize each
other in future."

"I don't suppose I shall come to Marseille again," she said
doubtfully. "My orders from the office are to go on elsewhere."

"A pity, Lise. Still it would be a good thing to meet Bernard."

"Yes, I should like to. One can always find a hotel, I suppose, where no questions are asked?"

"Oh yes. Marseille is full of hotels. Bernard knows the town
well and he can suggest a discreet place." He raised his glass,
smiling. "*A votre santé, Madame.*"

"*A la vôtre, Monsieur.*"

It was a queer thing to sit outside a café in Marseille and drink
an apéritif with a British officer while the soldiers of the Reich
walked the pavements of the town. Then she knew that she
must not think like that. The agent who saw him or herself
in terms of the romantic, the unusual or the grotesque, was
invariably a bad agent. Self-imposed glamour led one to
Dachau. She must learn calmly to accept her new identity
and her surroundings without conscious thought. But now and
again, in spite of herself, she couldn't help remembering, with
a momentary flicker of pure excitement, that she was Lise,
Lise, Lise . . . she was S.23 . . . and that this, all of this, was a
masquerade only rendered real by the knowledge of the penalty
of failure. It was hard to realize the final fact of that penalty . . .
when a smoky dusk was creeping over the cobbles, when green
shutters were closing over the yellow oblongs of the windows,
when a one-legged man tried to sell her companion a bright
cluster of mimosa and all Marseille undid its corsets and put its
feet up. It was hard to realize what one slip might mean, that
the soft white envelope of her body might be torn open by
bullets . . . when around her now the *mise-en-scène* was pure
René Clair, even to the extent of a hungry cat delicately sorting

a out pile of refuse and crooning over a fish's head. The
whimpering of an accordion slid into the dusk and a man sang
nasally in the gutter.

Parlez-moi d'amour
Redites-moi des choses tendres. . . .

She said blithely: "I like being in France."

"Yes," said Monsieur Vidal with a smile. "I expect you do.
You've now been here for how long? Thirty-six hours?"

"Just about."

"Wait till you have lived here for thirty-six weeks, then tell
me that again. Ah, here's Bernard."

He was a smiling, suave man in his early thirties who
regularly travelled between the widely separated units of the
Southern Group. He insisted that Lise join them for dinner. A
hotel? He knew a thousand hotels and, in each one of them,
he was *ami de la maison*. After dinner, he would telephone one
of his thousand hotels where it would not be necessary for Lise
to fill in any stupid forms. The matter was settled. Now he also
knew a restaurant where the oysters were delicious. First
they would dine and then he would arrange the matter of
the hotel.

They dined—and dined well. Bernard was a fountain of
conversation, influence and anecdote and the time passed
swiftly. At nine o'clock, Lise glanced at her watch. She said
to Bernard, "You were going to telephone a hotel for me," and
he immediately jumped to his feet. "I have been so distracted
by your presence, Lise, that I confess I forgot all about it.
Excuse me, I will arrange it at once."

He went away—and didn't come back for a quarter of an
hour. He sat down and bit his nails frowning. He said at last:
"It has been very difficult. Marseille is full of *sales Boches* and
not even I"—he slapped his chest—"not even I have been able
to arrange what I should have wished. Nevertheless it will not
be necessary for you to sleep in the station waiting room. I can
take you to a place where no questions will be asked and you
will be safe. You simply say that you were sent by Monsieur
Bernard. There are keys in the locks of the doors," he said drily,

"and, above all, no questions. It is not exactly the Ritz in the Place Vendôme, but it will be shelter."

She was Lise, and she was S.23; she was ready for whatever the gods might bring. She said, as her father had said before her:

"*Allons-y.*"

CHAPTER XV

"OTHER RANKS ONLY"

W ITH Bernard carrying Raoul's suitcase, they set out together in the general direction of the *Vieux Port*. Already the streets were emptying before the ten o'clock curfew and the wind that breathed off the sea had a jagged edge like a safety razor blade that has been used for sharpening a pencil. Bernard said apologetically:

"People who undertake work like ours must expect to find themselves in queer places and the thing is never to fill up an unnecessary form. All France to-day is honeycombed with official pieces of paper and each one of them is a little mouse-trap. It is a great art never to leave a trace. Still, I could have wished for something better. Next time, I will arrange it other-wise."

He stopped at a street corner. Odette noticed vaguely that the name of the street on the left was "*rue Paradis*".

"Here I leave you. It is better that I come no further. Go down the *rue Paradis* until you come to the sixth house on the right. Push the door and it will open. Inside is a woman. Tell her that you come from 'Monsieur Bernard' and that you want a room for the night—a room with a key in the lock. She will understand. I will wait here for exactly five minutes in case anything goes wrong. If you do not come back in five minutes, I will know that all is well. I hope we will meet again soon, Lise. My compliments to Raoul."

Odette was aware of a sudden cool disquiet. She said, looking along the dark street:

"What is this place where I am to sleep?"

"It is the only house where you will be absolutely safe in Marseille to-night. I am sorry, Lise." He shrugged. "It is a German soldiers' brothel."

"My God. . . ."

There was a long silence. Odette said in a low voice:

"Would . . . would it not be possible for me to sleep in the waiting-room at the station?"

"Possible—yes. But it would be risky. The Germans have the amiable habit of rounding up all passengers in the waiting-rooms and of transporting them to synthetic petrol factories in Germany—and we cannot afford to lose anyone so soon. You will be quite safe in this place, Lise."

She picked up the suitcase. With an odd detachment, she noticed again that the name of the street was the '*rue Paradis*'. She was sure that . . . somewhere there was an epigram to be made about that name but it eluded her. She twisted her lips into a smile.

"*Au revoir*, Bernard."

"*Au revoir*, Lise."

She walked slowly along the pavement, counting the houses. She stopped at the sixth door and glanced around her. The street was deserted. Then she pushed the door open and walked in. She found herself in a brightly lighted vestibule. A middle-aged woman was sitting at a table. She was darning a sock. She put the sock down and stared at Odette. She wore a gold crucifix on the horizontal plateau of her vast bosom and it flashed in the light. Her ageless eyes were as hard and as bright as two brown boot-buttons. Suddenly, like a snake's tongue, they flickered over Odette from the tips of her shoes to her hat. They missed nothing. Each separate stitch of each separate garment was seen and assessed and calculated in that lightning, X-ray glance. She said, hardly moving her lips:

"*Que désirez-vous, Madame?*"

The last word cracked in the air like a whiplash.

"I come from Monsieur Bernard. He said that"—she faltered "he said that I could have a room here to-night, a room with a key."

The woman looked at her with a face of stone. Then the stone swam and became alive and moved as her eyelids drooped like mauve curtains, shrouding the timeless glitter of her pupils.

"You know what manner of house this is?"

"Yes. I know."

"Have you any money, Madame?"

"Yes."

F*

"A room with a key will cost you fifty francs." She painted the swift caricature of a smile on her mouth, wiped it away. "I am always proud to be associated with the friends and the colleagues of 'Monsieur Bernard'. You need have no fears, Madame. I will see that you are not disturbed."

"I am most grateful."

"One is a Frenchwoman," she said drily.

Odette opened her bag, counted out fifty francs in notes. The woman took them without interest, put them in a drawer, rang a little hand-bell, picked up the sock. Odette looked around her. The carpet on the tiled floor was threadbare. At the end of the vestibule hung dark red curtains and, through them, she could see dim stairs. From the depths of the house, an old, old woman shuffled through the curtains and stood patiently.

"You rang, Madame?"

"Marie, take this lady to room number 10. She is not to be disturbed."

"*Bien, Madame.*" The old woman picked up Raoul's suitcase and half turned. The woman at the desk said to Odette: "You will need this." She slid a large key off a bunch at her waist and gave it to her with a brief, painted smile. "I trust that you will have a pleasant night."

"Thank you. I wish you good night."

Laboriously, the old woman began to climb the stairs. At the first landing, she put the suitcase on the floor and leaned, panting, against the banisters. Even more slowly, she climbed the second flight, opened the door of a room and switched on the light.

Odette gave her a twenty franc note. She muttered and put it down her blouse. She said: "There is a bell. If Madame desires anything, she only has to ring. I will hear and come."

"Good. I will ring if necessary." She stood by the door, "And now—good night."

"Good night, Madame."

Odette locked the door. She stood leaning against it until she heard the old woman's steps creaking down the stairs. Then she looked around the room. The shutters were closed. There were dirty lace curtains draped over the windows. In the middle stood a tarnished brass bedstead with one grey blanket folded over a striped mattress. There was a divan, a wardrobe, an armchair and a wooden cabinet with a cracked marble top by the bed. On this was an ashtray with a crushed-out cigarette stub and three hairpins. There was a smell, a hot, dry smell, laced with some indefinable scent whose name she had never known. She opened the wardrobe. Inside hung a dirty dressing-gown and a crumpled handkerchief, smeared with lipstick. She shut the door again. Somehow she managed to drag the divan over to the locked door and put the arm-chair on top of it like a barricade. Then she took off her hat and her shoes and, after one more glance around the room, turned off the light and lay down on the bed, her hands clasped behind her head.

*

Lying fully dressed on the bed of a Marseille brothel, Odette began to take again the road that led from Red Ball to the Tippings. Autumn would be over the woodland path by now and there would be mist by Culmstock Beacon. Gazing into the darkness, she cleared the woods in sunshine and crossed the wet field to the Tippings where the heifers used to graze—a million years ago. In the stillness of the night, she talked silently to her children in England and told them that they ought to be good girls but that if they weren't, it didn't matter as long as they washed their faces for tea. Underlining the sound of her children's voices, she heard the banging of doors and muffled talking and laughter of men. The moon threw a tracery of light through the slats of the brothel shutters—and Odette remembered the orchard at the bottom of the garden in Somer-set and how the moon made pools of light between the apple trees. She must have slept for a little while for she suddenly opened her eyes and sat up to see that dawn had already hung a dirty dish-cloth over the shutters. She peered at her watch. It was five past six. She yawned and ruffled her hair. Then she washed sketchily and put her feet into her shoes and looked in the cracked mirror. Her face was pale and stretched and she felt as though she would give all the world for a bath. She moved the chair and the divan away from the door as quietly as she could and unlocked it and listened. The house was as silent as the tomb. She looked once more round the awful room where she had slept. Then she put on her hat and, with Raoul's bag in her hand, crept quietly downstairs.

To her astonishment, the woman in black was still at her table in the hall. She looked round at Odette. She said, drooping her lids:

"*Bonjour, Madame.* You are very lucky, I congratulate you."

"Oh. Why?"

"Because at three o'clock this morning, a patrol of German *Feld-polizei* came to the house to search for a deserter from the Army. There are many Germans who desert their beloved Führer, Madame, and it is in houses such as these that they are sought."

"Nobody came to my room."

"I am aware of it. I told the sergeant that my niece slept there and that she was suffering from smallpox." Her face hardened. "You had better go now."

Odette walked out into the street. The early sunshine was a glory about the town and she breathed the cool air deeply into her lungs. To a morose policeman on the corner, she gave a cheerful "good morning" and he answered her with a surly grin. The station was crowded with people. Odette joined the queue at the ticket office, was lucky enough to find a corner seat in a second class carriage of the Cannes train. She was back in the *rue du Canada* in time for lunch.

★

"Well," said Raoul, "how did you get on?"

"Very well. I delivered our friends at the garage, collected your suitcase, met Monsieur Vidal and another man called Bernard."

"You gave Vidal the money?"

"Yes. Then it was getting late and I had to find somewhere to sleep." She said with exaggerated casualness. "I finally slept in a soldiers' brothel in the *rue Paradis*. There was a search during the night but the ... er ... proprietress said that I was her niece and nobody came to my room."

"Good." He dismissed the events of the night with a pre-occupied air which Odette found subtly irritating. He said: "Can you ride a bicycle?"

She had never ridden a bicycle in her life. But she said coolly: "I think that if one can spend a night in a Marseille brothel, the riding of a bicycle should be a comparatively easy matter."

He smiled. He said: "I confess that the connection between a *bordel* and a bicycle eludes me for the moment. Still . . . now I want you to cycle up to the Villa Diana and deliver this note to Baron de Carteret. Then, when you come back, I've got another job for you."

*

Half an hour later, Odette was sitting in a ditch with the bicycle lying across her, its back wheel still spinning. The knee of her left stocking was ripped and, through the torn silk, a thread of blood oozed and spread. Her attention from the serious business of steering had been diverted by the comical sight of a platoon of Italian soldiers on the march. A mule brought up the rear, to whose tail a magnificently-uniformed officer clung. When the column passed in dust and derision, Odette took off both stockings, remounted the detestable iron-mongery and grimly continued her journey to the Baron's villa. As she wobbled precariously along the sea-road, she had reluctantly to agree with Raoul that the connection between sleeping in a brothel and riding a bicycle was indeed remote.

CHAPTER XVI

NURSERY SLOPES

As the days went on, Odette found that the temporary work for which she had asked Raoul was becoming more and more absorbing. There was still no sign of the papers she needed to go on to Auxerre. Renard said with truth that such things took time to arrange. He was in the hands of people less efficient than he was himself and, because of that, Lise must have patience.

Meanwhile, Odette, already a reasonably safe if erratic cyclist, was able to take a great deal of work off Raoul's hands. She fitted smoothly and well into the organization, she was beginning to know—and to be known by—its members and she had begun to grasp the broad, strategic plan. She disliked Cannes wholeheartedly. She was reminded again and again of Boccaccio's Florentine youths and maidens who fled to the hills and passed their days and their nights lute-playing, love-making and telling indecorous stories while plague ravished their city. One evening Raoul spoke to her about it. He asked her casually how she liked working in Cannes.

She considered the question for some time before replying. "You ask me two separate things in one question," she said frowning. "I'll try to answer them separately. First of all, Cannes has nothing to do with the real France, the France I came to find. I expected a hard, resentful, smouldering France and I came to live in and to work in that France. It is my misfortune that I came to the one bit of my country where the war doesn't go on. I wanted very much to be with my true compatriots and to fight the Germans." They were sitting looking over the sea. From the sands below came the sound of feminine laughter and squealing as a circle of sun-worshippers merrily tossed a coloured ball about. "These people may be my compatriots but I can't feel that they have anything to do with the France I know. They make me sick. If you ask me if I like

" Le carab d'or fait sa
toilette de printemps."

" RAOUL "

Captain Peter Morland Churchill,
D.S.O., Croix de Guerre.

being in Cannes, the answer is 'no'. I even prefer the queues of
Kensington to"—she smiled—"to the 'sunlit sands of the
Côte d'Azur'. But if you ask me if I like working in your group
and with you, the answer is 'yes'. I think that you work very
hard and I know that I could do much of that work and leave you
free to get on with the more important things. You don't play
and you don't waste time. You are very much in the war—as
I want to be. Because of that, we could get on well."

"But you don't like Cannes?"

"No, I don't like Cannes. I didn't want to leave my children
but, having left them, it is, in a way, cheating for me to be
here." She smiled. "It's easy and silky and sophisticated. I
am none of those things. The thing I seek is reality—and I
don't think it is to be found in this . . . this decadent sunshine. Please don't think that when I use the word 'reality' I
mean danger. I don't particularly want to get into danger. If
I did, I should be weak and frightened. But I do want what I
can't define by any word other than 'reality' and it is only when
I have known this reality that I can return home and look after
my children in peace. That is really my *métier*, not this. I am
far better at blowing little girls' noses for them than sleeping
in Marseille brothels. I am a much better cook than I am a
British agent. I prefer *bouillabaisse* to Bren-guns. I am a very
ordinary woman."

"There I disagree with you profoundly, Lise." He smiled.
"No very ordinary woman would have set out along the
Corniche on a completely unfamiliar bicycle, fallen off, cut her
best silk stockings and her knees to ribbons—and completed
the journey. Why didn't you tell me that you didn't know how
to ride?"

"Because you seemed to take it for granted that everybody
is as . . . competent as you are yourself. It is most irritating.
Why should I give you the satisfaction of admitting ignorance?"

He shook his head. "It wouldn't have given me any satisfaction. You misjudge your fellow-men. Sometimes you are
rather like one of those little girls whose noses you are so expert
in blowing. You should be in navy bloomers and cotton stockings and a sulky look. Lise, would you like to stay here and
work for me?"

"If you and the office think I can be more useful here than in

Auxerre, I will stay. I am under orders. But I warn you, I don't like Cannes."

"Last night I had a radio message from Buck. He wants to know where you are and why I have not sent you on to Auxerre as previously arranged. I should like to reply saying that I want to keep you here. Do you agree?"

"I am under orders."

"That's not very gracious."

"No it isn't. You're quite right. I'm sorry. If Buck agrees, I'd like to stay—in spite of the wartime austerity of the *Côte d'Azur!* It's silly to think that reality belongs to a place. It belongs to the mind." Like a swallow, a thought darted into her head and she giggled. "If I do stay, what will Arnaud say?"

"Arnaud! Oh, you and he will continue to quarrel—and get on with the job." He gazed over the sea for a long time. He said slowly: "Accepting the fact that you do stay and work for me, the first thing I'm going to do is to try to send you back to England on a job. That sounds like a paradox but it isn't. You know Renard? Well, though I know he's honest and sincere, we don't get on as I should like. I dare say it's my fault but whatever it is, we're allergic to each other. It's a hell of a pity but there it is. I'm arranging to send him—accompanied by no less than five distinguished French Generals—to London for consultations. It will be a bomber pick-up in a field near Vinon. What I want you to do is to accompany these distinguished characters to London and give the office a detailed report on the situation here."

"And then?"

"And then I hope you will come back to France. That's up to the office and Buck. I'll get Arnaud to push out a message to Buck to-night saying that you're working here and suggesting that you be a sort of glorified air-hostess to these birds as soon as we can fix up a bomber. Are we agreed?"

"Yes. We're agreed."

"Good. Now I don't mind taking you to dinner *chez Robert.*" He grinned. "Up to this moment, I've kept it as my own private hideout but if we're going to work together, I'll let you in on the *entrecôte bordelaise* and the *crêpes Suzette. . . .*"

★

Radio message in code, transmitted to BUCKMASTER. 0830 hrs. G.M.T. 5.12.42.

FROM RAOUL STOP SUGGEST LISE WHO WORKS HERE GETS ON PLANE WITH RENARD AND HIS FIVE PASSENGERS STOP LISE WILL EXPLAIN DIFFICULTIES OF SITUATION ENDS.

*

Radio message in code, transmitted to Raoul. To be taken on his schedule at 0845 hrs. G.M.T. 6.12.42.

REQUIRE YOU RETURN WITH RENARD STOP SEND LISE TO AUXERRE AS ORIGINALLY PLANNED STOP SURELY RENARD CAN PROVIDE MEANS OF CROSSING DEMARCATION LINE STOP SHE SHOULD CONTACT TAMBOUR PARIS STOP BOMBER CAN ONLY TAKE SEVEN ALTOGETHER ENDS.

*

Radio message in code, transmitted to BUCKMASTER. 0940 hrs. G.M.T. 10.12.42.

FROM RAOUL STOP REQUEST PERMISSION KEEP LISE HERE TILL MY RETURN STOP SHE IS INDISPENSABLE ENDS.

*

Radio message in code, transmitted to Raoul. To be taken on his schedule at 0845 hrs. G.M.T., Friday, 11.12.42.

OK LISE ENDS.

*

"Well," said Raoul, "that's that."

"Yes," said Odette, "that's that. Now for the bomber pick-up."

*

"My dear Raoul," said Renard with an air of a governess talking to a recalcitrant child, "there is no need whatsoever for you personally to inspect the field. My subordinates—my subordinates, I repeat—all of whom are distinguished aviators, have already satisfied themselves that it is in every way suitable

for the reception of a bomber. For you to insist on inspecting
it would be an insult to the knowledge, the experience and the
integrity of my men. *Tout est organisé!*"

"I trust so indeed," said Raoul. The proposed field at Vinon
was some two hundred miles away from Cannes and a visit
would involve him in a railway journey with two changes
followed by a car ride which, in its turn, would involve false
car permits. For these, he would have to call on Renard's
assistance and this it would hardly be discreet to invoke. In
short, it would not only be tactless to force the issue: it would
be impossible. Before bowing to the inevitable, he made one
more desperate foray.

"How long is the field?"

"A matter of sixteen hundred metres."

"How broad?"

"Eight—nine hundred."

"What is the surface like?"

"The surface, my dear Raoul, has been examined by my
aeronautical subordinates. It is flat, as flat as a grilled sole,
and as hard as the heart of a well-bred Englishwoman. There
are no trees at either end. In it, you could land an airborne
division. It is the French edition of Croydon airport. It is
Prestwick in miniature. Have no fears. Summon your bomber.
I will do the rest. *Tout est au poil!*"

How many times was that beguiling reassurance to be the
prelude to disaster?

It was Odette's first operation and she looked forward to it
with mounting excitement. The auguries were good. The
B.B.C. message came up punctually. "*Joseph embrasse Nicole.*"
The train journey to Vinon was uneventful and the cars were
waiting. Standing in a group with Renard at the corner of the
field, the five Generals—one of whom had been dissuaded with
difficulty from bringing his parrot—scanned the dark sky and
thought of the steak-and-kidney pudding they would be eating
in a few hours under the shadow of Big Ben. These five Generals
had been collected from various hideouts and brought secretly
to the field. It was almost a miracle that they had all managed
to arrive at the same place at the same time but there they were.
The reception committee was all present and correct. Although
the night was bitterly cold, Odette had a rucksack with sand-

wiches and—more important—two bottles of Armagnac. The
Generals toasted the success of the operation and Renard
remarked airily to Raoul that the whole affair was a matter of
organization, a simple matter of forethought and planning.
The time had come to pace out the field and station the ten
members of the reception committee at hundred and fifty yard
intervals. Raoul gave his orders in a whisper. At all times, the
men should point their torches at the aircraft whether it was
circling or on the ground. Was that clearly understood?

One of the men scratched his head. He said in a deep,
rumbling voice:

"Torches? What torches?"

"You have no torches?"

"No, Monsieur. We have never had any torches."

"A moment." Raoul walked over to the gesticulating
Renard and asked him gently what had been arranged about
the trivial matter of torches to guide the bomber down. Renard
looked at him as Napoleon might have looked if questioned
about the correct number of buttons on a private soldier's
greatcoat on the eve of Waterloo. "I do not concern myself with
such details," he said with acerbity. "Torches are a matter for
my staff."

"*Tout est au poil,*" said Raoul philosophically. He called
Odette and together they distributed the ten torches she had
brought. Renard feigned an absorbed interest in the rising moon.

The field lay in a hollow. In some trepidation, Raoul began
to pace out the ground. After the first hundred yards, he stopped
dead. Standing nearly six solid feet high, a bank ran diagonally
across the field from corner to corner. It was a bank that would
capsize a jeep; it would even daunt a Meath-bred horse at the
Grand National. In stunned silence, Raoul clambered over it
—to stumble into a broad horizontal ditch some two feet deep.
The going was easier for him after that for the field ran steeply
downhill to lose itself in a wood of high trees. It was, he
decided with detachment, the nearest thing to a stiff point-to-
point course he had yet seen in France. As a place to land a
twin-engine Hudson, it was a joke, a satire; it was the blue-
print of an airstrip, drawn by a lunatic surrealist in his cups.
At that moment, the faint drone of the Hudson bomber itself
wove into the silence.

Pandemonium broke out on the field. Renard shouted to Raoul to line up the reception committee. The R.A.F.—the wonderful R.A.F.—could land anywhere. Get the men out! Flash the torches! Unless you flash the torches and give the signal, the aircraft will go away. Raoul, I command you to guide the bomber in! Jules, Charles, Anton, Pedro—do your duty! Raoul, order the men to do their duty. I, Renard, command you!

Odette took a deep breath and handed Raoul one of the bottles of Armagnac. If alcohol was not the antidote to catastrophe, it was at least an anaesthetic. Raoul took a deep swig, standing stock-still in the freezing field and together they watched the bomber circling against the pattern of the stars. It came so low that Odette could see two tongues of orange flame licking from the exhausts and the earth seemed to quiver under the roar of its engines. Round and round it circled— while Renard danced about the grass, cursing, cajoling and pleading. It was strange for Odette to look up to the sky and to know that English eyes were peering down waiting for the first, reassuring flash of a single lamp to be followed by a necklace of lights in the darkness. . . . It was strange to think that English voices were talking in that aircraft, checking navigation charts and asking each other what the hell had gone wrong. . . . Once more the Hudson circled, then it swept up towards the stars and flew high to the north-east. Raoul said in a flat voice:

"You see, Lise. This is one of those things. That aircraft took off in England to come here. It may have been attacked by Messerschmitts over the Channel and it certainly came through a curtain of Flak. Now it's got to face the same bloody thing again—and all for nothing. It would have been suicide to bring it down."

"Yes, I know that. I'll go and soothe the Generals while you cope with Renard."

*

Nearly two thousand years ago, the already ancient town of Arles was pillaged by the envious tribes who infested the *Bouches du Rhône*. It was restored and embellished by Constantine who saw, not with his eyes but with his vision, that a Roman glory could arise from the sunlit rubble. Though he planted stone that was to last for all eternity, Arles was to remain the envy of the barbarian. Visigoth and Saracen came in turn to plunder and to slay but over the centuries, Constantine's Arena, Theatre and walls stood fast to become the haunt of antiquaries, the inspiration for Mistral, sweetest of Provençal singers, and the backcloth for the blossom, the sunflowers and the cypresses of van Gogh. Treading in the footsteps of pope and prelate, emperor and king, legate and legionary, Goth, Moslem, painter, poet, and monk, Raoul, his courier Lise and a number of Gallic patriots came to Arles in December, 1942. They came to arrange for the reception of an up-to-date British bomber and they found the resurgent Goths of the twentieth century already in occupation.

The *Wehrmacht* Officers' Mess was on the ground floor of the hotel in the *Place du Forum* and these gentlemen's rooms were scattered about the first and second floors, the bed in which Napoleon had slept being occupied by no less a person than the Town Major. Because of this, it was a source of some sardonic amusement to Odette to ring up Arnaud in Cannes every morning and have a conversation with him by prearranged code while, through the glass panels of the telephone box in the hall, she watched the German officers strut past with the consequential mien of assured victors. After a day or two, she became used to the sight of them until sharply reminded by a would-be gallant salute or a heavy *"Pon-jour, Mademoiselle"*. She ignored these advances with dignified discretion.

The general purpose of the operation was similar to that at Vinon. It was to receive an R.A.F. bomber on a field some eight miles outside Arles, exchange its cargo of stores and explosives for the five long-suffering French Generals and remove all traces of the visit. This time, Raoul had himself inspected the field and it was suitable in every way. Four or five members of the reception committee lived in the hotel and others were scattered about the town. Owing to the presence of the Germans, Raoul had arranged with three different sympathizers who had receiving sets that they should be visited in turn for the B.B.C. message that would announce the advent of the bomber. Night after night, one or other of the reception committee listened in. Still the magic words failed to come up. A week passed and then ten days. There were messages galore each

night but no mention of the fact that "*le ciel est gris*". The young
men who had arrived in Arles full of enthusiasm began to shrug
their shoulders and mutter. Where was the wonderful R.A.F.?
It was easy enough for Raoul to promise a bomber but no
bomber came. Why not? Patiently Raoul explained. Though
it was true that the weather in Arles itself was perfect, there was
no reason to suppose that the weather in England was anything
other than characteristic. Had they never heard of the famous
English fogs? They should be patient. Soon the moon would
be round again and then they would see. But, said the young
men, Christmas was coming and a man's place at Christmas
was at home with his family. It was not sitting in Arles, gaping
at *sales Boches* and waiting for non-existent bombers. Raoul
discussed the matter with Odette who was equally sensitive
to the growing discontent. She pondered the matter and gave
the judgment of a Frenchwoman. What was needed was "an
Occasion". The men were scattered and therefore lacked
cohesion. Somehow, they should be brought together and,
as it were, rewelded. But how could this be done in a town
whose pavements were threaded with the soldiers of the
Reich? Again Odette supplied the answer. The German mind
was a highly organized one; it was subtle, suspicious and
tortuous. It could be beaten by one quality—audacity.

The baker's wife was a sympathizer and from her, by devious
ways, a cake was ordered—with the hint that, when the British
liberated Arles, that cake would stand to her credit. Madame
set to work with a will and with a chuckle. It was the sort of
cake that had rarely been seen in France since the outbreak of
war. A dozen eggs went into the bowl, a mountain of white
flour, a pound of butter, a Niagara of sugar and milk. On the
afternoon of Christmas eve, the cake was delivered to Raoul's
room. An hour later, a dozen bottles of *Côtes du Rhône* were
smuggled in by the back door. As twilight fell, the men slipped
unobtrusively into the hotel and made their way upstairs. They
had been asked to bring candles with them if possible and so,
by Black Market candle-light, the feast was spread. Odette sat
at the head of the table, dispensing conversation, cake and wine.
Slowly, the party fused, began to take hold. Somebody stood
up and, raising his glass, proposed a diffident toast to the
R.A.F. It was drunk with reserve and—half an hour later—

with gusto. A taciturn little man from Marseille told a story of
Marius and Olive and the party rocked with indelicate laughter.
Raoul winked happily at Odette as he drove the corkscrew into
the fifth bottle. Only one thing was missing—and that Odette
proposed to supply. Quietly she slipped out of the room and
downstairs to the proprietress.

"Please, because it is Christmas eve, could we have a piano?"

The proprietress—a good friend—spread her hands.

"Madame," she said, "it is my opinion that it is a very great
foolishness to hold this gathering at all. With the Boches in the
hotel, it is little short of madness. As to a piano, it has been
commandeered long ago and moved into the German Officers'
Mess."

"Thank you, Madame," said Odette. A smile suddenly
transfigured her face and she laughed, her eyes dancing. "I will
go and get it."

De l'audace, et encore l'audace, et toujours de l'audace....

Odette tapped on the door of the Officers' Mess. A gruff
voice shouted "*Entrez*" and, composing her features, she walked
in. She saw three officers in uniform. They scrambled to their
feet, buttoning their tunics. One of them was the Town Major,
the man who saluted her every morning. He said in some
surprise:

"*Pon-soir, Mademoiselle.*"

Odette gave him a flashing, sidelong glance. She said:
"Gentlemen, please forgive this intrusion. The fact is that it is
Christmas Eve and, though this terrible war has separated
many friends and families, I am fortunate enough to have around
me to-night some of the playmates of my childhood. As far as is
possible, we are for a brief hour, attempting to forget the war
and the misfortunes of my country. If you are indeed as generous
as one occasionally hears, you could do us a very great service
to-night."

The Town Major adjusted the skirt of his tunic and smirked.

"Mademoiselle, the German Reich seeks only to co-operate
and to be the friends of France. How can I be of assistance?"

"Gentlemen, you have in the corner a piano, the property
of the hotel. Among my guests is a pianist, a young man who
has had to forsake the profession of his choice and become a free-
lance journalist. It would give us all very great pleasure if he

could once again play to us songs of Christmas and of France."

The three officers looked at each other and mumbled. The Town Major said with a bow:

"Mademoiselle, my colleagues and I will be very pleased for your friend to play the piano—in view of the German policy of co-operation and because it is Christmas Eve. Perhaps you would inform him of our decision."

Odette shook her head sadly.

"You will not misunderstand me if I say that it would be most embarrassing for him to play within these intimate walls. True it is that he bears no permanent resentment towards your country, but frankly gentlemen, your presence would tend to deprive him of that fire, that *nostalgie*, that tenderness which he could only feel when surrounded exclusively by his compatriots."

"You wish the piano to be removed upstairs, Mademoiselle?"

"Please."

There was a further, muttered conference. The Town Major said stiffly:

"Very well, Mademoiselle. Though it would have pleased us to hold the concert in this Mess, the piano may be taken upstairs—provided it is returned by eight o'clock to-morrow morning. May I express the hope that actions such as this will indicate to your friends the sincere wish of the Führer and of the German Reich that they may win the collaboration and co-operation of your countrymen in their struggle against the arch-enemy of civilization, of France and of the New Order. I refer to England. *Heil Hitler!* The piano is at the disposal of your friends."

Odette said gently:

"You are very kind." She traced a demure pattern on the carpet with her toe. "I do not know the relationship existing between the rations consumed by the Armed Forces of the Reich and those of the French civilian population—but the piano is very heavy and my friends no longer have that physical vigour which was their birthright. I trust I make myself . . . clear?"

The Town Major stood up incredulously.

"Am I to understand, Mademoiselle, that you wish to suggest that my brother-officers and I carry the piano upstairs?"

"Gentlemen, you are more than kind. . . ."

There was a long silence. Then the Town Major said sharply:

"Captain Hartmann, Ober-Leutnant Staub, remove your tunics and roll up your sleeves."

*

The tinkling notes of the piano floated in through the Mess window, soft as single snowflakes. Muffled by laughter, a man's voice sang guardedly:

> *Près de la caserne*
> *Un soldat allemand*
> *Qui montait la garde*
> *Toute en pleurnichant*
> *On lui demande*
> *"Pourquoi pleures-tu?"*
> *Il nous répond*
> *"Nous sommes foutus. . . ."*

The Town Major put down yesterday's edition of the *Völkischer Beobachter* and scratched his greying head.

"There are one or two French words in that song that I don't understand," he said, "but the melody is pretty. I seem to have heard it before."

"So have I," said Captain Hartmann drily. He stood up and limped to the mantelpiece. "I heard it, *Herr Major*, when I was a subaltern attached to 90th Light Panzer Division outside Tobruk. It used to be the song of the Afrika Korps before the English stole it from us and before Rommel sailed . . . for home. It is called *Lili Marlene* and, with due respect to your rank, sir, that Frenchwoman is a she-devil."

"You forget yourself, my dear fellow. Both she and the melody are charming. You have been for too long in Africa. You do not understand the feminine French character as I do."

*

"*Le ciel est gris*," said the radio at long last from London "*le . . . ciel . . . est . . . gris.*"

From house and hotel, the reception committee made its way to the field. The moon rose and shone over the long levels of the grass. Torches were distributed and each man knew his exact position. The long period of waiting was over and excitement was intense. The bomber should arrive any time between ten o'clock and two a.m. and then, the job finished and the explosives hidden, the men could return to their homes. On this occasion, Odette remained in the hotel. Somebody had to stay to look after the men when they returned and the lot fell on her. She knew that she would be sure to hear the sound of the bomber and she strained her ears, lying in bed with the window open.

The little sounds of the town died away and a deep silence came over Constantine's ancient stone, pillar and terrace. All Arles seemed to be sunk into a timeless sleep and midnight melodiously chimed. The bomber would come at any moment now. But the minutes crawled by and still there was no distant drone to ruffle the waves of quietness. At one o'clock, she began to frown, thinking of the men crouching coldly under the moon. Surely it would come now. But still there was no sound. Half-past one. . . . A quarter to two. . . . Two o'clock. Still she listened, aware that Raoul would certainly allow half-an-hour's grace for wind, weather and flak. But the silence remained profound. At half-past two, she knew that something must have gone seriously wrong. She could imagine the scene at the field, the group of angry, disappointed men and their contempt. She wondered what Raoul would say before he sent them in their various directions, how he would explain that a fortnight had been wasted for nothing. She could only suppose that the bomber had been brought down on its way from England and already she mourned the loss of its crew.

Odette's estimate of the situation on the field was accurate in every detail. Raoul waited till half-past two before dispersing his team. They went their several ways, grumbling but far less resentful than he had imagined. It was the fortune of war and Raoul—whom they trusted—was obviously as disappointed as they were themselves. He tidied up the corner of the field where they had waited, even picking up and burying a cigarette end. He took a last look around an empty sky before mounting his bicycle. He was a good mile away from the field and the members of the reception committee were nearing their different hideouts when he heard a drone in the north. Louder and louder came the drone. It swelled to a roar and a single light fled like a firefly across the stars as the bomber accurately circled the field again and again. Then it flew swiftly away up the moonlit breast of the Rhone.

CHAPTER XVII

"FROM A FIND TO A CHECK. . . ."

In his book *Louise*, Carpentier said of early twentieth century France and particularly of Paris:

"Le rêve des grands-seigneurs, c'est d'être des artistes; le rêve des artistes, c'est d'être Dieu. . . ."

Translated into any other language, this would be both ludicrous and pretentious. Of some of the French, it is plausible and sincere. During the days of waiting at Arles, criticism of Renard's leadership had become articulate and the members of the Southern Group had split into two warring factions— those who voted for his retention and those who were determined to choose a new leader. Neither Raoul nor Lise took any part in these discussions nor did they, either by word or by deed, seek to influence the decision. Both sides sought to make them allies. Their neutrality remained absolute. It was a matter for the French themselves to decide. Whatever the final outcome, they would continue to work for the liberation of France and give either Renard or his successor all the support of which they were capable. Discussions went on and finally came to a head at a sort of unofficial court martial at which Renard was put on trial. This court martial was presided over by a General and, after much hot-blooded evidence had been given, the General announced that Renard had been deposed. In future, the Southern Group would be under the control of the reliable Marsac and of one Paul Frager. Raoul and Lise accepted the decision of the court without overt comment.

As for Renard, he paid little heed to the unfavourable findings of the assembly. He was first and last a patriot and he burned to go on serving France. He collected those of his followers who were still loyal to him and, with them, proceeded to carry on as if nothing had happened. Mistakenly convinced that Raoul had been a secret opponent of his, he opened up a long-range propaganda offensive against Raoul and all his works and laid certain plans. During the time when he had commanded the whole Southern Group, he had, of course, been informed of London's plans for the coming moon-period. Not only did he know the place and date of every proposed *parachutage* but he also knew the B.B.C. *message personnel* which would announce each operation. Now it was too late for Raoul to change them. The arrival of the bombers was therefore awaited with considerable curiosity.

What Raoul had feared came to pass. As the containers parachuted down the sky, Renard's zealous followers rushed forward from the hedges and, on the moonlit fields, the scene was reminiscent of an Irish race-meeting. A tug of war started as Frenchmen tried to snatch arms from Frenchmen. Feeling in the small hours of the morning was apt to run high and what began as a scramble ended on several occasions as a free fight with torn skin and cracked ribs. It was clear that the situation could not be allowed to continue indefinitely. Renard should go to England with the utmost speed and, when he went himself, Raoul would go by another route and take with him Paul Frager, new joint-commander of the Southern Group. After a personal report, Buckmaster would surely devise a way of restoring order out of what threatened to become chaos. In his absence, Lise could take over his job. He was by now completely confident of her ability to do so for she was already as much a part of the organization as he was himself.

*

The devil obviously had his hoof on bomber landings as far as Raoul was concerned and by this time it was decided to pick up him and Paul Frager by Lysander. This should be a less complicated affair in every way. The size of the field need only be eight hundred by four hundred yards; three lamps placed in the shape of the letter "L" will serve as a flare-path and the run needed for take-off is comparatively short. If less commodious than a Hudson bomber, a Lysander is also less noisy. The R.A.F. had themselves pin-pointed a small aerodrome which appeared eminently suitable. It was at Basillac,

a small village some ten kilometres from Perigueux and report
had it that the aerodrome was disused. Would Raoul please
find out if this was indeed so and if he considered the operation
feasible? Subject to his overriding approval, the R.A.F. would
send a Lysander and the *message personnel* would be: "*Les
femmes sont parfois volages.*" It all seemed very simple and
straightforward—from Baker Street.

Methodically, Raoul began to plan the operation. Paul
Frager, his fellow-passenger, was at the moment in Lyon so
a courier was sent to that city to summon him to a rendezvous
at Perigueux which Raoul decided, should be operational H.Q.
Not only was Perigueux the obvious place but its *foie gras* was
famous throughout France. It would be pleasant to bring home
a jar for Buck who had a cultured palate. . . . The next thing
was to inform Marsac, then in Marseille, of the plan and to ask
him for the loan of a receiving-set to pick up the B.B.C. message
on the spot, so another courier was despatched hot-foot to
Marseille. In case the field proved on inspection to be useless,
Arnaud was consulted and two alternative innocent-sounding
code messages were devised by which London would know
whether to carry on or to call the whole thing off. He—
Arnaud—would transmit the chosen message immediately he
received a telephone call from Lise from Perigueux. That disposed of Cannes. Raoul packed cheerfully and set out with
Odette by train for Perigueux—a distance of some three
hundred and twenty miles.

At Marseille, the always reliable Marsac was waiting on
the platform. Through the window of Raoul's second-class
compartment, he passed a receiving-set to Odette—who
graciously accepted the assistance of a German officer in placing
it on the luggage rack. It was, she said, very kind of him and
he said that it was a pleasure. "Your suitcase, madame, is
heavy enough to be a radio set," he said with a guffaw and
Odette smiled a little wanly. At Toulouse, Raoul and she
changed trains and travelled uncomfortably through the night,
arriving at Perigueux in time for an early lunch.

Neither of them had ever been in Perigueux before nor had
they any contact there. It was always unwise to indicate that
one was a stranger by asking questions and it was thus with a
completely false air of assurance that they entered the town.

In the main square stood the Grand Hotel and, to their surprise and gratification, rooms happened to be available—albeit in the attic. As it would be necessary to listen in to the B.B.C. in the hotel, the humble position of their rooms suited them admirably. The fact that the dining room was cluttered up with German officers was compensated for by the excellence of lunch, and Raoul wavered a little in his decision to present Buckmaster with a jar of *pâté-de-foie-gras*. His aim was to eat all he could get himself. A glass of *Marc* merely confirmed this gluttonous wish.

Immediately after lunch, he and Odette hired two *vélo-taxis* and told the muscular cyclists that they wanted to go to Basillac. Though she disliked *vélo-taxis* on principle because a human being took the place of a horse, she sat with composure in the trailer while the sweating young man pedalled up the hills. She had time to reconsider her view. There was, after all, about a *vélo-taxi* a refreshing absence of noise—if one could ignore the gasps and grunts of the rider. Surely the majority of the world's ills sprang from the invention of the internal combustion engine. While musing idly on this sad and well-worn theme, she had noticed and marked down for future reference the exact position of an aerodrome on the left—the philosophical and the practical being nicely mixed in her blood. Arrived at Basillac, she and Raoul paid the exhorbitant sum demanded by their *conducteurs* and dismissed them. They had, they said, decided to take the bus back after a walk to settle their over-taxed digestions.

They had not only noticed the airfield. They had also remarked on the disturbing presence of a hangar, a building that looked remarkably like a barrack-block and a control tower. The great question was still to be solved. Were these ominous buildings occupied or not?

Arm in arm, Raoul and Odette sauntered round the field. To the casual observer, they were merely a flirtatious couple taking the air. In the intervals between calculating the field's layout and the distance from the road to the hangar, Raoul gave her an occasional bucolic nudge and Odette produced in reply the traditional rustic giggle. The buildings were definitely if sparsely occupied. On the other hand, flowing behind a clump of trees, there was a river with a bridge on the far side of the airfield and this bridge would make an excellent escape route after the operation, leading, as it did, to dense woods. Weighing up the merits and drawbacks of the field—and not forgetting the three hundred miles they had travelled to get here—Raoul and Odette decided that the operation stood rather more than a fair chance of success. They walked the ten kilometres back to Ferigueux and, after dinner, Odette put through a guarded trunk call to Arnaud in Cannes. The operation was on.

Next morning, a new difficulty arose. Somehow a plug had to be found to fit the wire of the receiving set into the electric light socket. This essential part—like every other radio part— was illegal to sell, and any attempt to purchase it might lead to arrest. Without it, it would be impossible to listen in to the B.B.C. Odette used her lipstick to best advantage, put on her smartest hat and her air of damsel-in-distress and sallied forth into the town. She was back within half an hour with the plug in her handbag. When they met Paul Frager and his lieutenant Jacques Latour punctually to the minute in a café, it seemed that fate at last must be with them.

It was agreed that Paul and Jacques should dine together on the terrace of the hotel while Raoul listened in upstairs to the B.B.C. As he plugged in to the electric light switch, it occurred to him that the walls were remarkably thin and it was little comfort to remember that only that morning, the Vichy police had arrived and arrested the man who had slept last night in the next room. He found considerable difficulty in getting the B.B.C. at all on the new, unfamiliar set and, when he did get what he thought must be their wavelength, a fearful caterwauling and wailing sounded all over the attic. He switched it off and wiped his forehead. He must try again because, in three minutes, the transmission would be over. Hopelessly, he moved the needle to another station. The first words he heard came through, clear as a cow-bell.

"*Les femmes sont parfois volages.* . . ."

It took Raoul about three minutes to pack. He strolled leisurely downstairs, cancelled dinner and his room and explained that he had met some old friends who had asked him to stay with them. While Odette paid her bill and told some equally plausible story, Raoul sauntered out to the Terrace where Paul and Jacques were studying the menu and wondering what to have after their *pâté-de-foie-gras*. His news decided them and all they asked for was the bill. By a quarter past eight, all four conspirators were marching gladly along the road to Basillac at a steady four miles an hour, their heads high and their eyes on the moon that was rising like a gigantic blood-orange behind the jet-black fretwork of the trees.

At ten to ten they reached the road leading to the airfield. Over the grass a white mist lay waist-deep under the moon and the night was very cold and still.

A whispered conference was held at the field's corner and, by the shaded light of a torch, Raoul indicated the general layout and where he had decided to place the flare-path. The first thing to do was to circumnavigate the field so that Paul and Jacques should get the feel of the ground. Then, having marked down the angles of the "L"-shaped flare-path, they should all four rendezvous at the fringe of the copse and wait. As soon as the Lysander appeared, Raoul and Paul should run to the top of the "L's" upright, Lise should station herself at its right angle and Jacques at the end of the horizontal. Once the aircraft had touched down, Raoul and Paul would scramble in and take off while Lise and Jacques would meet again by the copse and together make their way across the river bridge and through the woods, rejoining the main road to Perigueux lower down. Speed was the absolute essential, for the moment they heard the aircraft coming in to land the guards would be out. With any luck, the Lysander's wheels would not have to rest on French soil longer than ninety seconds and Raoul sincerely hoped it wouldn't come in until after midnight when some, at least, of the guards might be expected to be in bed and, as it were, temporarily, *hors de combat*.

By twenty past ten the flare-path had been marked out and white handkerchiefs left on the ground to indicate each person's position. The mist was rising and soon the airfield would be as light as day. Odette opened her rucksack and produced her invariably first-class supper of smoked ham, Camembert and Armagnac. Sitting shivering in the shadow of the trees, she asked Raoul to give her messages to Buck and to her friends in the Section. With his mouth full of smoked ham, he said he would. It was disquieting to realize that, in a few brief hours,

G

this living being beside her in a French field could pick up a telephone and ask for a number in Essex and be connected and then ask to speak to her children and then talk to them freely. Though she very much wanted to send her love to them, she was silent. By now they would have settled down and become used to her absence and news of her, given by a stranger, would only distress them. It was at that moment that the faint grumble of an aircraft slipped into the silence.

Quickly, Odette collected the remains of the picnic into her rucksack and stood up. Raoul and Paul Frager melted into the half-darkness and Jacques ran along the shadow of the wood to his appointed position. She walked to where the white handkerchief lay on the ground at the angle of the "L", picked it up, felt the button of her electric torch. The first sound of the Lysander had now swelled to a roar and suddenly, she saw it, skimming in low from the north-east. In the moonlight, she could see a bright light begin to flash and blink as Raoul's lamp gave the "Q" sign again and again. Dash-dash . . . dot . . . dash. Dash-dash . . . dot . . . dash. The Lysander was like a black dragonfly in the sky and its shadow flowed over the field. Right over her head it sped in thunder to disappear beyond the hills. The sound of it grew fainter and fainter and died away. Soon in the quietness she could hear again the cold whisper of wind in the grass.

Raoul turned to Paul Frager. He said in a low voice. "I don't know what's happened, but she may come back. You'd better lie low here while I warn Lise and Jacques. I'll be back in a moment."

Stepping lightly on the grass, he walked over to where Odette stood. He told her to crouch down and wait where she was for ten minutes. If the Lysander hadn't come back by then, she should go to the copse and he would join her. She nodded. He smiled cheerfully and shrugged and tip-toed on to Jacques. Then he went back to Paul and lay down on the freezing ground. Dimly he saw two men crossing the field towards him. He nudged Paul and together they pressed their bodies flat to the earth. The two men passed within a few yards, so close that he heard the sharp sound of an iron-shod heel on a stone and the rumble of their voices. They faded into the sheaves of mist and he breathed again.

He heard a distant drone and listened intently. In a moment he was sure. The Lysander was coming back. Quietly he stood up, felt for his torch. The sound of the aircraft rose to *crescendo* and he was just going to flash the "Q" sign to the sky again when, not three hundred yards away, an Aldis lamp suddenly blazed whitely and began to signal the control tower at terrific speed.

The trap was sprung.

The meaning of the Aldis lamp signal was immediately clear, for the dark barrack-block burst into light and life. A man's voice shouted furiously in French and Raoul heard every word of his bellowed orders.

"Put out those lights, *imbéciles*. Wait until the plane lands and we'll grab the whole lot!"

There was the sound of confused shouting and the lights in the barrack-block faded into darkness. Steadily and coolly Raoul flashed his agreed dispersal signal towards Odette and Jacques, got a momentary blink of "message understood". Then he and Paul Frager broke to the left.

Odette stood stock still for a moment. Though she knew instantly that she was in extreme danger, the beat of her heart was unhurried and calmly, she saw the field, the copse and the river spread out before her like a relief map. She walked lightly towards the edge of the airfield, away from the buildings. Over her head, the Lysander was humming round in circles like an angry hornet and she found time to wish it God-speed and a fair wind to England. Jacques came running up to her and she said: "You make for the right and I'll meet you on the back road to Perigueux." He grinned and vanished into the mist. Slowly Odette walked on. The Lysander lifted its wings and soared upwards and away. Quietness fell like rain. She reached the edge of the trees and listened. Then she heard a terrible sound. With a trickle of ice-water spreading over her heart, she knew what that sound meant. It was the savage yelping and whining of a police dog.

She walked a few yards towards the copse and peered into the dim field. She saw or thought she saw a shape like that of a wolf casting and casting near to where she had stood. There are many people whose dreams are made horrible by snakes; the sense of blind falling will drive blood from the heart of the bravest and, over the grey hinterland between sleeping and waking, waters will rise and ooze and flow and slowly fill the lungs of the sleeper so that he awakes, gasping and crying for breath. These are some of the phantoms that haunt the nurseries of our childhood. There are many others—and the plateau of Odette's half-consciousness had always held in it a peculiar breathless fear. It was that she should be hunted by an animal.

With a yelp of triumph, the dog hit the line and moved towards her, snuffling. She slipped between the trees of the wood and half ran into their dark depths. Once she caught her heel and fell headlong. She heard the dog crash through the freezing bracken and stop. Wide-eyed and scarcely daring to breathe, she got to her feet and moved on into greater darkness. The dog followed and she could hear its body in the undergrowth, coming nearer and nearer. It stopped where she had fallen and whined eagerly, lurched on. Odette stumbled out of the copse and ran swiftly across the moonlit space of grass to the river. It was, she knew with desperation, her last chance and she took it, sliding down the bank and into the freezing water. The coldness of it drove the breath from her body so that she gave a shuddering moan. She waded into the stream and the water rose above her knees to her waist, gripping her cruelly with fingers of ice. The river bed shelved steeply upwards and she plunged through stiff reeds and climbed the far bank, making across a field of frozen stubble to the road. There she stopped to listen and to wring out the dripping hem of her skirt and spill the water out of her shoes. From the airfield, she heard a piercing whistle and the far away sound of a man's voice calling, "Frizi, Frizi". With her teeth chattering and her sodden clothes clinging to her, she set out to walk the ten kilometres back to Perigueux.

A few hundred yards down the road, she met Jacques Latour. Two of the four, at any rate, were safe.

*

When Raoul and Paul Frager had run a hundred yards, Paul suddenly stopped. He said that he had left a rucksack where he had been standing and that he was going back for it. He was cool and excited and he said: "There are twenty beautiful reports in it for Baker Street and we can't leave them for the Gestapo. I'll go back and get it." He had begun to saunter leisurely back when Raoul overtook him in a sprint and said breathlessly: "Make for the side of the road and wait for me." Raoul tore back over the grass, snatched up the rucksack and found Paul who appeared to be taking an almost academic interest in the progress of the chase. Using the cover of the woods and hedges, they made a wide circle to the west and finally settled down in a thicket between half-past three and four in the morning. Both men were used to night work and wore thick clothes. It was well that they did for before dawn, the temperature had sunk to 10 degrees below zero. By that time, Raoul's flask of Armagnac was empty and he and Paul were dreamlessly asleep under the stars.

It was about seven o'clock in the morning when Raoul and Paul re-entered Perigueux. As far as was possible, they had tidied themselves up, even to the extent of shaving in a stream by the roadside with the help of a pocket torch. With handfuls of grass, they had cleaned the mud off their shoes. This was of importance. Raoul was reasonably sure that news of last night's happenings would by now have certainly reached both Gestapo and Vichy police in the town and it would be indeed difficult to explain away muddied shoes to a sharp-eyed *flic*. They found a small restaurant and ordered coffee, keeping a sharp eye on the road. By nine o'clock, they had briefly visited every café that was open that Sunday morning. There was still no sign either of Lise or of Jacques and Raoul, as he chose a table on the terrace of the Grand Hotel overlooking the main square, was conscious of considerable anxiety.

At ten past nine, Odette walked serenely up the steps of the Grand Hotel. She looked as if she had that moment stepped out of the pages of *Vogue* and she greeted Raoul and Paul with grace. She wore her hat with an air and her frock was immaculate. There were no wrinkles in her silk stockings and the buckles of her high-heeled sandals caught and held the frosty sun. She was followed by Jacques who gave Raoul a cheerful "Good morning", as he drew up a chair. The four members of the party looked at each other in affectionate silence. Then Raoul's eyes laughed behind their spectacles as he summoned the waitress and said gaily: "*Quatre cafés, s'il vous plaît.*"

Lunch was interesting—and instructive. Not only was the food admirable, but it gave considerable pleasure to Raoul to sit back and listen to four members of the Gestapo at the next table as they discussed the curious goings-on that had been reported from Basillac last night.

"No doubt," said one of them, "the swine are still hiding in the woods—if indeed they failed to freeze to death. We shall get them by to-night, never fear, for the cordons are out now beating the coverts."

"There is a rumour that one of them was a woman."

"Nonsense, my dear fellow, nonsense. Frenchwomen are not the sort who consent to stay out all night in a freezing field."

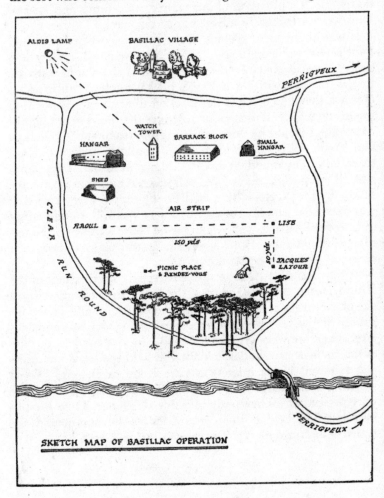

SKETCH MAP OF BASILLAC OPERATION

CHAPTER XVIII

"FROM A CHECK TO A VIEW. . . ."

RAOUL and Odette left Perigueux by the evening train for Toulouse and for Cannes. The journey was to be interrupted by some very disquieting news.

Arrived in Toulouse, Raoul immediately got into touch with Eugene. Eugene was a young man, a British officer, who had been landed by *felucca* in France some months before, and who engaged in training the autonomous units of French saboteurs in the Toulouse sector. As gay as he was brave, he was eventually to be caught in the net of the Gestapo and, after the usual bestial interrogations, was sent to the Concentration Camp of Buchenwald. To describe a man as being "an example to others" has become a trite phrase. Of Eugene, it was true and real. His bearing and his behaviour at Buchenwald were such that they even earned the grudging admiration of his gaolers, anaesthetized as they were, to all gradations of light and darkness in the human spirit. To his fellow-prisoners, he gave heart and courage by his patience, his dignity and his unquenchable faith in the essential goodness of man. A few days before the end of the war, the hangman came for him and his body died far away from home. But Eugene himself survived through the words of the poems he had written with a stub of pencil in his cell. These scraps of paper were found and brought home. They are the poems of a sensitive man, transfigured by forgiveness, and in them is the very breath of the winds that blew in freedom beyond the barbed wire of the camp. He called his slim collection *Leaves of Buchenwald*, little knowing that they would ever see the light of day. His triumph over Buchenwald was complete for he even saw the wooden uprights of the gallows that hanged him as a tree in bloom. His name was Captain Martin Perkins and his age, when he was murdered, was a bare twenty-two years.

On this February morning in 1943, Raoul and Eugene met

in a back-street café in Toulouse. It was a very fortunate thing
that they did meet, for Eugene was able to warn Raoul that his
flat in Cannes had yesterday been visited by the Gestapo.

The heat was on and the hunt was up.

Exactly how and why the Gestapo had got on to his trail,
he didn't know. But it was hardly surprising that they had
when he considered the general air of lurid melodrama that
obtained along the coast where men swore terrible oaths in
cafés and childishly showed each other their revolvers. Sun
or wine or a combination of both induced volubility and display
amongst the dwellers in the Mediterranean basin and it was
impossible to restrain either. He had tried often enough, warning men again and again that their lives and the lives of their
comrades depended on discretion in word and deed. In spite of
all that he could say, the curtains were rung up the moment he
had finished speaking and the show went on—with the patient
Gestapo in the rôle of cynical critics in the stalls.

Raoul's first thought now was for the safety of Arnaud. His
wireless operator's well-being must be cared for—both for personal and for professional reasons. Arnaud was still in Cannes
and should be got out immediately. Only when he was safe
would Raoul begin to consider his own position and that of
Lise. As far as he knew at this moment, the attention of the
Gestapo was exclusively directed towards himself but it could
well be otherwise. To speak to Arnaud on the telephone might
be dangerous, so one of Eugene's couriers was sent to Cannes
with instructions to gather what information he could on the
new situation and to bring Arnaud to Toulouse forthwith.

The next afternoon, Arnaud arrived. Cannes, he said, was
up and boiling and it looked as if the whole circuit had been
blown. If Raoul considered returning there, then Raoul was a
bloody fool. The Gestapo had been to Baron de Carteret at the
Villa Diana, asking for information about "Monsieur Pierre
Chauvet", and his whereabouts. de Carteret had sent them off
on a wild-goose chase to one of Raoul's empty flats, believing
that he—Raoul—was already half-way to England. As far as
Arnaud knew, de Carteret was not under suspicion nor was
Lise. He helped himself to a pickled onion and produced from
his pocket, a stump of garlic sausage. Even if Raoul was bloody
fool enough to go to Cannes, the Gestapo now had the address

of his flat and he would be arrested anyway. "You should have caught that Lysander to England last night," he said genially, "and cleared out for good. If I'd been there, I'd have shot the bastards and made it."

"If you really were to shoot all the people you've threatened to shoot," said Raoul gently, "we'd have run out of ammunition long ago. You are verbally the most homicidal character I know. Now listen to this. I'm going to Cannes or rather to la Bocca where I can hide up for a day or two in the farm, clear up one or two things and warn everybody to lie low. You can stay here and work for Eugene until I can get a new circuit going elsewhere. Then, when I've got everything fixed up in the new place, I'll send for you."

"Where will you go to?"

"A town called Annecy. It's in *Haute Savoie* and it has a lake and a lot of mountains."

"I don't like mountains," said Arnaud the single-minded, "they interfere with my transmissions."

*

As Raoul suspected that the Gestapo and the Vichy police would be as thick as green plover at Cannes Station, he returned by way of Antibes. In taking this precaution, he was wise for there had been a continual identity-card check during the last two days. He had decided to stay with a farmer at la Bocca, a silent and reliable man from whose farm Arnaud had frequently sent out his transmissions. It was an old tumble-down building and there was no accommodation for a guest. With many expressions of regret, the farmer offered him the best he could provide, a loft over the stable, and Raoul accepted gratefully. There he left his luggage before catching the autobus to Cannes.

The news everywhere was the same. Somebody had given the game away and the quicker he, and everybody who had been concerned with him, cleared out the better. The whole closely-woven fabric was being torn to shreds and every hour more and more people were being arrested and held for interrogation. Raoul should go.

Lying in darkness on a truss of sweet-smelling hay while the
G*

horses stamped and coughed beneath him, Raoul pondered the situation and planned his movements for the next thirty-six hours. He could not suddenly desert without a word, the men and women who had worked with him over the dangerous months and leave them to face the music. Even in their most extravagant moments, they had been loyal to him, and as far as it was humanly possible, he proposed to look after them now. Lise, up to to-night anyway, was unsuspected and she would be invaluable for she could move about Cannes with reasonable freedom. There was no mission to which she did not bring a beguiling mixture of reserve and audacity and he knew that she could be relied upon to bluff or charm her way out of any normal difficulty. Not altogether light-heartedly, he had wired Buckmaster at the outset of their association that she was "indispensable". It had since proved to be an under-statement. Turning this and to-morrow's problems over in his mind, he settled down more comfortably on the hay and slept as soundly as always.

When Odette arrived at the farm next morning on her bicycle, she brought very little news and most of it was bad. Only one thing was satisfactory. Suzanne had found the elusive aircraft engineer called Charles Roubier from Clermont Ferrand. He had turned up, complete with his ten-year-old son from whom he had refused to be parted. If England wanted his services, then his son must come too. *Père et fils* had both left by *felucca*. For the rest, the interrogations continued and he, Raoul, was definitely on the black list. "Monsieur Pierre Chauvet", free-lance journalist, would have to vanish into thin air. All that had been coped with. She had last night contacted the forged document expert and here was a beautiful new identity-card for "Monsieur Pierre Chambrun". He said, laughing: "You think of everything," and gave her a list of people to see if they were still at large and as much money as he had to distribute. He was himself going into Cannes to do one or two things but he would promise to keep away from the main streets. They arranged a discreet meeting place for lunch and she cycled away to carry out his instructions.

Next morning, they left Cannes for Annecy. The identity-card check was still in force and it was in considerable trepidation that Raoul approached the barrier to the platform alone.

Odette was several yards behind him so that, in the event of his being stopped, she would see what happened and act accordingly. There was a uniformed member of the Vichy police standing there looking at all identity-cards—while behind him, scanning the face of every passenger, was a civilian in a dark grey suit and a soft hat. This, Raoul knew, was the man he had to fear. He shuffled slowly forward in the queue, handed the policeman his new identity-card and looked the Gestapo man full in the face. He knew that any attempt at concealment would be fatal and that the only way to get through was by sheer effrontery. For a moment, he and the Gestapo man looked into each other's eyes. Then the policeman said sharply:

"*Voici, Monsieur.* There are others waiting to board the train."

"*Oh pardon, Monsieur.*"

Raoul picked up his suitcase and walked on to the platform. He felt a little sick as he turned round and saw Odette smiling and saying something to the policeman. The next moment she was putting her identity card back into her bag and politely refusing the offer of a would-be railway platform gallant to assist her with her luggage and find her a corner seat in his compartment.

As the train slid slowly out of the station, Raoul looked through the window. This was good-bye and he wondered when he would see Cannes again. Very soon, the sun would be setting behind the *Alpes Maritimes* and the sea, suddenly drained of its colour, would be flat and grey in the brief twilight; the air of the *Croisette* would become cold from one moment to another and the sun-worshippers would hurry back to the synthetic warmth of their rooms; soon the *boîtes* would be opening their sophisticated doors, the fiddlers would be tuning up and the saxophonists trying out a tentative note. *La ville des fleurs et des sports élégants* would be spreading its fly-paper . . . as the Gestapo had unsuccessfully spread theirs.

Odette came into his compartment, sat down beside him. He said in a low voice:

"Now we start all over again. New contacts, new faces, a new life." He yawned. He was very tired. "We're very lucky. What do you think about it?"

"I never liked Cannes.   I told you that a long time ago."

"Will you like Annecy?"

"I don't know. We'll see. Why don't you try and sleep for a little while?"

"You must be tired too."

"I'm all right."

As Raoul slept and the train raced and jolted through the night, Odette gazed straight ahead of her into the darkness. She was conscious of deep distress because, for no reason at all, she felt as she used to feel walking the Normandy cliffs as a young girl, that she was alone and lost and solitary and that she was entering the mouth of a tomb.

CHAPTER XIX

COW-BELLS OF SAVOY

THE ancient town of Annecy stands at the north-west end of the lovely lake that bears its name. It is a town so veined with canals that the great early seventeenth-century traveller Fodéré called it "The Venice of sweet waters". Over the jumbled roofs and the limpid canals, the bells of *Notre Dame de Liesse* chime and linger with a gentleness that has come to them over two centuries of time. The pavements of the old town run under cool arcades and there are dim wine-shops under the vaulted stone.

The lake is a mirror for the mountains of *Haute Savoie* and its waters are haunted by swans. Around its shores, villa and chalet seem to have alighted as haphazardly as white butterflies on the fringe of blue. Looking south from the acacia-lined promenade of the town, the wooded Semnoz rises darkly along the right shore and, on the left, the high fangs of the *Dent de Lanfon* take a jagged bite out of the sky. In the dawn, the mountains are dark blue and the lake, bled of its leaping life, lies flat and white and still. The young sun spills a chaos of colour over the mountains and the waters and, in the evening, the high rocks, rose in the first sunset, darken to jet as they retreat into the night.

Along the right bank of the lake under the Semnoz, the main road from Annecy to Albertville touches, leaves and retouches the water's edge. About five miles from Annecy, it widens into the cross-roads of St. Jorioz. This tiny village was to become Raoul's headquarters and in and around its quiet byways were to be many desperate comings and goings. Here, before spring had even painted the fields, Odette's long tribulation was to begin.

*

Raoul and Odette were met at Annecy station by Madame Marsac. As the town is situated four hundred and ninety-

eight metres above sea-level, Odette had taken the precaution to obtain from an accommodating physician in
Toulouse a medical certificate which stated that it was
necessary for her health that she should live at an altitude of
five hundred metres above sea-level. It was considered
that the difference of two metres would not do irreparable
harm. . . .

The drive to St. Jorioz was done in the suffocating autobus.
During the five mile journey, there was hardly a moment when
the driver did not have his finger on the ear-splitting klaxon.
Battered and deafened, Raoul and Odette fought their way out
of the bus at St. Jorioz crossroads and, putting down her bag,
Odette looked about her. Grouped round the four corners of
the crossroads, she saw the *Hotel de la Poste* with its own café
opposite; the *Hotel des Terraces* and the post and telegraph
office. The main road ran roughly north and south. At right
angles to it, one road struggled westwards to the cemetery and to
the mountains, another ran down to the lake and to the *Plage*.
It was a good place to get away from in an emergency—
and there was a balcony that encircled the first floor of the
Hotel de la Poste with an easy drop to the road. She picked
up her bag and followed Madame Marsac into the restaurant.

It was a large room with a number of small tables. A bar—
with the inevitable coffee machine—was on the left and
behind it, rows of bottles with imposing names. In the far
corner on the right, a piano badly needed tuning. There was
an entrance at either end of the room. Marsac himself was
sitting near the door. He rose, shook hands cordially with
Raoul and with Odette and led the way into the office where
Jean and Simone Cottet, proprietors of the hotel were
waiting.

Jean Cottet glanced at Raoul and at Odette with shrewd
eyes. He was a man of about thirty-five, dark, uncommunicative, watchful. The movements of his hands were deft with the
certainty that springs of controlled, muscular strength. The
bones of his face were set in a curiously oriental mould, rendered the more striking by the utter inscrutability of his glance.
Long ago, his integrity had been sifted and proved by those
members of the Southern Group whose business it was to assess

ANNECY

" The Venice of sweet waters "
(*Fodéré*)

the reliability of their compatriots. Jean Cottet was sound; *un homme de confiance.*

In days to come, he was to be more than that.

"These are my friends," said Marsac.

"I will do my best to see that they are comfortable," said Jean Cottet. He glanced indifferently at the two names in the visitors' book. He and his wife Simone were well aware that these entries meant precisely nothing. They also knew that this man and this woman were engaged on dangerous and secret work directed towards the enemies of his country; more than that, they knew the punishment meted out by the Gestapo to those who knowingly harboured such people. They were well content—even proud—to give them shelter.

Jean Cottet smiled his slow, infrequent smile and showed them upstairs to their rooms.

*

Many lessons had been learned in Cannes. The first of them was the vital necessity for dispersion. In St. Jorioz this proved to be impossible for the only suitable house was a large villa facing the station called "*Les Tilleuls*"—the Limes. The Limes was a bare quarter mile away the Hotel de la Poste and, with some misgivings, Raoul accepted it as the rendezvous for the groups—with the proviso that nobody should ever come to the hotel or make public contact with them or with Lise. The next thing to do was to find a special courier and a man called Riquet was detailed. Riquet was an ex-sergeant instructor of the French Air Force, a man in his middle twenties. He had three essential qualities for the post of courier. The first was his appearance. He was the epitome of the normal. It would be almost impossible to pick him out of any identification parade, for there was nothing outwardly to distinguish him from a hundred of his fellows. He was of medium height, blue-eyed, imperfectly shaved. His glance had in it that half-nervous obsequiousness that was so pleasing to his conquerors. His two other qualities would have been less gratifying to his enemies had they known that he possessed them. Riquet was as resourceful as an Irish horse-coper and as brave as a lion.

Raoul's primary needs had been satisfied. Now—Arnaud.

The first and most urgent task was to find him a safe house. That, said Riquet, had been arranged. In the little town of Faverges, twelve miles south of St. Jorioz, there were reliable people who would take him in and assist him in every way. Raoul need have no fears. *Tout est organisé.*

Raoul looked at Odette with philosophical resignation and she gave him the glimmer of a smile. Vinon. . . . Arles. . . . Basillac. . . . The familiar teaching came back. The wireless operator's comfort and safety was paramount. Arnaud's was the breath in the living body; only through the touch of Arnaud's fingers could that body be made to move and to function. With Arnaud safe, well and working, the body would live. Without him, the eager flesh would die.

Raoul stifled a yawn. He said to Riquet. "Can you get me a bicycle?"

"Surely. But I assure you that it is unnecessary. *Tout est organisé.*"

"I know, Riquet," said Raoul, "but I'd like to meet the Faverges people all the same."

*

With Riquet riding a girl's bicycle beside him, Raoul started out on the first of his many journeys to Faverges. Before long, both he and Odette were to know every stone and every curve of that weary road.

Riquet had spoken truth. *Tout était organisé.* The men of Faverges were bred the right way. Raoul first met Milleau, a tough, truculent short-horn bull of a man with a lowered head and a vast crown of crinkly hair. He was a rock of strength and it was a joy to work with him and to drink with him. Milleau and his comrades were resourceful, aware and determined. Theirs was a strong sense of reality. Where the gallants of the *Côte d'Azur* demanded footlights, the men of Faverges only asked for shadow. Their word, given after reflection, was their bond. They were as good a Group as existed in France.

The first problem—the human one—was solved and Raoul turned to consider Arnaud's practical requirements. Now to seek a house where Arnaud could work freely at all hours of the day and night. If he could find a house that commanded a gap in the mountains, a gap that opened in the general direction of London, it would very greatly help both transmission and reception. Raoul thought bitterly of the grotesque distortions of the *Alpes Maritimes*, of how the mountains mangled and soured the sensitive waves of sound. He explained his problem simply. One more point; given this house whose windows looked towards London, could one find a nearby post or tree to which a discreet aerial could be fixed?

The answer lay in the tiny hamlet of *les Tissots*.

There, three and a half miles in the hills, the forest warden owned a villa. He was a reliable man—again *un homme de confiance, un gonflé*—and his villa overlooked a north-west gap. Would Raoul care to come and see? There were trees in plenty and only a few cows and chickens to tell the tale. With Riquet, Raoul mounted his bicycle and pedalled towards the darkening hills.

Two hours later, they rode leisurely back to St. Jorioz. Riquet accepted a *Cinzano* in the bar as he waited for the packed auto-bus to Annecy. When he had gone, Raoul yawned copiously and went to bed.

Tout était au poil!

*

Long after Raoul slept, Riquet was sitting hunched up in a third-class carriage *en route* for Toulouse. He was on his way to a back room in a back street where Arnaud waited, cursing gently as he cleaned his Colt .38 and occasionally fingered his transmitting set.

*

The February moon period was coming up and it was to be a time of immense activity. Riquet returned from Toulouse with Arnaud, each carrying one of the two transmitting sets camouflaged as a suitcase. On the journey, a trivial incident had occurred, the sort of silly, unpredictable complication that can—and frequently does—spell disaster. The conductor of the autobus from Annecy to Faverges told Riquet gruffly that he must put his suitcase on the roof of the bus with the other luggage. Riquet refused politely. The conductor seized the handle. Riquet clung on. The two men glared at each other, each with a hand on the transmitting set. The prestige of minor officialdom was at stake and Arnaud—violent as ever—slid his hand to the butt of his Colt. The conductor shouted that he would call a *Gendarme*—now, immediately, this instant. Still Riquet held on—and, with his thumb, Arnaud eased over the safety catch. *Impasse!* The irresistible force of the conductor met the immovable solid of Riquet. . . . The problem was suddenly solved by the arrival of a stout woman from Faverges who carried two live hens. The conductor let go of the transmitting set, wrenched his features into a scowl of diabolic fury. Did Madame possibly imagine that the Annecy-Faverges autobus was a travelling zoological garden? *Oui ou non?* Somebody rang the bell and the driver let the clutch in with a jerk that threw everybody off their feet. Reluctantly, Arnaud pushed the catch back to safety, the conductor said *"Merde!"* and the incident was over.

Now, with Arnaud installed above Faverges, work began. During February, over forty suitable parachute grounds had to be listed and pin-pointed for London. Each one of them had to have its limit of dates between which its own B.B.C. *message personnel* would summon the faithful out on the actual night of the operation; more than that, each field had its own code-signal to be flashed to the pilot. London, furthermore, had to be informed exactly what each reception committee required in the way of material. Some asked for Sten-guns; others for explosives, medical supplies, clothes, radio sets, boots, commando knives, food, .36 hand-grenades. Attached to each container was a reward and a consolation for the reception committee's vigil. This was a parcel of coffee and cigarettes and— as patient grass-widows must not be forgotten—chocolate was also included. These parcels were eagerly divided and there was more competition than ever to join the reception committees. "The Limes" hummed like a dynamo. Couriers arrived from Nice, Antibes, Cannes, St. Raphael, Marseille, Arles, Toulouse; from Agen, Aix-en-Provence, Lyon, Clermont-Ferrand, from Paris, even from Belgium, the couriers came cheerfully to the villa opposite the station at St. Jorioz. They left again with instructions, money, explosives. Plans were laid for large-scale sabotage of railways. D-day was coming—sometime—and France should be prepared. A B.B.C. message was circulated which would serve to warn all informed listeners that they should wreck their particular sector of permanent way forty-eight hours after hearing the magic words. The actual destruction should be timed to take place between one and three in the morning when French passengers would be clear of the doomed trains—for the sorcerer of Baker Street had not only a taste for claret and burgundy but a care for French lives.

It was in the midst of this activity that the inscrutable Jean Cottet asked permission to join Raoul and Odette after dinner one night and drink his cognac in their society. For a little while, he dwelt on the decline of the drama, the price of pigs and the current scandal concerning the baker's wife at Albertville. Then, looking reflectively into the corner, he said:

"I am naturally unaware of—and incurious about—your politics. You are guests in my hotel. But it might interest you to know—academically—that there are a number of my compatriots who have, for reasons of their own, decided to resist being drafted to forced labour camps in Germany. These men —most of them are young, hunted, energetic and determined— have joined together to form an organization called a 'Maquis'. The war throws up some curious names and as these men live in the undergrowth, they have chosen the name of the scrub in which they lurk." He paused. "You are tourists, here for your health. Because you are much in the fresh air, it is possible that you have a map to assist you on your walks abroad. On that map I could place a pin on the exact spot where these rebellious young men have congregated. Suppose—only suppose—that an unscrupulous person wished to assist these impatient Maquisards, I could indicate to that unscrupulous person—or to his representative—what their needs are." He blinked like a Mandarin. "One cannot fight steel with flesh, Monsieur Chambrun. . . ."

Odette looked at him sharply. Was she in St. Jorioz, listening to Jean Cottet—or was she in Room 238, Hotel Victoria, Northumberland Avenue, London, W.1, listening to Captain

Selwyn Jepson as he gazed at a crack in the ceiling and
soliloquized on war?

"I think," said Raoul drily, "that I know a man unscrupulous
enough to wish to assist this . . . er . . . Maquis and these
Maquisards in every possible way."

"I thought you might," said Jean Cottet blandly. "Possibly
you would care to take a cognac in my room? It might be of
assistance if you were to bring a map. It aids the digestion."

★

More work for Arnaud. By an acacia tree near Duingt,
Odette handed him a message for immediate coding and transmission. It stressed the natural impatience of the French for the
advent of D-day and the stimulus that a delivery of arms and
ammunition to these rebellious men would give to other
hesitant Maquis. The iron was hot. Would London please
strike—now?

Within twenty-four hours, London's answer chimed like a
fox-hound.

FOR RAOUL: FROM BUCKMASTER
 WELL DONE STOP THIS IS WHAT WE HAVE BEEN WAITING FOR
STOP WARN MAQUISARDS PREPARE THREE LARGE BONFIRES AT
HUNDRED YARD INTERVALS IN STRAIGHT LINE OF WIND AND
LIGHT THESE ONLY AT SOUND OF SQUADRONS APPROACH STOP
EXPECT DELIVERY OF ONE HUNDRED AND TWENTY-SIX REPEAT
ONE HUNDRED AND TWENTY-SIX CONTAINERS BETWEEN MIDNIGHT
AND 0200 HOURS FROM TO-MORROW NIGHT STOP NO B.B.C.
MESSAGE STOP TALLY HO STOP ENDS.

The accident ambulance of Annecy hospital—an accommodating vehicle that was above suspicion—rushed the joyous
news to the hungry Maquisards in the hills. Men slipped
into the woods with pocket knives to hack down the
branches of trees and to prepare cans of precious paraffin.
Men sang as they flung the branches down, for the R.A.F.
was coming to *Haute Savoie* and there was jubilance in their
song.

The tempo quickened. Next day Raoul went home. A radio message in code instructed him to go to a field near Tournus where a Lysander would pick up him and Paul Frager and fly them to London. He handed over the direction of the whole, vibrant organism to Odette, blessed her and ran for the autobus to Annecy. At Tournus, a further message came at the last moment, telling him to go to a field near Compiègne. He and Paul Frager made it with minutes to spare. They found that the faithful Marsac had come to see them off. The Lysander came skimming down and a passenger jumped out. This was Roger—Lieutenant-Colonel Francis Cammaerts, D.S.O., Croix de Guerre, Médaille de la Résistance—a newcomer and a man who was to be the cause of many a headache to the Gestapo. Raoul welcomed him briefly and, with Paul Frager, scrambled into the aircraft. Less than sixty seconds later, he was airborne and climbing steeply in the moonlight towards the northwest and towards London.

Roger lit a Players—and then remembering that he was in France and not in Baker Street—buried it carefully and lit a *Gauloise* instead. Together he and Marsac set out for Paris where, fortunately for Roger, they parted at the Gare du Nord and arranged to meet later. But the gates and the guards of Fresnes Prison were to prevent Marsac from keeping the appointment.

*

Odette lay in bed in the Hotel de la Poste at St. Jorioz. Although it was after midnight, she was wide awake and listening. The night was very still. Just before one o'clock she heard a faint surging sound and jumped out of bed and opened her window. At first, it was little more than a drone in the silence but, as she stood there in her bare feet, the sound swelled and became constant. It became a roar and it turned into thunder, thunder that rolled off the flat waters of the lake and boomed among the mountains, rolling and booming and echoing in her heart. There were tears in her eyes as the high squadrons of the R.A.F. passed overhead with the cool symmetry of grey-lag on the wing. They were on their way to the Maquisards of *Haute Savoie* and she knew that the beacons would blaze in the hills that night and that their fire would illuminate all France.

★

Next morning, Odette went into Annecy in the autobus. She wore a dark grey coat and skirt, a blue blouse and miniature clusters of forget-me-knots in her ears.   It was a beautiful morning, loud with the rising of sap, and she walked as if she were stepping on thistle-down. She kept an appointment at the third tree on the boulevard that overlooked the lake and gladly told the courier from Grasse that London now not only approved but encouraged active sabotage.   She went to call on "Tom" Morel, ardent patriot and martyr who, at the time, clothed his brave body in the uniform of the Vichy police. From him, she got a number of blank identity cards, the address of an expert in radio-technology and a warning that the comings and goings at St. Jorioz were beginning to interest the authorities.   She went blithely on her way to her hairdressers and, while being fanned by an electric drier, listened with simulated indignation to an account of how the insupportable R.A.F. had last night had the temerity to fly over Annecy —twenty, thirty bombers, Madame, in formation like wild geese in the moonlight. *Quelle audace, Madame!* All the town was talking of it—and the sound of their engines made a noise greater than that of a church organ. Madame had herself heard this music from the sky? No? A pity. It was, of course, *très impertinent* of the R.A.F. but one could not help wondering about their destination.

Odette had invited a guest for lunch at St. Jorioz, the mother of Marsac's secretary. She finished with her hairdressers at eleven thirty and, walking to the autobus, stopped to buy a bunch of living forget-me-nots. She pinned these to the lapel of her coat. The bus was reasonably empty and she got a seat. Before it started, several people were standing in the narrow passage. As she bumped along the lake-side, she glanced idly at the strap-hangers. For no reason at all, her casual glance rested on a man, a man in a dark suit. The pulse of her blood suddenly quickened and she looked at him from under her lids with a sharp, instinctive sense of danger. Like a hare in the corn, she cocked her ears to the soundless presence of a poacher. He was of middle height, aged about forty-two or -three; his face was oval, his nose longish, his eyes brown and benign behind his spectacles. He caught her glance, looked away. Though he had made no sign and moved no muscle, Odette was aware that he was aware of her.

Hugo Ernst Bleicher of the Counter-espionage Section of the German Army was on his way to St. Jorioz to bring off the coup of his career.

PERSONAL PARTICULARS

Name: Bleicher
Aliases: Monsieur Jean
Lt.-Col. Henri
Henri
Jean Castel
Jean Verbeck
Gottschalk
Henri Botherau

Christian Names: Hugo Ernst
Date and Place of Birth: 9.8.1899,
Tettnang, Wuerttemburg

Nationality: German

Occupation: Manager of Export firm

Weight: 12 stone 5 lbs.
Height: 5 feet 10 inches
Build: Well built
Hair: Brown, receding at forehead
Face: Oval, longish nose, wears spectacles
Eyes: Brown
Physical peculiarities:
Four vaccination scars, upper right arm; hairy back and chest

Last Permanent Address: Poppenbuttel, near Hamburg
Languages: German, French, Spanish
Parents: Karl Bleicher; Emma––née Vogel
Brothers: Two, aged 43 and 48 years
Wife: Luzie; one son, aged 10 years
Identity documents: Abwehr-Ausweis No. 3933, issued Berlin, 16th of July, 1943, in name of Hugo Bleicher.

CHAPTER XX

PORTRAIT OF HENRI

HUGO ERNST BLEICHER sprang of "good sound" German stock. For several generations, his ancestors had lived in Tettnang, a small town on the shore of Lake Constance where they had always been held in proper respect by the bourgeoisie to which they themselves belonged. A great-grandfather had been *Posthalter* to the Count of Thurn, another had been chief of the Postal Service. When Hugo was born on the eve of the new century, the family had taken to trade and his father was owner of a large and prosperous cycle store. He was a genial, slow-thinking sentimentalist—and a fanatical admirer of the young Kaiser Wilhelm II who was already busily engaged on his deliberate policy of bullying and brow-beating Europe. Karl Bleicher was a perfect example of that sinister schizophrenia which splits the German soul. In relation to his own domestic circle, he was an affectionate father and a man of high moral principles; as a servant of the state, there was no dishonest or bestial act to which he would not gladly put his hand without conscience, guilt or remorse.

Home life for Hugo and his two brothers was a very happy one. There were boats to sail on Lake Constance and fine walks in the pine-woods. He was sent first to the local school and then to High School, completing his education at the Senior School at Ravensbourg. When the question arose as to how he should earn his living, his father naturally suggested the cycle shop. Blinking behind his spectacles, the boy Hugo calmly announced that he had decided to do one of two things —either to enter the Navy or, if that failed, he would fulfil the dearest wish of his heart and become a concert pianist.

As he had half-hoped, he was rejected for the Navy because of his defective eyesight. He applied himself with passion to the piano and practised unceasingly. Only after months did it become manifest that the profession he loved more than all others was beyond him. His talent, though considerable, was not enough in a country that had bred some of the finest musicians of all time. It was a bitter disappointment to him and, more than that, he took it as a personal humiliation. He was a boy of boundless social ambition and it is possible that he was not uninfluenced by the thought of the advancement that the concert would have automatically brought. It would have meant escape from the cycle shop and entry into a fabulous world peopled by the rich, the great and the sophisticated. With melodious fingers, he could render real and pliable those scented, feminine phantoms who haunted his adolescent dreams. Now all that was gone. He became morose and resentful and at last accepted ungraciously the offer of a two years apprenticeship with a firm of bankers at Ravensbourg. When the two years were up, he stayed on. There was no point in doing anything else for the Great War was raging and he would be called to the Colours on his eighteenth birthday. In 1917, he was flung casually into the infantry as a private and became a minute cell in the gigantic frog-spawn of the German Army. Transferred to a Pioneer Gas Corps, he moved up to the bloody welter of the Somme and slyly succeeded in getting himself captured by the British without further ado. Private Bleicher found life within the wire of 165 P.O.W. Camp near Abbeville to be unpalatable. More for the purpose of pitting his wits against those of his captors than for that of rejoining his comrades in the line, he escaped four times. He either failed to reach Germany or did not want to for, having devised the perfect escape method, he allowed himself tamely to be recaptured each time. He had, after all, had the intellectual exercise he needed and was now content to sit down in safety and wait for the war to end. He was repatriated by the British in 1919 and returned to Tettnang.

By this time, a little fire was smouldering in his loins whose heat was never to be quenched. He followed a woman to Wiesbaden and worked there for a year on the railways, laying siege to her body. When she fell, he left and pursued another woman to Mainz, getting a job there as interpreter in the local taxation office. Carnal victory again brought boredom, and, though he had become head of the office, he left Mainz in 1922, travelling to Hamburg where his Aunt Marie was working as a lady's maid to the wife of General Levinski. It was galling indeed for the suave and cultured Bleicher to have to own to an aunt in domestic service and even more galling to be forced to accept the General's good offices in getting a job. He would have preferred the approach to have been through the drawing-room rather than via the servants' hall but he took the post offered him and immediately severed all connection with his aunt. He joined an export firm called the *Afrikanische Handels-Kompanie* which soon after amalgamated with several other Hamburg export houses under the name of the E.L.K.A. Company. Though he found the ladies of Hamburg most accommodating and co-operative, he was glad to sail to Tetuan in Morocco as manager of the Bazar Aleman and looked forward keenly to the sunshine, the palms and the golden-skinned girls of the Mediterranean.

In October, 1927, the E.L.K.A. Company went bankrupt. Bleicher was forced to close down the Bazar Aleman and returned to Hamburg. Almost immediately, a man named Max Friedrich, whom he had met in North Africa, obtained for him the post of foreign correspondent in the Jewish firm of Bodenheimer, Schuster & Co., Hamburg, exporters of chemical goods. Here Bleicher became chief clerk, and his amatory wanderings temporarily over, married a simple, healthy girl called Luzie and settled down to found a family and to play the piano. A son was born a year later and Bleicher, now nearing forty, saw the future in terms of domestic and musical tranquillity.

Just as Kaiser Wilhelm II had led Germany to damnation a generation ago, Adolf Hitler was doing it now. Father and son were both led by the nose. Alas for Hugo's dreams of the future as a perpetual musical soirée, interrupted only by the laughter of his children. . . .

As the name of his firm was Jewish, it had to be changed to Friedrich & Co. All the Jewish agents had to be sacked forth-with so that the brown-shirted louts of the S.A. could hound them into concentration camps. Though they had been good and loyal servants of the firm; though it was to their work that the firm owed its prosperity; though many of them were Bleicher's personal friends and faithful colleagues, Hugo did not hesitate. Years ago, when he had exploited his Aunt Marie to the full, he had thrown her overboard. Now he tipped his Jewish friends off the raft and cynically became a member of the Nazi Party.

How much he actually believed in Hitler is hard to say. Some of his subsequent actions indicated that his was merely lip-service and that he was ready to hitch himself—and his piano—to any star that happened to be in the ascendant. It is difficult to believe that a cool, subtle and intelligent man such as Hugo Bleicher could sincerely worship at the throne of a creature possessed. Eva Braun was still shrouded in the *triple ninon* of the future and the Führer, surrounded as he was by the glandular gorillas of the S.S., moved in a sort of homicidal chastity that was far from the taste of Hugo. Nevertheless, he went through the Party motions with the requisite fervour and made the correct, corrupt contacts—with the result that, at the outbreak of war, his was at once made into a reserved occupation. Possibly, that musical twilight would come true after all.

In the triumphant turmoil of victory, however, local bosses and Party demi-gods were being uprooted and replanted elsewhere. Bleicher saw the red light—and answered an advertisement for those with knowledge of languages to join the Postal Censorship. He was engaged at once and found to his joy that the job gave full rein to a latent passion for peering and prying into the affairs of others. He had great fun for a little while and was beginning to compile a list of interesting persons and addresses when the blow fell and he was called up and made a member of the *Geheime Feld-Polizei*, the German equivalent of the Field Security Police.

Group 312, G.F.P. were under training at Duisberg. There Bleicher learned the technicalities of spying on his fellow-soldiers. He took to the work like a duck to water and when the Group was sent to the conquered Hague for a month in May, 1940, he had already been earmarked for promotion to Sergeant. After a short spell at Rugles, near Verneuil, the Group was transferred to Paris—with the task of assuring security of part of the route along which the victorious Führer was to make his triumphal entry. In spite of the magnitude of the German victory and the much-publicized benefits of the New Order about to be conferred on France, it was not unwisely decided that it would be the height of folly for the Führer to expose his

person to the plaudits of the French populace. Triumphant
entries were off. That was a matter of small importance to
Sergeant Bleicher who had not failed to profit from his fortnight's stay in Paris. More moves. This time he went to Caen
in Normandy. The little, stoked fire about his loins was
smouldering away merrily and it burst into flame when he
encountered buxom, sloe-eyed Suzanne L., a lady who ran a
bar in the town and dispensed her favours and her champagne
with impartial discretion. After a brief and tumultuous courtship,
Suzanne sold her bar and became Bleicher's mistress. Though
he was to stray occasionally from her side and sleep in other
beds—"it was only for the purpose of getting certain information, *chérie*," he would say with a pseudo-repentant sigh—
he remained reasonably faithful to her until 1944.

Caen, St. Lo, Cherbourg—everywhere that Bleicher went,
Suzanne was sure to go.

By October, 1941, he was becoming more than a little tired
of the Field Security Police. His duties were purely those of a
military policeman, a glorified hush-hush redcap, and he saw
no hope of getting that commission for which he was intel-
lectually equipped and for which he considered he was socially
entitled. It had become almost an obsession with him, the
obsession of the son of the cycle shopkeeper of Tettnang. To be
an officer, even the most junior officer, would be balm to the
remnants of his *bourgeois* soul. The social chasm between
commissioned and non-commissioned rank was, to his mind,
a vast one and, if he could only jump it, it would more than
compensate for his many disappointments. He had failed to
join the Navy; he had failed to become a concert pianist. If
only he could one day walk the pavements of Tettnang wearing
the uniform of a German officer, his cup would be full. He
began to make application through various channels to get a
transfer to the mysterious and sophisticated "*Abwehr*".

*

The *Amtsgruppe Auslandsnachrichten und Abwehr*—usually simply
called "*The Abwehr*"—was the foreign intelligence and counter-
espionage service of the German Army. It was a purely
military instrument and came under the direct control of the

High Command who, sometimes openly and sometimes covertly, had always preserved a steady antagonism to the upstart Hitler and all his works. The *Abwehr* prided itself on the fact that it had nothing to do with the Nazi Party or with Himmler's various "Security Services" and a perpetual battle raged between it and the regimented thugs of the S.S. So strong was the *Abwehr* in 1940 that one of its senior officers, Colonel Pieckenbroek, when asked by an intermediary of Keitel's to arrange the murder of General Giraud, coolly replied: "It is about time that Keitel was clearly instructed to tell his Herr Hitler that we, the military *Abwehr* are no murder organization like the Sicherheitsdienst or the S.S." Pieckenbroek's deliberate choice of the words "Herr Hitler"—i.e. Hitler the civilian—was a calculated insult to the Führer and indicated the strength of his position. In 1943, however, Himmler at last achieved *Gleichschaltung* and the organization was submerged in the slime of the S.D. Its director and chief was Admiral Canaris who, for his alleged part in the anti-Hitler plot, was arrested and vanished into one of the S.S. Concentration Camps. There he died—according to one report—by the genial process of slow strangulation.

The *Abwehr* was very much Bleicher's cup of tea. In the pleasant society of the upper classes, he could put his intellectual and social talents to full use and—even more important—the commission for which he longed might well be within reach. By a curious roundabout way, he was to become a member by the end of the month.

*

In Cherbourg, there was a certain underground organization of saboteurs, mainly composed of Poles. Its leader was a gentleman known as Kiki, and this Kiki was unwise enough to pick a quarrel with one of his subordinates. The subordinate, smarting under the lash of Kiki's tongue, sidled along to the offices of the Field Security Police (Luftwaffe Section) and denounced his master. The F.S.P. thanked him politely and sent a report to the headquarters of *Abwehr* III in Paris. It was passed to the St. Germain section of the *Abwehr* "for action", and from there, one Captain Borchers, a clever, ruthless Intelligence officer, was sent to Cherbourg to investigate. He went into the matter with care and decided that Kiki might eventually prove to be useful to the Germans in the rôle of double-agent. He should therefore be arrested and grilled and, provided he could be induced to switch his loyalty, he should be released again to get on with the job of betraying his friends. Captain Borchers desired not the death of the sinner but rather that he should transfer his wickedness and live. It happened, however, that there was no suitable person at the headquarters of the Luftwaffe Section to make the actual arrest and the matter was again passed "for action" to Field Security Police (Army) to which Bleicher was attached. He was more than delighted when he happened to be detailed to do the job. This, he knew, was his big chance and he seized it with both hands.

Accompanied by the traitor who had denounced Kiki and by a contingent of his own men, Bleicher followed his quarry from Cherbourg station. Kiki was on his way to pay a call on his mistress and suspected nothing. At a street corner, he stopped to light a cigarette. Bleicher closed in—and Kiki looked round to see half a dozen sub-machine guns trained on his body. It was a fair cop and he went quietly. In handing him over to Captain Borchers, Bleicher was smooth, suave, ingratiating. He was enchanted to have been of assistance to the *Herr Kapitän* over this trivial matter. With consummate skill, he managed to convey the impression that he was indeed a flower that blushed unseen and was wasting its sweetness on the Cherbourg air. Though no hard suggestion was made or implied, both men understood each other perfectly, and when Captain Borchers left for Paris with Kiki in handcuffs, Bleicher went back to his billet and, with a slow smile, began to pack.

These things take time to find their way through the usual channels and it was some days before a telegram arrived summoning Sergeant Bleicher to St. Germain. He was all packed and ready to go and he took leave of his comrades with touching regret. They had been such very good friends and he loved them dearly. To the faithful Suzanne, he said that it might be a week or two before he could send for her but she should be ready to follow him to St. Germain in the near future. Gently smiling, he left by train. Before his spectacled eyes danced the vision of the commission for which his soul lusted.

"Lieutenant Bleicher," sang the wheels of the train,

"Captain Bleicher, Major Bleicher, Lieutenant-Colonel
Bleicher. . . ."

He was received at St. Germain by Captain Borchers—
Bleicher wondered idly how soon he too would have to be kicked
overboard—and at once introduced to Major Eschig, head of
the St. Germain section of the *Abwehr*. The interview was a
brief one. As a result of his assistance in the arrest of Kiki,
Sergeant Bleicher was to be transferred at once from the
Geheime Feld-Polizei to the *Abwehr*. Captain Borchers would
make the necessary arrangements. Sergeant Bleicher might
now dismiss. *"Heil Hitler!"*

"Heil Hitler!" said Bleicher, putting into the hackneyed
phrase exactly the same mixture of adulation, cynicism and
contempt as that used by Major Eschig. He and Eschig were
obviously going to get on.

"Captain Bleicher," tootled the motor-horns of St. Germain,
"Major Bleicher, Lieutenant-Colonel Bleicher, Colonel
Bleicher. . . ."

*

Throughout 1942, Bleicher applied himself with diligence to
counter-espionage. The field of his activities covered all France
and he found no shortage of lambs for the slaughter. He was
appointed to the position of expert adviser to *Abwehr* III (F.)
and was always prepared to go anywhere as ordered. Sometimes he went alone. When he was in Paris, he dined on equal
social terms with his superior officers and cultivated a nice
discrimination in claret. He moved always through a fine web
of intrigue and, genuinely a humane man, tried to convert his
captures to his own cause. Those who proved intractable—or
worse still, boring—were turned over to the S.D. In spite
of the fact that he used the S.D. much as a High Court Judge
uses the services of the common hangman, he felt himself to be
on another plane. His was the verdict, theirs the execution.
Several factors—one of them strongly personal—may have
influenced his seemingly inexplicable behaviour during the
early months of 1943.

By then, Goebbels' "law of the pendulum in war" had begun
its slow swing away from the Reich. The freezing shambles of
Stalingrad had ended in defeat; the church bells of England

had rung for el Alamein and Rommel licked his wounds to the echo of the pipes, the drums and the cannon of the 8th Army; sawdust was dribbling out of the *Duce* and the invasion and collapse of Italy was only a matter of a few months. It had become manifest to any thinking German—and Bleicher had not only a clear brain, but access to files—that victory for Germany was out of the question. How soon would the sombre tragedy come to an end? How long would Hitler's sexual frustration be allowed to find its gratification in the flow of Nordic blood? These problems may have worried Bleicher to the extent that he found it desirable to stretch a tentative toe into the other camp. It may be that his increasing dislike and contempt for the S.D. influenced him. Certain it is that he was moved, as always, by a not at all academic appreciation for a most elegant ankle.

*

Assuming the socially gratifying role of "Lieutenant-Colonel Henri", Bleicher arrested Marsac as he was taking a cup of *ersatz* coffee in the spring sunshine of the Champs Elysées. He was moved to Fresnes Prison forthwith and spent the afternoon in agitated speculation as to who had betrayed him. To his cell that night came the same distinguished Lieutenant-Colonel who had arrested him—with an astounding proposition. It was a proposition which seemed to Marsac to be capable of meaning the difference between war and peace and it was as a result of it that Hugo Bleicher found himself strap-hanging on the autobus between Annecy and St. Jorioz. Always ready to combine duty with pleasure, he found time to admire the profile and the forget-me-not earrings of a slim, unescorted young woman on the front seat.

H

CHAPTER XXI

"CEASELESS PURSUIT AND FLIGHT WERE IN THE SKY...."

IT was in no way a surprise to Odette when the benign man in spectacles got off the bus at the St. Jorioz crossroads. She saw him stand there and look about. Then he asked somebody the way to a house by the railway station, a house called "*les Tilleuls*", and set off down the road. Odette's eyes narrowed. She walked on a hundred yards and turned down a narrow road parallel to the one he had taken. She crossed a field, climbed a fence that enclosed the patch of garden and crept to the window of the living-room. As she had suspected, he was there talking to Marsac's adjutant. The window was open at the top and she could hear snatches of their conversation. She listened, straining her ears. When she had heard enough, she slipped away and recrossed the field to the road. Her face was set.

Her luncheon guest was waiting. She would have far preferred to lunch alone but now this was impossible. She wanted to have time to think, to sort out the astonishing implications of what she had heard, to decide coolly on a course of action. She chose a table facing the door and began to order. While she was still discussing the relative virtues of *escalope de veau* and *poulet garni*, she saw one of the couriers from "The Limes" come in and look round. He saw her and came immediately to her table. He said in a quick rush of words:

"Lise, there is a man here who wishes to speak to you."

She looked at him icily. "You know Raoul's orders—that you should never come and speak to me here."

"Yes, I know. But this is urgent and. . . ."

"You see that I have a guest. Please leave immediately."

He stood irresolutely. She turned deliberately to her guest. The courier walked away. Out of the heel of her eye, she saw him return to his companion, shrug helplessly. The other smiled with a sort of ominous, genial patience and leisurely

ST. JORIOZ

and the Lake of Annecy

picked up the menu. Then he sat down and beckoned to the waiter.

Somehow Odette managed to keep the bright bubbles of conversation flashing in the air. She and her guest talked of trivial things—and it seemed an age before she finally took her departure. Odette returned to her table alone. The man stood up and walked across to her. He bowed and said in almost accentless French:

"Mademoiselle Lise?"

She gave him a cool, upper-class look.

"I am she."

"May I be permitted to take my coffee with you, Mademoiselle? I would not intrude if I had not things of importance to say."

"You will forgive me, Monsieur. I do not know your name."

"My name is Henri and I am an officer in the German Army."

"I fail to understand what an officer in the German Army can have to say to me."

"I am the bearer of a letter, Mademoiselle, a letter from your . . . colleague, Monsieur Marsac."

"Please sit down."

He offered her his cigarette case and, after a split second's hesitation, she took one. It was the first cigarette she had smoked for months and she took it deliberately, not to soothe her nerves for they were steady and taut, but to have something in her fingers, something at which she could look, something she could pretend to consider while she adjusted her mind to the tenor of his words. He said, carefully watching her:

"I came from Annecy on the *autobus* this morning."

"Oh did you, Monsieur," she said with polite interest. "As a matter of fact so did I."

He frowned. He knew that she had not only seen him on the bus, but that she had noticed him sharply. He also knew that she knew that he was aware of the fact. Up to this moment he had regarded his job as being comparatively simple. Now he wasn't quite so sure. He looked at her with both professional and personal interest.

"First let me give you my letter of introduction from Monsieur Marsac."

She skimmed it quickly. It was fairly short. It said that he had been arrested and was in Fresnes Prison. He was well but hungry. He had not been ill-treated. Since his arrest, he had had several conversations with "Colonel Henri" of the German Army who he believed to be trustworthy. Colonel Henri would himself discuss an important matter with her. That was all. She folded the note and put it in her bag.

"I would like now to give you the circumstances of Monsieur Marsac's arrest—and some very confidential information."

"I am all attention."

"I have told you that I am an officer in the German Army. I am a member of the military *Abwehr*, that is the counterespionage department, whose allegiance is solely to the General Staff. We of the Military *Abwehr* are, as it were, a race apart. Because of this, we are ourselves watched by the Gestapo—whose allegiance is to the Nazi Party. It was I who arrested Marsac, in order to save him from arrest by the Gestapo and in order that I might make a certain proposal to this brave and patriotic Frenchman. Within the limits of his duty to France, Marsac is prepared to further my plan. Marsac, however, is in prison. You are in freedom." He said with startling irrelevance. "Tell me, Mademoiselle, do you care for music?"

"Very much so."

His brown eyes smiled with genuine pleasure. "I am so glad," he said. He shook his head as if reluctantly dismissing a subject about which he would have preferred to talk. "What I have to say now may be surprising to you. It is this. Germany is split. On the one side stands Adolf Hitler and his bloodthirsty satellites, on the other stands the High Command of the Germany Army—and between the two is a vast and ever-widening gulf. It was not the High Command who made war, Mademoiselle, but Adolf Hitler. He had success as you know, such success that the Generals, wise and experienced as they were in the art of war, began to wonder if this lance-corporal could not indeed be the greatest commander of all time. These doubts are now dispelled. Hitler's greatness was merely the sum of the littleness of his enemies—and these enemies are no longer little. The descendant of Shickelgruber is dwarfed by the descendant of Marlborough and, even though we hold half a continent in chains, Germany's ultimate doom under Hitler is sure. We of the Germany Army love our country, Mademoiselle, and only we can save Germany from destruction."

"Nothing can save Germany from destruction."

"There I think you are wrong. If Germany is destroyed, Europe is destroyed. With Adolf Hitler out of the way, Germany could sue honourably for peace with the West. Of the East, I do not speak. You, Mademoiselle, could be the intermediary between those who think as I do—and London. It is not an unimportant rôle," he said drily, "for a young woman of wit and discretion."

"What do you want of me, Monsieur?"

He drew up his chair.

"I want you to give me a transmitting set and code whereby I can get into direct touch with the British War Office."

Odette looked at him with detachment while her mind raced and darted like quicksilver. This was too big a proposition for her to tackle alone and she knew that she urgently needed the guidance of London. She had learnt to distrust over-simplification and the situation, as outlined by Henri, was far too candid. Only Buckmaster would see the labyrinth that was spun behind. The first thing to do was to play for time. She gave him a smile in which interest, regret and suspicion were smoothly blended.

"I am unable to give you a transmitting set, Monsieur, for the simple reason that I haven't got one. Without that, a code would be useless to you. On the other hand, I have got means of communicating with London myself and that, subject to certain conditions, I am prepared to do."

"Does it not strike you as a little odd," said Henri gently, "that you, a British agent in France, should seek to impose conditions on a German officer—who has got powers of arrest?"

She laughed. Her laughter was infectious and full of gaiety.

"Come, Monsieur, it is unworthy of the great issues at stake that you should remind me that I am at your mercy. We are both adults. May I speak freely?"

"Please do." A brand-new thought slid into his mind and stayed there. What a recruit she would make for the *Abwehr!*

"You know my name, Monsieur, and you have told me yours. You will forgive me if I say that your occupation, that of German officer, does not automatically recommend you to me. You have given me a note from Marsac who is in prison. In what circumstances was it written? Was it written freely or under duress? I don't know. I do know that Marsac is hungry. I suggest this, that you allow me to send a man with you to Paris and that you take him into Fresnes Prison with you and that he talk to Marsac—by himself. He can then report back to me and I will decide what to do—in the light of his report."

"I agree to that."

"Good. Perhaps—as Marsac is hungry—you will allow me to send a parcel of food as well."

"Yes, I agree to that too. You wouldn't run away, would you, Mademoiselle Lise?"

"It is hardly likely that I would deliver a man—however unimportant—into your hands and then run away. No. I assure you that I will wait for his report on Marsac."

"I believe you." He smiled. "You are wholly French?"

"May I ask why this interest in anthropology?"

"I could have wished for a dash of Teutonic blood."

She shook her head. "Should I say that I am sorry to disappoint you?" She stood up. "If you will be here at five o'clock, I will present to you the hostage, and the food parcel. Your country, I know, has a care for hostages but the man I send will not be worth arresting in view of the importance of your proposal. One does not catch flies with vinegar, Monsieur."

He said slowly. "I suppose I couldn't induce you to come to Paris yourself—to see Marsac. Next week, they are giving Mozart's *Magic Flute*."

"No, Monsieur Henri. My health is delicate and I must remain at an altitude of five hundred metres above sea-level."

"I quite understand. I have no doubt that we will meet again." He bowed and walked leisurely into the sunny afternoon.

*

Odette wrote a brief report and gave it to Arnaud for coding and for transmission to London. When he learned that she had that afternoon sat in the Hotel de la Poste talking to a German officer, he scowled and said that if he had known, he would have shot the bastard. She laughed. She said: "Working with you makes time stand still because it's always the

Fifth of November. Arnaud, you know that English officer 'Roger' who arrived in the Lysander that took Raoul away? He's staying at the Hotel de la Plage at the moment and I think he'd better go. Things are getting a little too involved for a newcomer and I've decided to send him to a safe place in the south. How soon could you move, if necessary?"

"Any moment. But don't be a bloody fool all your life and think I'd go without Raoul and you."

"That's as it may be, but I should pack. We may have to make a very rapid getaway. My impression is that zero hour is very near."

She rode her bicycle back to St. Jorioz. She knew that it was a question of waiting until the man she had sent away with Henri came back from Paris after seeing Marsac. Only when she had the whole story could she report fully to London and ask for instructions. She had sent Jules (the name "Jules" cloaks the identity of a man subsequently arrested on a charge of high treason. He awaits trial in Paris as this book goes to press) and all she could do until his return was to make tentative plans for possible evacuation. This would be difficult for couriers were flocking in and out of Annecy from the four corners of France, coming to her for instructions, advice and money. It would be no easy matter suddenly to wave a wand and dissolve the whole, elaborate organization into smoke. She wasn't Mr. Jasper Maskelyne and her rabbits were allergic to top-hats. . . .

Jules returned from Paris. He said that he had been admitted into Fresnes Prison and had talked to Marsac alone. Marsac was well and he thanked her for the food parcel. Jules lit a cigarette. Henri, he said, was absolutely trustworthy. Of that he was convinced. Now Henri had an even more ambitious idea. If Lise could arrange a bomber pick-up on one of three fields, he, Henri, would somehow get Marsac out of prison and himself fly with him to London. It would be quite a happy little party. Henri—and, of course, the faithful Suzanne—Marsac and his lieutenant, Lise herself—all of them would fly to London, Lise would introduce Henri to Buckmaster and between them, they would work out peace terms on behalf of the German High Command, peace terms which would be acceptable to the British War Cabinet. Henri would then be returned to Germany—leaving Suzanne as a sort of svelte Dr. Watson in Baker Street—and he would get on with the puny problem of blowing up Adolf Hitler and his evil associates. In brief, all Lise had to do was to summon a bomber and the war would be practically over.

Listening to this proposal, Odette was more and more deeply conscious of one dominant belief. She did not know what lay behind this elaborate façade; she could not begin to understand the Macchiavellian workings of Henri's mind; of only one thing she was sure. Jules had come back from Paris to betray her and her comrades.

She said, hating him and his shifty, dishonest eyes:

"You have done very well, Jules. Go back to Paris, see Henri and tell him that I am trying to arrange a bomber. This moon period ends on 18th of April and that is the date I'll try to work to. I'll let you know the position of the field later."

"Excellent, Lise." He asked with exaggerated unconcern: "What news of Raoul and when is he coming back?"

"I don't know, but if he comes before the 18th, I'll let you know so that you can tell Henri. Yes, I say again that I think you have done very well indeed."

She mounted her bicycle and rode off towards Faverges to meet Arnaud. She decided not to tell him about Jules because if she did, Arnaud would certainly use his .38 Colt at last.

*

London's orders were terse and were what she had expected. She should have no more negotiations with Henri, but dissolve the circuit and clear out with the utmost speed. She was in mortal danger and every day added to it. Raoul was ready to come back and would jump by parachute. Would she please indicate a suitable ground? He sent his love and was prepared to jump anywhere, absolutely anywhere.

*

The Semnoz rises some six thousand precipitous feet over the right bank of the Lake of Annecy. It is heavily wooded with oak and elder and pine and there is a stony path that struggles up its mighty flank, twisting and zig-zagging through the scented gloom of the pine woods, bisecting hewn rocks, crawling like a snail's track to the windy summit. In summer, it is a strenuous day's climb and descent; in winter and spring, when the wind is about the woods, when the path is deep in snow and the rocks veined with ice, the people of Annecy are well content to leave the Semnoz to the hawks and to the spirits that dwell in high places.

In the early afternoon of the 14th of April, Odette and Arnaud rode their bicycles along the lake's edge under the Semnoz. Arriving at *Le Crêt*, they hid the bicycles behind a stone wall and took the path to the mountain. When the snow was knee-deep, they left the path and climbed up through the bitter woods, scrambling over the freezing rocks. It took them over two hours to get to the top and they stood at last on the summit, breathing deeply and looking around them.

"Well," said Odette at last, "will it do?"

Arnaud paced a good hundred metres right and left. He said:

"Yes, it'll do—provided the navigator is dead on. But it's a hell of a place to jump. On the other hand, if we light a fire under the lip of the hill, it can't be seen from Annecy."

"We'd better get some branches now and make ready."

Between them, they hacked off enough wood to make a big bonfire and laid it in a heap. Dusk was beginning to shadow the valley far below before the job was done. They had a last look around and started the journey down the mountains. It was dark by the time they reached the fields where their bicycles were hidden, and Odette's legs were aching. At St. Jorioz, she gave him a message for transmission to London, pin-pointing the tiny flat space on the top of the Semnoz. When Arnaud rode on to Faverges, Odette walked down to "The Limes". Jules was there. He asked her eagerly is she had any news of the bomber pick-up for Henri, and she said that she was doing all she could to arrange it for the 18th of the month.

"And, Raoul—what news of him?"

"None," she said. "I doubt very much if he will return at all."

"Oh. One more thing, Lise. That British officer, Roger, who was in the Hotel de la Plage, he's suddenly vanished."

H*

"I know," she said calmly. "I sent him away."

"Where's he gone to?"

"To an address of some friends. Why this sudden interest?"

He shrugged. She didn't hate him any more. She was only conscious of pity for him, pity and contempt. He said lamely: "I only wondered where he had gone to, that's all."

"He's quite safe," she said easily, "quite safe."

★

The next day, the 15th of April, was a terribly busy one. She went into Annecy and warned as many people as she could either to lie low or clear out. In no circumstances should anyone come to St. Jorioz. She was on tenter-hooks all day, knowing that she could expect no B.B.C. message until 7.30 in the evening and that, if it came, she and Arnaud would have a desperate climb to reach the top of the Semnoz in time to light the fire and to welcome Raoul. The hours of the afternoon took an interminable time to pass and she kept looking at the clock and yawning. At about a quarter past seven, Arnaud arrived at the hotel with some very welcome news. He had managed to get hold of an old car driven by gas but it would at least save them a bit of a climb. At half past seven, Odette, he and Jean Cottet clustered eagerly round the radio and tuned in to the forbidden wavelength. They hardly heard the news bulletin in their impatience for the *messages personnel*, and the announcer seemed particularly leisurely to-night. At last, the laconic announcement came:

"Le carabe d'or fait sa toilette de printemps."

Raoul was on his way back to *Haute Savoie* at last.

It was a perfect night and towards ten o'clock, the half-moon would flood the high snows with light. In breathless excitement, they started off. The asthmatic old car trundled slowly along and turned unwillingly to the hills. At the first steep incline, it stopped dead. No power on earth could make it move upwards. Arnaud took the can of paraffin and Odette the torches and, after Arnaud had delivered a kick and laid a fearful curse on the inanimate car, they started up the path. It was likely that the aircraft would arrive any moment after moonrise, the night was as dark as pitch and the wind was getting up. Sweat ran into Odette's eyes as she stumbled upwards, slipping and sliding on the crusted snow. Time that had crawled by that afternoon was racing now and she drove her aching legs forward until each separate muscle was a separate spear of pain. Unconscious of the intense cold, numbed to everything except the determination to get to the top and set the beacon alight, she fought her way through branches and clambered up the rocks. Sometimes she could hear Arnaud behind, crashing and cursing, but the sound of his voice was like the dreary mouthing of an idiot. Though her mind roved dizzily in a nightmare, in a spiral within a spiral, her body remained obedient to her will and her eardrums were keyed and alive and waiting for the complaint in the sky that would tell her that she was too late. The wind dropped and the moon rose. Flies crawling up the flanks of an elephant, she and Arnaud made the last thousand feet. There was the plateau and there were the heaped-up branches. She swayed where she stood and spat a thread of blood from a mouth that burned like a furnace. Arnaud said, gasping: "Suppose he doesn't come," and Odette said, "He'll come." The moon cast blue shadows on the snow and, below in the valley, the little outrider fringe of fir trees looked like hooded nuns shuffling into the woods. An anthem of cow-bells chimed with sudden, unbearable sweetness from the moonlit pastures below and the sky was as clear as spring water. . . .

Blinking and calling, blinking and calling, the Halifax bomber flew insolently over the mountains in a roaring waterfall of sound. The drenched branches exploded into flame, licking and blazing and leaping to the frosty stars. Priest and priestess of the cult of fire, Odette and Arnaud gazed with exaltation at the thunderous sky. The Halifax wheeled over the lake, drove down for the low run-in, passed over their heads in triumphant *crescendo*, slanted up and away into the zone of the moon. The chime of cow-bells laced the silence delicately . . . until it was lost and drowned by a strong human voice singing.

Floating down the infinity of the sky, Raoul threw back his head and laughed as he sung the words of the *Marseillaise* to the mountains and in a moment of time, he was at her feet and in her arms.

CHAPTER XXII

APRIL 16th, 1943

"To-morrow we clear out."

"Yes. We've only got until the 18th before Henri catches up with us."

"You should have gone before, Lise."

"I tried to—but there was such a lot to do. Couriers kept coming in, wanting money and orders and all sorts of things. We've been busy since you've been away, you know, not just sitting around. I couldn't run away and leave everything."

"I still think you should have gone. You're an obstinate woman. My God, you're an obstinate woman."

"I know. But we're all set to go to-morrow. I've arranged for a boat to take us across the lake and I've even found a new hideout for Arnaud." Odette yawned. She said, half-smiling, "I may be an obstinate woman but I'm also a very tired one. I think I'll go to bed now."

"Right. And it's good-bye to St. Jorioz in the crack of the dawn—whatever happens."

"It is. That's a promise."

*

The promise was to be fulfilled.

Dimly, in the veils of sleep, she heard somebody knocking on her door. She switched on the light and glanced at her watch. It was a few minutes after eleven and she could only have been asleep for a matter of minutes. She called out:

"Who is it?"

"Jean. Jean Cottet."

"What do you want, Jean?"

"There's a man here, one of the couriers from 'The Limes'. He says he must see you immediately, and that it's terribly urgent." He paused. "Lise, there's something about this that I don't like."

"Tell him to wait. I'll be down."

She dressed quickly, looked around the room. She had no premonition of danger but only a weary irritation at being woken up when she was so very tired. She walked along the hotel corridor and down the wide curving staircase that led into the restaurant. As she reached the bottom, blinking in the strong light, she saw a man step out from the side of the stairs. She stopped—for in his hand he held a ten shot Lüger automatic pistol and it was pointed at her heart. She looked at him with calm curiosity, as if he were a strange thing, seen under a microscope. Then she looked to the left. There was another man on the other side of the stairs and he held a Lüger as well—and two more men behind. All of them were strangers to her. Jean Cottet stood in the middle of the room, his friendly face strained and dismayed and incredulous. She felt as if she were in a cinema, as if she had been watching a swift, flickering film that had unaccountably stopped, freezing the moving actors into absurd, etched immobility. Suddenly, the projector started working again and the shadows quickened into life. With fascinated interest, she saw another man stroll forward. This was no stranger to her. The bland, bespectacled figure of Bleicher was only too familiar. He said quietly:

"You have played the game with great skill, Lise. I congratulate you." He shrugged. "Escape, by the way, is out of the question because the hotel is surrounded. Please don't make things difficult for us and for yourself." He spoke sharply to one of the men in German and she only understood the single word "Raoul".

She was marched upstairs, the muzzle of an automatic pistol pressed against her spine. The corridor along which she had walked in freedom five minutes ago looked just the same. That was queer. Henri opened Raoul's door and switched on the light. She saw that he was in bed and sound asleep. There was nothing she could do, absolutely nothing. Or was there? His coat was hanging over the back of a chair and she knew that his wallet with its utterly damning contents was in his inside pocket. Henri cocked his pistol and nodded. As the taller of the men shook Raoul's shoulder roughly, she half staggered into the room and swayed and lurched into a chair and shut her eyes weakly. She heard Henri's voice say:

"You. What's your name?"

Raoul sat up. "My name? Chambrun. Pierre Chambrun. Who are you and what do you want?"

"You are under arrest. You are Peter Churchill, alias Raoul, British agent and saboteur. Get up."

With infinite care, her fingers slid the wallet out of the inside pocket of his coat, transferred it to a place where—failing a feminine search—it would be temporarily safe. She opened her eyes and moaned slightly, as if recovering her consciousness and her strength. Raoul, covered by the three automatics, was dressing. He gave her a look of oblique meaning and she heard Henri say:

"I must insist that you wear handcuffs."

"How the hell can I wear handcuffs when I'm dressing?"

"All in good time, my friend. You are aware that this district is in occupation by our allies the Italians?"

"Yes."

"Which would you prefer, to be the prisoner of the Italians or of the Germans?"

Raoul laughed shortly. "That's a damn silly question. Even if you did hand us over to the Italians at this moment, you would always be able to demand our bodies. Hitler struts on the manure heap, not Mussolini."

"Which would you prefer?"

"To be with the Italians, of course. . . ."

The answer obviously did not please him. He said, as Raoul put on his coat: "Now you will be handcuffed." The steel bands snapped. The Gestapo men were searching the room, pulling open drawers, opening cupboards. There was nothing incriminating and the search was soon over. One Gestapo man took Odette's elbow and the sombre procession started downstairs. Jean Cottet stood still in the middle of the room. He had been a good and trusty friend and he could have known nothing of this. Raoul stopped. He said deliberately:

"Jean, I'm sorry to have caused all this bother in your hotel. How could you possibly have spotted that I was a British officer? Sorry, Jean."

There were two cars waiting and a ring of Italian troops.

Raoul and Odette were hustled into the back of the first car, separated from each other by a Gestapo man. Henri had vanished. When the car started, Odette leaned forward as if adjusting the top of her stocking, and slid the wallet from its hiding place and pressed it deeply between the cushions of the car. Then, her last duty done, she sat back. Now she was in the Hands of God.

The lake of Annecy glimmered with the track of the moon. Above the high, cold line of the Semnoz the night sky and the infinite spaces of the sky were clear. There the winds could rove in freedom, there the birds could fly with great speed from the steeps to the steeps. In a few hours, the sun would rise and fling broad rays of light from the mountains to the mountains, leaping the little hills with scorn and in the glory of the sun, water would tumble and splash in the hills and human feet would walk and run and go freely from one place to another.

One grey door opened in a line of grey doors and Odette walked into a cell. The grey door shut behind her with a crash and a key turned in the lock.

PART THREE

"True courage is to do without witnesses everything that one,
is capable of doing before all the world. . . ."

La Rochefoucauld.

CHAPTER XXIII

FRESNES

THE *domaine de Fresnes* lies some ten to twelve miles from the heart of Paris, to the south past the *Porte d'Italie.* Just on fifty years ago in what were then pleasant fields, the *maison de Correction* raised its forbidding head to become the biggest criminal prison in Europe. Over the bare half-century, hundreds of thousands of men have entered its gates to shuffle along its endless corridors and to count the leaden hours to freedom. Some, the impatient ones, have flung themselves screaming from the high landings; some have died in the prison hospital; many, the shackled ones, have left to keep a dawn appointment with the polite gentleman in evening dress and his dreadful wicker-work basket. When France fell the whole teeming labyrinth of Fresnes, cells, chapels, kitchens, dungeons and corridors was ready for the eager hands of the S.S.—and for those of their sisters, the women in grey, *les souris*, the mice. As the *Wehrmacht* marched down the Champs Elysées, the new prison staff moved in and the timeless twilight of Fresnes deepened.

It was about mid-morning on the 8th of May, 1943, when the night train from Marseille came into the Gare de Lyon and a curious little band descended stiffly from a third-class carriage. Passengers hurrying to the exits glanced at them and then away, crossing their fingers as if to avert the evil eye. Between two uniformed Gestapo, a dark, broad shouldered, bare headed man was being hustled along the platform, and beside him, her arm held firmly, a slim young woman walked along the platform with an air of dignified distaste. At the barrier another man—a civilian—was waiting. Hugo Bleicher, punctilious as always, had come to meet his guests at the station. As the little group approached, he had the grace to bow. He gave an order and the bare-headed man was handcuffed. He then followed the group out of the station to where three Gestapo cars were waiting. He himself got into the front car and, followed by the other two, led the sombre cavalcade through the sunny traffic to Fresnes.

The iron gates were opened and the three cars swung into the inner courtyard.

*

To the left of the main hall is a nest of wooden cupboards, each of them large enough to hold one erect human being. Odette was locked into one of these, Raoul into another. Though hidden from each other they could hear through the wooden walls and they talked until the guards shouted the only French word they seemed to know. It was a word Odette was to hear a million times in the months to come. *"Silence!"* they bellowed. *"Silence!"* An hour dragged by and then another hour. A scowling S.S. woman unlocked Odette's door and she was led to a bare room to go through the humiliating panto-mime of official admission to prison. Since her arrest a month ago, she had already been subjected to this sort of thing so many times that it had ceased to mean anything. One prison was dirtier than another, one guard more truculent, the food better or worse but the dreary pattern was roughly the same. She gave the name shown on the identity card she happened to have in her bag when she was caught. One had to have some sort of name in prison and this one was as good as any. For the Gestapo, she would have another name and another story, but that would come later. As regards the *Maison de Correction de Fresnes*, Chambrun would do. She was, therefore, Madame Odette Chambrun, aged thirty-one, married, Roman Catholic, French, born at Dunkirk in 1912. That was all she had to say. She was ordered to strip naked and to stand facing the wall. She shrugged. Impersonal nudity meant nothing. Decency was not clothing but state of mind. She undressed, faced the wall, raised her arms obediently, let them fall again, walked six paces to order, about-turned, walked back. With beady, envious eyes, the shapeless omnesexuals in grey scrutin-ized her body, groped in her hair with dirty fingers, probed in her ears. *Nichts versteckt! Kleider wieder anziehen!* Odette dressed again, was given one blanket and a coarse grey sheet.

FRESNES

The Third or " Women's Division " of Fresnes Prison, Paris

She wrapped her one change of underclothes in the blanket and waited.

"Cell one hundred and eight, third division. No concessions of any kind whatsoever—by order of the Gestapo."

One of the S.S. women unlocked a door, pointed downwards and snarled her dreary parrot cry.

"*Heraus! Los! Schnell, schnell!*"

Odette walked down a flight of steps. She found herself at the end of an underground passage which seemed to stretch to infinity. Occasional electric lamps were set high in the vaulted roof and between their pools of light lay chasms of darkness. Parallel rails were set in the concrete floor and there were doors set into the wall.

"*Vorwärts. Schnell.*"

The smell of the prison, a sour dirty smell, curled in her nostrils like a wind that had come from a place that was sunless and corrupt. She took two or three steps forward into the gloom. She was suddenly conscious of fear. It was not fear of pain or of mutilation or even of death. Over the last weeks she had had time to contemplate the shadow of those grisly brothers, and her mind was adjusted to their advent. She had silently sounded a *reveillé* to her reserves of fortitude and they were ready for battle. But this was another and more terrible fear. Here was the negation of the soul. She saw nothing but alternating blobs of abysmal darkness and pitiless light. She walked forward because her legs moved but she didn't know how long she walked or why she was in this fearful place. After what had seemed an age, she saw steps leading upwards and she quickened her pace. She almost ran up the steps into a flood of white daylight and gazed around her. This was the heart and the core of Fresnes. Before her, gallery built on gallery, were lines of cells, each door as flat as a tombstone. Even the rays of the midday sun were broken and repulsed by the huge frosted glass window at the end of the block.

"*Schnell, schnell. . . .*"

She walked the length of the gallery, past the line of tombstone doors, climbed a scrubbed flight of steps to the first floor. At the top a man was waiting, a civilian in a dark suit and spectacles. Either with reluctant grace or derision, he bowed. The S.S. woman muttered some command and Odette stopped

In the presence of Bleicher, the grey unit beside her had suddenly become a woman. She fawned on the official and the man, giving him a little, slanting female smile.

"*Hier ist Frau Chambrun, Herr Hauptmann.*"

Odette looked at him coolly. With a sudden gesture, she thrust out her bundle. Bleicher took it automatically and held it in his hands, frowning. She said:

"In civilized countries, it is usual for men to carry things for women. I see no reason why the courtesies should not obtain in prison. We are still in France, Monsieur."

She marched along the landing, her head high. Bleicher followed carrying her bundle. Outside cell number one hundred and eight, he gave it to her without a word and walked on. The S.S. woman opened the cell door with her master-key, pushed Odette inside. She put her bundle on the rusty slats of a bed and turned round. The S.S. woman said harshly:

"We'll soon clip your wings for you. You are for interrogation immediately. *Heraus! Schnell, schnell.* . . ."

⋆

Bleicher sat at a table in a little room at the end of the landing. When Odette came in he stood up and indicated a chair. Mouthing deferentially, the S.S. woman sidled out. Bleicher offered Odette a cigarette. She shook her head. He said:

"As you wish." He gave her a long, frowning look. "Lise, I am truly sorry to see you in this place. Fresnes is not for . . . for people like you."

Odette said nothing.

"I would far prefer to see you in St. Jorioz, against a tapestry of mountains. But I was forced to arrest you. You already know that there are two distinct organizations, the Gestapo and the Military *Abwehr* and it was to save you from the Gestapo that I decided to arrest you myself."

"I remember how you told me that you arrested Marsac for the same altruistic motive. The number of persons you claim to have 'saved' from the Gestapo would fill a landing at Fresnes. *Abwehr* or Gestapo, steel trap or foxhound, the end appears to be much the same. Here I am."

"Yes," he leaned forward and said earnestly, "but there is no need for you to stay here, Lise."

"No?"

"No, Lise. It is in my power to get you out of Fresnes, to restore you to a life of human dignity." He looked frowning at a typewritten sheet. "I see that you spent a week in jail at Annecy and were interrogated by the O.V.R.A., by the Italian Secret Police. You told them nothing. Then you were taken to Grenoble and to Turin where you spent a night in a cell with two prostitutes. After Turin came Nice for ten days, Marseille, Toulon and now Fresnes. It has not been a pretty *grand tour*, and it is time it came to an end. If it has served to indicate the squalor to which you are unnecessarily subjecting yourself, then it has not been in vain."

She smiled. He said, "Does the possibility of freedom amuse you?"

"I was wondering what bargain you were going to suggest. I am afraid that I can't offer either a radio set or a bomber pick-up from here."

"You are in many ways a very foolish woman, Lise. I have no bargain to offer. Here are some facts. Here in Fresnes, for example, you are under the name of 'Madame Chambrun'. It is not your name. You told the Italians that you and Raoul were married and that your real name was Mrs. Peter Churchill. That is also untrue. I know a great deal about you, far more than you think. I know that you are the mother of three small daughters, that you are a member of the French Section of the War Office, that your headquarters are in Baker Street, London, and that your chief is Colonel Maurice Buckmaster, a tall, alert man, clean shaven, educated at Eton, speaking perfect French and good German. Those are some of the things I know about you. You must yourself admit their truth."

"I have nothing to say."

"You are also a very obstinate person. Because of a curious twist in your nature you are willing to give to others what they are unwilling to give for you. In some ways you are very much of a realist, in other ways you are quite incredibly naïve. You remind me a little of those English officers who rally their troops with a hunting horn and advance into battle with a walking stick. In war, chivalry went out of fashion when the tank came in. Do you think self-sacrifice is noble? You are wrong. It is merely childish and out of date—and anyway, yours is misdirected. You are a mother and your duty in this chaotic world is to your children. It is not to a collection of amateur spies and saboteurs from the French Section of the War Office. Do you really think for one moment that your friends Arnaud and Roger—or even your so-called husband Peter Churchill—would do as much for you as you seem to be ready to do for them?"

"Yes, I do. But the point is unimportant. I do not barter loyalty against loyalty. I am no shopkeeper, Monsieur, and I sell nothing by the pound. If these 'amateur spies and saboteurs' as you call them, were indeed prepared to betray me—which I don't believe—that would not influence my decision in any way. I am only responsible to my own conscience."

He looked at her for a long time without speaking.

"What would you say," he asked slowly. "If I were to tell you that I am trying to arrange an exchange for Peter Churchill. If the British Government will release a German prisoner of equal rank and status, he will be sent home. What would you say if I tell you that he is more than eager to go—if necessary leaving you here to rot?"

She laughed. She said: "I would say that you were a liar, Monsieur Henri."

He sat back, stroking his chin. He thought, in spite of her transparent disbelief that he might have sown a tiny seed of doubt in her mind. If he had, it would have plenty of time to grow—in the eternal solitude of cell one hundred and eight. Unlike other seeds, it would germinate more freely in shadow than in sun. With the skill of a trained interrogator, he changed the conversation. He said easily, conversationally, as if he were in a drawing-room:

"You told me in St. Jorioz at our first meeting that you cared for music. I heard, the night before last, Mozart's divertissements for string quartet and two horns. It was quite enchanting—with two minuets in the French manner." An iron food trolley rumbled along the landing, drowning his voice and he smiled in mock helplessness. "Yes," he said at last, when the din had stopped, "it would give me great pleasure to introduce to you some of the almost unknown masterpieces of Mozart. At his best, he is exquisite, at his laziest, he is always lively and delicate and charming. There is a symphony concert in about a fortnight." He stood up. "It still grieves me to see you here, Lise. I shall visit you again—very soon."

The beady-eyed S.S. woman took Odette's arm and led her along the landing, opened the door of her cell.

"*Herein! Schnell, schnell. . . .*"

The door slammed. Odette sat down on the edge of the bed for a long time. Then she stood up and walked slowly round the cell, fingering the walls. The window, made up of little frosted glass panes, was hermetically sealed. She looked very carefully at each pane and saw at last that there was a tiny hole, no bigger than a pin-prick, in the bottom pane on the left. She dragged her rickety chair over to the window and stood on it. By pressing her head hard against the sloping stone, she could just see through the hole and she saw what she wanted to see more than anything in the world, a minute segment of the sky.

*

The long twilight deepened. Only when the first stars were sure, did Odette step down from the window. She had not realized the passage of time, but now her cell was already dark. By touch more than by sight, she spread her blanket on the lumpy palliasse and lay down. Imperceptibly but surely, the last remnants of light drained from the window and a terrible silence brooded over the prison. She shut her eyes and found after a little while that the darkness under her lids was less opaque than the darkness of her cell. With a sustained effort of will, she found that she could project what were at first formless shadows on to the screen of her mind. They were blurred and jumbled and disobedient to her will, and it was only by almost painful concentration that she could etch them into clarity and see them as living beings. Though they moved slowly and with uncertainty, though they were like shy ghosts poised on tip-toe for instant flight, they were friendly ghosts and she watched them entranced. She opened her eyes and they vanished like wisps of smoke. The physical blackness of her cell rushed at her and pressed like a vice on her spirit. Her body was in prison, human and vulnerable to humanity. She had thought that her mind could preserve its freedom for ever but now she was less sure. For how long in this awful place could she retain the power to separate mind from matter? For how long could she continue to find strength to summon visions of light and cleanness and normality and gaze on them through the transfiguring lenses of her lids? Again she shut her eyes. For a long time the screen refused to come, and then, very slowly, it formed in an oblong that was less dark than the void from which it had emerged. With every muscle tense, she waited for the screen to fill with friendly faces and, feature by feature, a face formed. It was the scowling, beady-eyed face of the S.S. woman in grey. Odette shook her head fiercely in the darkness and the face grinned and dissolved into the blackness from which it had come. The night was cool but there was sweat on Odette's forehead. She stood up and groped her way to the far wall, feeling the stone with the tips of her fingers, groped back to bed, lay down. A new problem, terrifying in its implications, oppressed her soul. It was the problem of selectivity. She had established that it was possible to project phantoms to bear her company but was the choice of spectre hers? "In smooth water," wrote George Herbert, "God help me; in rough water, I will help myself." That's what she had to do now, to help herself. Hers and hers alone was the strength or the weakness.

With her face puckered in the darkness, she caused the screen to form. There it was, the blank grey oblong in the black. Fearful of what might come she silently called her daughters to come and throng it, and after an intolerable time, they came, running and laughing in sunlight and stayed there to fill the screen with joy. Every muscle of Odette's body relaxed and she smiled, breathing easily in the silence of the prison. She knew that the others, the ugly ones, were lurking in the gloom, waiting to sidle on and banish her children, but between them she cast a line of light over which they could not pass. Just as her presence used to bring them peaceful sleep, so would their presence give her peace—for as long and as often as she had strength to ward off the mouthing spectres of the women in grey. Theirs was the advantage, for they moved and breathed in the present, actual, venomous, exuding reality from their living skins. For this hour she had achieved victory, utter and absolute. But she knew from the wearying rhythm of her blood that the victory had cost her dear and that she was becoming drained of will. Soon, please God, she would sleep and ask that the fountain of strength be refilled for the battle that would recur with every dusk and only declare brief armistice with every dawn.

A scream rent the silence. Odette sat up in bed, gasping. There was another scream and then another. Somewhere locked in the dark honeycomb of stone, a woman's screams pierced the walls of her cell and romped in freedom along the corridors. Heavy footsteps ran along the landing and, as they came nearer, the scream exploded into laughter, laughter that tangled itself in the roots of Odette's hair and ran like fire along her spine. She heard a key rattle in a lock, heard the shout of "Silence! Silence!" and then the high-pitched shrillness became a piteous wail and she heard another reiterated sound, the thick sound of blows rained on a human body. She shrank against the wall whining as if it were her own flesh that received each stroke. The fearful tempo became slower, stopped. Some final abuse was shouted and a cell door slammed. Around her, Odette could hear women stirring and muttering. The footsteps of the guards, unhurried now, passed her cell door leisurely. The muttering died away and soon there was only one sound, a ceaseless, stifled sobbing that went on and on and on, threading the darkness with ungovernable grief.

Never in her life had Odette known such a delight as the pallid morphia of the dawn.

CHAPTER XXIV

ODETTE could only have slept for a few minutes. She woke to the rumble of a trolley outside and the rattle of a key in the lock. She scrambled off her bed. Her door opened and an S.S. woman grunted in the bastardized jargon of the prison:
"*Donne ta gamelle.*"
"*Je ne comprends pas.*"
"*Donne ta gamelle. Là.*" She pointed to a tin bowl. "*Gibt schnell.*"
Odette held out the bowl. The S.S. woman half filled it with some tepid brown liquid from a large can, swung the door to with a crash. Odette sat on her bed and tasted it. It was acorn coffee, thin, watery, without sustenance. She swallowed it to the last drop. Then she folded her blanket and sheet and began a general examination of her domain. First she paced it. It was roughly twelve feet by eight. She decided that she was *chatelaine* of some ninety-six square feet of valuable leasehold property in the vicinity of Paris. *Quelle propriété!* The furniture was naturally utilitarian rather than decorative but it was, at least, fashionably sparse. There was a bed made of rusted iron slats, two of which were missing. She had a chair with a broken back, a shelf to serve as a table and a lavatory in the corner. There was a cold water tap, a brown enamel basin, a tin bowl and a spoon. Set in the door was a spy-hole from which she could be watched from outside. The walls were of plaster and an outcrop of fungus grew in patches on the ceiling. High on the left wall was a cobwebbed grating about six inches square, the *bouche de chaleur*. She began to examine the walls with care. On one of them she saw some writing scratched with a pin. This was treasure trove indeed. With such a find, one should exercise patience. She would return to it later and decipher it bit by bit, tasting each word like a grape. Opposite it, she saw a faint series of numbers, each one bisected with a scratched diagonal line. She considered it for a long time before she saw

what it was. It was a calendar, the sort of calendar that home-sick children make at school, and the last date to be struck through was the 17th of February. On that date had the fingers that made it moved into freedom or were they stilled in death? Odette would never know, but she decided to keep a similar chart. It too, like the still unread scribble on the wall, would be something to think about in the interminable hours to come. She tried the point of a hairpin on the plaster and found that it left a faint mark. This was more than treasure trove; this was real, lasting wealth. She had something to read and the means to write. Within an hour, she had achieved the tracery of a calendar and, with joy, had drawn a line through the first day, the 8th of May, the day of her arrival in Fresnes, was now banished into eternity. She sat down on her bed and smiled in triumph.

It must have been at least an hour before she heard a call repeated monotonously again and again. It seemed to come from low down outside her window and she heard it faintly and insistently. She listened, not realizing it could have anything to do with her and then, frowning, she walked towards the window and stood on her chair and put her ear to the tiny hole.

"*Allo*," said a woman's voice from below. "*Allo! La Nouvelle.*"

"*La nouvelle*", the novice, the newcomer? The voice took up the patient summons again.

"*Allo! La nouvelle* in cell one hundred and eight, can you hear me? If you can hear me stamp on the floor. Hullo, hullo."

Odette got off the chair, stamped heavily on the floor, listened at the window again.

"Listen carefully. I am Michèle, in the cell directly under yours. In your cell is a grating high up in the wall, the *bouche de chaleur*. We can speak freely through this for it connects with my cell. If you understand and wish to speak, use the grating."

Odette stood still for a moment, looking round her cell. Then she took the blanket and folded it into a solid, flat lump. On this she put her chair. Then she took her palliasse of straw and rolled it into a bundle and put it on the chair. Clinging on to the shelf, she managed to climb the wobbling edifice and found that, by stretching, she could just bring her mouth to the grating. She called softly:

"Allo. Hullo. Michèle."

A voice answered immediately in a resonant whisper:
"Ah! *C'est la nouvelle!* Welcome to Fresnes. *Comment t'appelles-tu?*"
Odette hesitated, still wary. She said: "*Je m'appelle Céline.*"
"*Bonjour Céline.*"
Eagerly, with avidity, came the inevitable question. "What
news outside?"
"I don't know much. I was taken on the 16th of April and I've
been in many prisons since then, Annecy, Turin, Nice, Gren-
obles. But when I was taken, things were going very well."
Whispering into the heating vent, she told Michèle of the pro-
gress of the war. Africa was all but clear of Germans, Italy
would soon fall. Every day the R.A.F. became stronger and
mightier. The American Armies were pouring across the Atlantic;
men, cannon and tanks. Victory was certain, absolutely certain.
"And you, Céline? Who are you and how have you come to
join the ranks of the *mortes vivantes*, the living dead?"
"I am English, a political prisoner."
"English! *Oh là là!*"
She told Odette about Fresnes and the dreary round of the
prison day. She was herself a Communist and an incriminating
letter had been found by the Gestapo. She had been inside for
four months without trial. One day she would either walk out
into freedom or be taken to the Gestapo and shot. "If it is the
latter, I hope to die bravely and with dignity. It is the best
weapon against the Boche, dignity, because they do not understand it." For the rest, there were three divisions in Fresnes,
three cell-blocks, each of five floors. The first was for German
deserters, men. The second was also for men, political prisoners,
Frenchmen and those who had worked in the underground.
The third was mixed, women and men, political also. Among
the prisoners the Gestapo had planted "*des moutons*", "the
sheep", women whose business it was to induce others to talk.
Most of them were known for what they were. On the top
floor were German women prisoners and their cell doors were
left open when the R.A.F. came so that they could get away if
the bombs fell. The R.A.F. often came over Paris. It was
wonderful. Food was very bad and one was perpetually in
pain from hunger. The S.S. women, *les souris* were bitches
and whores. The men guards were a little better but not much.
The Commandant of the prison was a German officer who was

"correct". When one was taken to the Commissars of the Gestapo, the S.S. women told you in the early morning by shouting the word "Tribunal" into your cell. That meant that you would be taken in the *"panier à salade"* to 84 Avenue Foch and grilled. Sometimes you came back, sometimes you vanished. The Commissars were fiends of hell. What was the *panier à salade?* The salad basket, the *voiture cellulaire*, the Black Maria. The best times to talk were in the early morning after coffee, between twelve and two when half the S.S. women were at lunch and between four and five in the afternoon.

Odette asked a question. Michèle said scornfully:

"There are women here who scream every night and then they are beaten. *C'est de la canaille* without self-respect, those who can scream before the Boches. Sunday is a bad day because the prison is very quiet and quietness makes them scream all the more. Also Sunday is our day for suicides. Céline, I called you for a long time before you answered this morning."

"I couldn't hear. My windows don't open."

"Break a pane. You will be punished by being given no soup but you are new and you don't know hunger yet. It is worth it—to exchange one bowl of stinking soup for the sight of the sky. We will talk again this afternoon. *Au revoir*, Céline."

"*Au revoir*, Michèle."

One said "*au revoir*" to a person one had never seen, to a disembodied voice. Odette climbed down and put the palliasse back on the bed. Then, deliberately, she took her chair and swung it and crashed it against her window. One pane splintered. She heard the tinkle of broken glass on the ground below. Michèle's voice floated clearly into her cell.

"Bravo, Céline."

Then Odette sat down on her bed and waited calmly for the S.S.

*

The food trolley rumbled past her door. Michèle was right. It was better to do without a meal now while her body was still strong than later when her stomach would yawn with hunger. She stood on her chair and watched a wisp of cloud come up from the south. It had come from over the Mediterranean and the snows of the *Alpes Maritimes* and the olive groves of the south, drifting high over the bountiful breast of France on its

way to Paris and Fresnes. She watched it as if she had never seen
a cloud in her life before, marvelling at the changing shape of it,
and its lightness, its beauty and its freedom. When it passed
the orbit of her window, she was cast down as if a friend had died.

★

"Michèle."
Hollowly, but clearly, the voice of her unseen friend echoed
in the heating vent.
"Oui, Céline?"
"I have found something written on the wall of my cell."
Odette chuckled. "It is something wonderful. I am the richest
woman in Fresnes, for now I have something to laugh about."
"Tell me, Céline. Please tell me."
"Ever since I found it, I have been waiting to share it with
you. It is a thing that has made me very happy. Listen.
Scratched on the wall are these words. *'Quand j'étais petite, je
gardais les vaches; maintenant ce sont elles qui me gardent. . . .'* "
There was a long silence, then a sigh.
"Thank you, Céline. Oh my God, thank you. All night I
shall be happy. *A demain*, Céline."
"*A demain*, Michèle."

★

Around Odette, each locked in her numbered box of stone,
the women of Fresnes breathed in the darkness. Waking or
sleeping, all these women shared one common denominator—
hunger. Superimposed on this basic "desire" for food was a
host of other desires moving in a dizzy spiral, advancing and
receding, climbing and sinking, merging always into the
tantalizing vision of full plates of food, food that was hot and
plentiful and rich, food that was bursting with goodness to be
tasted and swallowed and absorbed and transmuted into living
tissue. Only when this recurrent craving was briefly anæsthe-
tized by the arrival of the food trolley could other desires take
shape and, in the intervals between acute hunger and temporary
satiety, women longed for their own normalities. All their
bodies were attuned to the idea of love, some to its physical
manifestation. To be shown affection, to be recognized as a
human being and as an individual, was the fundamental need
and from it all else sprang. If their stomachs craved for food,

so did their skins crave for the friendly touch of human hands, the hands of husbands or parents or lovers or children, any hands so long as they were personal and kind. The chaste thought of a kiss as a holy thing, of a caress as a benediction; the sensual groped in the past and relived obscenely what had transpired in strength and cleanness, smearing remembered passion with mental slime, conjuring nameless indecencies, wakening their starved glands to artificial tumescence. The fortunate, in being deprived of every courtesy of living, found God and pestered him unceasingly. They were the ones to be envied for they were never alone in their cells. All night long electric lights blazed from the vaulted roof, illuminating every corner of the lofty hall, shining pitilessly on the lines of tombstone doors behind each one of which a cube of darkness enclosed a woman. Every hour the guards strolled along the landings, sliding the peep-holes in the doors, flashing the light on in the caverns of blackness, peering to make sure that the occupants still drew living breath, strolled on. Hungry, frightened, brave, lonely, lustful, the women shrank back from the light and closed their eyes, to pray, to remember, or to sleep.

Odette watched a pencil of light wander round her walls, settle on her blanket, crawl up to her face, dart out through the peep-hole. She smiled. It was kind, she supposed, to use a torch rather than the light. All was well. She lived. To-morrow she could strike a whole day off her mural calendar. Though she was beginning to know the first symptoms of hunger, her mind was buoyant. She had been in Fresnes for little more than twenty-four hours. Already she had found a friend in Michèle the Communist, tough, truculent, as unyielding in her inhuman creed as the Germans were in theirs. A flag waved, a dictator spoke and Michèle happened to be on her side. Nazi or Communist, rat-catcher or rodent operator, the fell purpose was the same—the enslavement of unregimented humanity. How would the cells of the Lubianka compare with the cells of Fresnes? N.K.V.D. versus S.S., Slav versus Nordic, whoever won, mankind would lose. Odette stirred uneasily. She had, thank God, a more tranquil pastoral theme and she would go back to it.

"*Quand j'étais petite, je gardais les vaches. . . .*"

Pastures, green and wet and shining with spring rain; six

I

Devon red heifers coming through a five-barred gate and looking up at her incuriously with soft, fringed eyes as they raised their heads from the sweet grass. . . .

Somewhere near in the prison, a demented woman set up a doleful, lunatic chant, using a succession of dirty words and there was an angry murmur as other women stirred and beat their hands on their cell walls, resentful that their private dreams should be disturbed.

With an effort, Odette shut her ears to the present and listened to the past. The little tugging sound of the heifers cropping was loud enough to drown the reiterated misery of Fresnes.

★

With her S.S. guard, Odette walked along the landing to the interrogating room. As always, Henri stood up as she entered. He opened his cigarette case. She took a cigarette with alacrity and he lit it for her. After one puff, she stubbed it out carefully against her heel. He watched her. He said:

"Why do you do that, Lise?"

It was foolish to lie. She said: "It is for a friend."

"But how do you give it to a friend if you are in solitary confinement?"

"I have nothing to say."

"Obstinate as always, Lise. But I confess that I am human enough to admire your spirit. This morning I have been to see Peter Churchill. He is in cell number 220, in the second division."

"I know."

"How do you know?" he said sharply. "You have only been here for three days and it is impossible for you to know."

She shrugged. He considered her for a long time in silence. He said: "Peter Churchill is well and he sends you his love. I have given him some cigarettes. As you know, I am trying to arrange an exchange for him. But it is about you that I want to talk. I have already told you about the relationship between the *Abwehr* and the Gestapo."

"You have—twice. Once in St. Jorioz and once here. As outlined by you, the difference seems to be that which in England exists between the Gentlemen and the Players. You, I need hardly say, claim to play for the Gentlemen."

"I had hoped that three days and three nights in this place might have softened you a little, Lise."

"Did you, Henri," she said, deliberately dropping the "Monsieur". He looked at her in frowning silence, wondering why she had chosen to do that at this moment. It could be for one of various reasons. It could be to show that she resented the familiarity of "Lise"; it could, in certain circumstances, imply the start of a new collaboration; it could be—and very likely was—designed to put him in his place. He went on, picking his words with care:

"If you choose to stay here in Fresnes, the Gestapo will send for you. They want to know the whereabouts of your wireless operator Arnaud and of the British officer called Roger who lived for a time in the Hotel de la Plage at St. Jorioz. They know that you have this information and I frankly fear for you if you once go to number 84 Avenue Foch. They are not excessively scrupulous in their methods, Lise—nor are they as patient as I am."

"Tell me, Henri," she said with interest. "Are you about to offer to save me from the Gestapo again?"

"Yes," he said. "I am."

"I am not sure," she said, "which rôle I admire most—that of international airborne peace-maker or Teutonic St. George."

He said, blinking behind his spectacles:

"If you have to go to the Gestapo, you will regret it. I can get you out of here, and I am prepared to do so—without any onerous conditions attached. I am a reasonable judge of character and I know that I would be wasting my time in asking you either to give away your friends or to work for me."

"Then why," she said with disconcerting candour, "do you want to get me out?"

"I don't want you to have to go to the Gestapo, Lise."

As he said the words, he knew that they were only part of the truth. Looking at her, he was aware of a sense of frustration both unfamiliar to him and humiliating. He had, before their first meeting, been professionally interested in her, because she was a British agent and therefore an enemy. He had, during their conversation, become interested in her as a person. She was mentally as agile as he was himself—and as glib. He had sensed a background of breeding which, to the son of the cycle

shop keeper of Tettnang, was irresistible and possibly because
of that, he wanted her to be in his debt. He wanted both her
gratitude and her admiration—or if admiration was too much
to hope for—he at least wanted her to treat him as an equal.
Talking to her, he felt as if he were again in the presence of
General Levinski's wife, having been brought upstairs by her
maid—his Aunt Marie. Now he held all the cards. At his word
the gates of Fresnes would open. There was hardly a woman
in the prison who would not leap at the chance of freedom and
be prepared to pay almost any price demanded—as women had
in the past. He was the fairy godfather, wand in hand, and Lise
the reluctant Cinderella. It was most irritating to find that
she preferred the ashes of captivity to the glass coach of freedom.

He said bluntly, angrily:

"Why don't you want to leave this place?"

"I will tell you. I do want to leave it—physically. No
human being in her senses *wants* to be locked up and hungry
and encompassed by misery and cruelty. But as you seem to
know so much about the French Section of the War Office
already, there is one thing more that you should know. If one
of us is captured, then we've got to take what's coming to us.
We can't play games with you. I tried to once, and you beat
me. That's why Peter Churchill and I are here. You're too
strong. You've got everything on your side, battalions of
trained investigators, telephones, teleprinters, everything.
We've got nothing. I'm not clever enough to leave this place
under your . . . your protection so to speak and keep my
silence and my self-respect. So I choose to remain."

"I impose no conditions, Lise."

"No, but I do—on myself. Do you think I could ever go
back to England and look Buck in the face and say: 'I was
captured but they let me out again and I had a fine war—under
the benevolent wing of the *Abwehr* or the Gestapo'?" She stood
up. She said: "You will forgive me if I ask that this interview
now come to an end. I have a headache and anyway I have
nothing more to say."

"Are you hungry, Lise?"

"Very."

"I could order you extra food."

"No other women get extra food?"

"Some. Those who work for us do, the *Kahlfaktors*, the women who push the food trolley round and that sort of thing."

"No thank you. I can manage without extra food."

"Would you like books to read?"

"No other women get books?"

"Yes. Practically everyone does."

"Then I should like some books."

"I will arrange it. Is there anything else?"

"Yes, there is. On my cell door are a number of notices in German. I don't know what they mean and it would be interesting to find out."

He smiled wryly. "I will translate them for you."

"Thank you, Henri."

They stood outside the door of cell 108. With some embarrassment, Bleicher began. "That one means that you are '*grand secret*', most secret. Then these say 'no books', 'no showers', 'no parcels', 'no exercise', 'no favours' . . . and that sort of thing."

"Wouldn't it be simpler to have one notice only saying '*Nichts, rien,* nothing?' "

"It would be in a way," he said seriously, "but it might upset the administration. These things are part of a carefully planned system."

"Would it not upset the administration if I accepted your offer and walked out of Fresnes? How would that fit in to the carefully-planned system?"

"You are quite incorrigible, Lise. There is no point in my coming any more."

"As you wish. I am always, as you know, *chez moi* and it is beyond my power to add a notice saying 'no canvassers'!" She walked into her cell smiled politely and shut the door.

*

There was another flaw in the carefully-planned system, one which would greatly have upset the officers of the administration had they known that it existed. The flaw was a priest. His name was Paul Heinerz and he was a very good man.

He wore the uniform of the German Army and held the rank of Major. He was an ardent Catholic from the South, from Bavaria. He had been allowed into the prison at his own request to minister to the sick and to the dying. For some weeks he walked the landings with averted eyes as if he were ashamed of something that he alone could see. Then he applied one day to the Commandant for permission to say mass. The Commandant referred the matter to the Gestapo who took the trouble to inform the priest personally that his business was solely to listen to the last gabbles of the doomed. It was not to encourage the living in their idolatry. *Mein Kampf* was the missal of the twentieth century, and thou shalt have no other gods but Adolf Hitler. Application dismissed. It should not be put forward again. *Heil Hitler!*

One very early morning, long before the sun was up, Father Paul came to Fresnes. In the interrogation room, he silently made an altar of two chairs, a plank of wood and a prison sheet. He lit two candles and laid a crucifix on the sheet. Then, on tip-toe, he went from cell to cell unlocking the doors and beckoning to the women. Bewildered and frightened, they followed him along the lit landing and into the candle-light and sank incredulously on their knees.

Interibo ad altare Dei . . . .

Soon the sleeping prison would wake to the misery of another day. Soon the food trolleys would rumble along the landings, the chains would rattle and the keys click-clack in the cell doors. Soon the boots of the S.S. would sound on the stone flags, and their voices would echo their furious, passionless shout. "*H'raus, h'raus. Schnell, schnell.*"

Ad Deum qui laetificat juventutem meam. . . .

To God who made joyous my youth. . . . In pain and delight, the women received the forbidden mass, sobbing without restraint at the sound of the whispered, remembered words. The priest rose from his knees and said gently.

"*Mes filles* . . . there may be those amongst you who bear resentment against God that He, who is omnipotent, can let such things as this come to pass. It is not for us to question God, but to accept with patience, remembering the greater suffering of His Son. If you can think of your grief as an extension of that greater grief in the Garden of Gethsemane, then God will surely give you strength. *Ite, missa est. . . .*"

The women crept back to the darkness of their cells and Paul Heinerz, priest and gentleman, to his regiment.

CHAPTER XXV

"ON NE DOIT PAS FRAPPER UNE FEMME—MÊME AVEC UNE FLEUR." *17th Century French proverb*

AT about six o'clock on the morning of the 25th of May, an S.S. woman unlocked the door of Cell 108 and shouted *"Tribunal"*.

Odette's heart turned over and she drew a long, quivering breath. Though she had known that a summons to the Commissars of the Gestapo was inevitable, though she had expected it every morning since her arrival in Fresnes more than a fortnight ago and she had steeled herself to accept it with composure, the knowledge that it had now come drained her momentarily of strength. Other women had been called to 84 Avenue Foch. Some of them had come back, but even those had never spoken about what had happened there. Most of them had not returned and a new occupant had come to their cells. Sitting on her bed, Odette tried coherently to run over the points of the story she had decided to tell, testing each lie for a possible flaw. Her *ersatz* coffee was slopped into her bowl and she drank it greedily, for her mouth was dry. She told Michèle in a whisper that she had been called to the *tribunal* at last, and Michèle said that she regretted for the first time in her life that she didn't believe in God. "If I believed, I would pray for you, Céline. . . . I shall be in fear for you all day."

Odette was taken out of the prison at eight o'clock. The sides of the *panier à salade*, the Black Maria, were windowless, but from each compartment one could look through a wire mesh into the centre passage. There was an iron grill in the back door and, by laying her cheek against the mesh, Odette could just see through the grill into the street. In a jumbled blur, she saw people walking on the pavements and once, in a traffic block, she saw for a static, poignant instant, the sight of children playing. For no reason at all, she was reminded of her many journeys to Paddington when she had first tried to go to

France and how remote she had felt then from the people on the pavements. She had stopped her taxi in the Edgware Road to buy a bunch of violets. "Good luck, Miss," the man had said. "Good luck, Miss. . . ."

The Black Maria stopped. Her compartment was unlocked and the back doors were flung open.

"*H'raus, h'raus. Schnell, schnell.* . . ."

Good luck, Miss. Good luck.

*

She came back to Fresnes in the late afternoon. When the S.S. were out of hearing, she erected her improvised ladder and called softly down the *bouche de chaleur.*

"*Allo, Michèle.*"

"Céline. You are back?"

"Yes. I'm back."

"Tell me what happened. Tell me everything. I have been in fear for you all day."

"It was not necessary—this time. We went in the *panier à salade* to the avenue Foch and then I was taken upstairs to a small room and locked in. I waited there for two, three hours and then was given a magnificent lunch, meat, potatoes and thick gravy." Michèle sighed. "I knew the purpose of this feast—to make me sleepy before the interrogation, and I only ate half of it. I took a potato and hid it and I have it here. I will send it down to you by the *Kahlfaktor.*"

"A potato! My God. . . ."

"Then I was sent for by the Commissar. He is a young man, very clean and fair and correct. He smells of eau-de-Cologne. He asked many questions. He was quite polite—in spite of the fact that after two hours questioning, he had only been able to write three lines on a very big sheet of paper. At the end he said that he and I would meet again and I was locked up to wait for the Black Maria. That's all. I had had meat and gravy for lunch—and all for nothing. Now I'm going to my window to watch the sunset. I am a very lucky woman to have been to the Avenue Foch and to come back as I am."

*

"*Tribunal.*"

"But . . . but I went to the *tribunal* yesterday."

"You go again to-day. *Tribunal, tribunal.*"

The door slammed. If going to the Avenue Foch only meant meat and thick gravy and a stolen glance at free people walking the pavements she had little to fear. But she had a premonition that it was going to mean a lot more than that. They had told her during her training in England about these clean young Commissars of the Gestapo who lived in number 84 Avenue Foch. They were the hand-picked inner core of the Gestapo and their training in Himmler's No. 1 School was long and thorough. They wore no uniform and they had nothing to do with the ordinary bullies of the S.S. Their job was to make people talk. To their impersonal eyes, the human body, male or female, was merely so much raw material to be classified and sub-divided into varying zones of articulate pain; in their eyes Odette or Lise or Madame Chambrun or Madame Churchill was no longer a woman. She was a subject, a number, a unit. She was a cypher from Fresnes, a cypher with a tongue, vocal cords and a sensitive nervous system, the laceration of which would cause the tongue to speak. These Commissars were very efficient young men and a credit to their Master. It was rare indeed that they took "no" for an answer while the subject of their investigations continued to breathe. Sometimes, of course, death was kind enough to intervene and then the Commissars got a reprimand. They were very healthy young men and lived in a sort of muscular chastity with plenty of good music, P.T. and cold baths.

Odette told Michèle that she was going to the Gestapo again.

"*Oh là là*, that's not so good, two days running. I shall be anxious for you all day. If you get a chance, bring me back another potato, Céline."

"Somehow I don't think I shall be able to give my attention to potatoes to-day, Michèle. But if I can, I will."

"Try, Céline. The hunger in my belly is like a spear. *A ce soir.*"

"*A ce soir, Michèle.*"

Odette would far have preferred to stay in her cell all that day and rest.

It was not a good time for her, but the young gentlemen of

I*

the Gestapo could hardly be expected to take account of the feminine calendar. She drank her coffee and considered her pitiful wardrobe. She wore her coat and skirt—she had told Buck a very long time ago that it would be suitable for prison— a red blouse and her only silk stockings. A few minutes before eight, the guards came for her and she was marched out into the courtyard of the prison to the Black Maria. It was a lovely day and the courtyard was dappled with sunshine.

At 84 Avenue Foch, there seemed to be rather more activity than yesterday. Odette was taken upstairs to a room on the third floor. This time, she was sent for almost at once and went into the same interrogation room where she had been yesterday. The same Commissar sat at a table on which was spread his meagre notes. He looked very healthy and fresh, as if he had just come out of a cold bath, and she noticed again the faint not unpleasant scent of eau-de-Cologne. He indicated a chair and she sat down facing him, her back to the door. He said briskly, in very nearly perfect French:

"Lise, you wasted a great deal of my time yesterday. You will not be permitted to do this again. There are three questions to which I require the answers. The first is this. Where is your wireless operator, the man you call Arnaud?"

"I have nothing to say."

"We will see. It is known to us that you sent the British officer, Roger from St. Jorioz to an address in the South of France. I want to know the address to which you sent him."

"I have nothing to say."

"Again, we will see. It is also known to us that you obtained from a French traitor a day or two before your arrest the lay-out of the docks of the *Vieux port* of Marseille. As it is impossible that you could have had time to send this to England, I want to know the whereabouts of this document or the name of the person in whose possession it is."

"I have nothing to say."

"Lise, there is a parrot-like quality about your conversation that I find most irritating. Here again are the three questions. Where is Arnaud, where is Roger and where is the Marseille dock lay-out? I propose to give you one minute to provide the answers."

He looked at his wrist-watch. It was one of those watches

with a complicated dial that gave its owner a lot of trivial information about the sub-divisions of eternity.   From the busy
streets below, Odette could hear the *staccato* trumpeting of
motor horns, as urgent and as strident as the hunting horns of
the English shires.

"Well, Lise, I would now like the answers to my questions."

"I have nothing to say."

"It is very foolish of you.   We have means of making you
talk."

"I am aware of your methods.   Do you think we come to
France from England without knowledge of the sort of thing
you can do to us?   You must give us credit for something,
Monsieur."

There was another man in the room now.   He had come in
silently and he was standing immediately behind her chair.   He
caught her arms and held them behind the back of the chair.
The fair man who smelt of cold water and eau-de-Cologne
stood up and walked over to her and began leisurely to unbutton
her blouse.   She said:

"I resent your hands on me or on my clothes.   If you tell me
what you want me to do and release one hand, I will do it."

"As you wish.   Unbutton your blouse."

She undid the two top buttons.   The man behind her drew
her blouse back so that the corrugations of her spine, were bare.
On the third vertebra, he laid a red-hot poker.   Odette lurched
forward.   The fair young man's mouth moved and his voice
came from a long way away.

"Where is Arnaud?"

"I have nothing to say."

"You are more than foolish."   He opened his cigarette case
offered it to her and snapped a lighter.   From it sprang a small
sedate flame, like an altar candle.   Dumbly Odette shook her
head.   He said smiling.   "It's quite all right.   I can assure you
that the cigarette isn't poisoned.   If you look, you will see that I
am smoking one myself.   Did they tell you that in your school
for amateurs in the New Forest, to beware of poisoned cigarettes?   You know the three questions.   Are you now prepared to
answer them—after the *hors d'oeuvres* or do you want the full
meal?"

"I have nothing to say."

He came over to her and stood there, half-smiling. The cold bath and eau-de-Cologne smell was apparent. He said to her: "Perhaps you would prefer to take off your shoes and stockings yourself. If not, I can assure you that I am well experienced in the mechanism of feminine suspenders."

"I will do it myself."

To be tortured by this clean, soap-smelling scented Nordic was one thing. To be touched by his hands was another. She slid her feet out of her shoes and unrolled her stockings. The wooden floor was warm and rough to her naked feet. She automatically adjusted her skirt over her knees.

"My colleague here, Lise, is going to pull out your toe-nails one by one, starting at the little toe of your left foot. In between each evulsion—to use the correct medical term—I propose to repeat my questions. You can bring the ceremony to an end at any moment by answering these questions. There are those who faint after the third or fourth toenail, but I don't think you are of the fainting kind. If you do faint, we can always revive you with brandy and the ceremony will continue. Now, before we begin, where is Arnaud?"

. . . clamor meus ad te veniat . . . .

A man knelt at her feet. He was a young man, under thirty, very good-looking in a dark, Mediterranean handsomeness, and he glanced up at her with blind, brown eyes. He did not see her as a woman but only as a living, sensitive adjunct to a naked foot. His impersonality was terrifying. He took her left foot in his left hand and settled the steel jaws of the pincers tightly around the tip of her nail. Then with a slow, muscular drag, he began to pull. A semi-circle of blood started to the quick, oozed over the skin, flooded after the retreating nail. . . . He shook the pincers and her nail fell on the floor.

"Now would you care to tell me Arnaud's address?"

She tried to say the word "no" but no sound came from her mouth. She shook her head. *Clamor meus ad te veniat. . . .*

The Commissar nodded to the kneeling man and sat on the edge of the table, swinging his legs. The pincers clasped the next nail, gripped hard, were slowly drawn back. The enclosing flesh ripped and yielded in agonizing pain as the nail was dragged out. . . . The reiterated questions flew round her head like wasps as the agony leapt from toe to toe, from foot to foot.

She gave no cry. After an eternity, her torturer stood up, his pincers in his hands. He looked at the Commissar, waiting obsequiously for more orders. Odette gazed incredulously at the bloody furnace of her feet and at the red litter on the floor, litter of a diabolical chiropody. The sound of motor horns below sounded thin in the sunny air and she was aware of a subsidiary ache in the palms of her hands.

"Well, Lise, I think you will find it convenient to walk on your heels for some time. Now I would like to offer you a drink. A glass of wine, a little brandy—or, better still, a cup of tea." He smiled. "In England, the country of your adoption, a cup of tea is the cure for all evils. I will order you some tea. You are a woman of surprising endurance."

Sitting on a wooden chair, her body quivering, she drank her tea. He talked to her easily and she hardly heard a word he was saying. She felt as if she were drowning in recurring waves of nausea and she tried desperately to reach the shore. The nausea passed and the walls of the room took shape again and became solid. She leaned back in her chair and shut her eyes. Though her lacerated toes were ten separate hubs of pain, she was conscious of a sudden stab of elation. She was Odette and she had kept silence. Now she had an almost irresistible urge to talk freely and to laugh and to gabble with her mouth, anything to make sounds with her tongue. And then she recognized this sense of triumph for the danger that it was. This was how the Gestapo wanted her to feel. Her sense of relief and of triumph could easily be a better weapon to their hands than a pair of pincers. The Commissar watched her like a cat, as if aware of every thought process of her mind. She opened her eyes and looked at him. Just as he saw her as a mere nervous system, she now saw him not as a Commissar of the Gestapo nor even as a man. She saw him for what he was, a creature from whom human pity and human understanding had been deliberately drained and the hollow filled with blasphemy. He half-smiled.

"Well," he said, "how do you feel?"

"I have nothing to say."

"Conversationally we are becoming a bore to each other. I keep on asking the same questions and you keep on making the same replies. No doubt you see yourself as a heroine at this moment and me as a monster. I am not. I am a servant of my

Führer, Adolf Hitler, and I have no regret for what I do. You should know that I shall stop at nothing to get the information I require. Last night the charming R.A.F. dropped two thousand tons of bombs on Dortmund. I do not know how many good German men, women and children were killed or maimed or burned. If mass murder by the R.A.F. is considered to be a legitimate act of war, do you think I care for the sufferings of a single, obstinate, renegade Frenchwoman?"

"I am interested to see, Monsieur, that you consider it necessary to defend what you have just done."

"Nothing of the sort. We Germans have no need to excuse ourselves to subject races." He stood angrily over her. "Are you going to answer my questions?"

"No."

"Then I shall now cause to be done to your finger-tips the same operation that has just been carried out on your feet."

Odette stared at her hands and the living pink nails on her fingers and the quick of the nails. Then her eyes travelled down to the red pulp of her toes and her stomach turned over in sickness. She heard the door open and the sound of steps in the room. The young Commissar sprang to attention and snapped:

"Zur Befehl, Herr Major."

Another man in civilian clothes walked to the table glancing casually at the bloody *débris* on the floor. He said: *"Wer ist das Weib?"*

"Frau Churchill." He spoke rapidly, deferentially, in German and the other man shrugged, answered shortly and walked out of the room. The Commissar said:

"The Major says that I am wasting my time and that you will never talk. He has a higher opinion of the endurance of the French than I have. I do not agree with him, but he has ordered that you be taken upstairs. You are a very fortunate woman, Lise. I have no doubt that we shall meet again. One more thing. If you speak about what has happened to a living soul, you will be brought here again and worse things will happen to you." He gave an order, and the dark man laid the pincers on the table and spoke for the first time. Holding the door open he said in what Odette knew instantly and with horror to be his native tongue:

"Permettez-moi, Madame."

She gathered up her shoes and stockings and stumbled in agony to the door.

*

Cell one hundred and eight, Fresnes.

Odette feebly tore her prison cloth into strips and wet them and bound her feet. Then she leaned back on her bed and lay without moving. She could hear Michèle calling and calling. She wanted to go to the window and say that she was back and alive and she was sorry she had no potato, but she couldn't summon the physical strength to stir a muscle. The sun's rays turned from yellow to orange and greyness came into her cell. Sometime in the space between dusk and darkness, her door was unlocked and an S.S. woman brought a bowl of soup to her bedside. She was too weak to sit up and eat and it stayed on the floor untouched. Though she had kept silent, she was filled with sickness and fear for she had heard of some of the other things that the Gestapo could do to women's bodies and, alone in the darkness of Fresnes, she was afraid lest her strength might give way.

CHAPTER XXVI

8832 HOURS

Two or three days later, the priest came to her cell. She was sitting on the edge of her bed when he came in, looking with detached, absorbed interest at the scratched calendar on her wall. Father Paul was in uniform and she saw that his face was grey and drawn. She said formally: "You will please forgive me, Father, if I fail to stand up."

"*Ma fille* . . . what have they done to you?"

She didn't answer for a full minute. Then she said:

"You are a German officer and you must know that it is not permitted to discuss what happens at number 84 Avenue Foch."

"I am a priest."

She looked at him steadily and for a long time without speaking. Then she moved her feet forward and unwound the bloody rags that bound them. He stared with horror at the inflamed and lacerated flesh. He said at last, in a half-whisper:

"And your hands. What are those marks in your hands?"

"You will understand, Father, that when they were doing that to my feet, I clenched my hands very tightly, so tightly that my finger-nails bit into my palms. I was unaware of it at the time. These marks are nothing. They will disappear."

He stood up. He gazed at her with compassion and with shame. Swiftly he bent over her, kissed her forehead. Without a word, he walked out of her cell and shut the door.

*

Several days passed, days of advancing and receding pain. One sunny morning, the dreaded summons came again.

"Tribunal, tribunal. . . ."

Odette limped along the landing, down the scrubbed stairs,

along the hall past the tombstone doors, down the stone steps
to the underground passage through which she had first been
brought to her cell. One single phrase ran in her brain and she
repeated it again and again, trying with all her strength to
banish every other formation of words from her mind and from
her vocabulary. "I have nothing to say. . . . I have nothing to
say. . . . I have nothing to say. . . ."

Le panier à salade, la porte d'Italie; sunshine on the pavements
and free men sitting at the little round tables outside a café;
two laughing women waiting to cross the road, their silk
stockings as sheer as sunburn; Avenue Foch; number eighty-
four. . . . Good luck, Miss. Good luck.

"*H'raus, h'raus. Schnell, schnell.*"

Odette was taken upstairs—as far as the first floor. Guarded
by two S.S. men in black and silver, she was ushered into a
sort of ante-room. A chair was given her. Nothing like this
had happened on either of her interrogations and, with sick
apprehension, she wondered what was afoot. She did not have
to wait long. The tall double doors facing her were flung open
and a Germany Army N.C.O. shouted:

"Frau Churchill."

Flanked by her guards, she hobbled into a large, sunny
room. There were several officers there, all in uniform and all
wearing that pre-occupied and portentous expression which
indicated a formal occasion. The room had once been a drawing-room, and a beautiful cut glass chandelier caught the sun's
rays and flashed like spring water. She sat down, facing a plain
deal table. The officers looked at her with sidelong glances and
frowned and fiddled with their pencils. They were then
addressed for some minutes by a hard-faced civilian who
looked, to Odette's tutored eye, like a senior member of the
Gestapo. When he finished speaking, the officers huddled
together and spoke in undertones. As all the proceedings had
been conducted in a language she did not understand, she had
no idea what they were saying. That they were sitting in judgment on her was plain. But where was counsel for the defence?
Where was the interpreter? She considered the chandelier. It
was either Louis Quatorze or Quinze and the octagonal
lustres made limpid prisons for the sun. Now the officers had
obviously arrived at a unanimous decision, for there was much

solemn nodding of heads and then the huddle broke up as each man resumed his former position. The man in the middle—a colonel with the Iron Cross—stood up, coughed and recited something ponderously in German. His tunic was too tight for him. She only understood the first two words which were "Frau Churchill". When he had finished, she shrugged and, in French, spoke for the first time.

"I do not understand German, Monsieurs."

The colonel frowned. He said in slow, guttural French:

"Madame Churchill, you are condemned to death on two counts. The first is because you are a British spy and the second because you are a Frenchwoman. *Heil Hitler!*"

Odette looked around the court. These self-conscious creatures, showing off in their corsetted uniforms, set bubbling a hidden giggle of derision. It was all so pontifical and seemed to bear no relationship to reality. The words the colonel had made with his mouth were only sounds . . . and his French had been execrable. She had no fear of these marionettes as she had of the Gestapo upstairs. She said with a smile:

"Gentlemen, you must take your pick of the counts. I can only die once."

That night there was a new sign on her door. It was a small red mark in the shape of a cross.

*

She slept soundly that night, for the first time since she had come to Fresnes. On the rare occasions when, reading the newspapers as a girl, she had allowed herself to speculate about the reactions of the human being to the death sentence, it had been with sympathetic horror. She had imagined the condemned as being stricken with fear of what was to come, of the macabre formalities of judicial dying. Now this thing had happened to her. Mrs. Odette Sansom—in this hour she harked back through the maze of aliases to her true name—Mrs. Odette Sansom was herself *condamnée à mort*. Lying on her bed in her cell, she said aloud. "*Je suis Odette, Odette, Odette et je suis condamnée à mort*. This matter concerns me, me, me." She waited for a cold feather of fear to touch her heart but it failed to come. The realization of the phrase *condamnée à mort* in relation to her personal identity was not yet upon her and she thought more of the Louis Quatorze—or was it Quinze?—chandelier in the converted drawing-room than she did of the meaning of the words used by the colonel whose tunic had been too tight. How foolish they had been, those pompous gentlemen, to waste all that time on her—while others far more deserving of the subtle flattery of the death sentence continued to live and to breathe. Peter Churchill, for example, now languishing in the men's division of Fresnes, Peter was far more worthy of that honour than she was. What had she done? She had carried a few messages, attended a few parachute operations, made herself as useful as she could to the men who really ran the circuit. And Arnaud. Now that one was a real thorn in the German side, a thorn that the Germans would do well to pluck out and destroy. Yet Arnaud roved France in freedom and she, Odette Sansom, mother and housewife, courier and amateur agent, had the little red mark on her cell door. In the grand balance of the war, it was as it should be. She said a soundless good night to each of her daughters in turn and went to sleep in steady tranquillity.

In the night, the pendulum of thought swung strongly and she woke to a sharp sense of loneliness and fear. Around her, the prison was beginning to stir to the misery of another day. She wondered, with a feeling akin to panic, if she would see the day's end. From now onwards, every step outside her cell, every unlocking of her door, might mean that they were coming to take her out and to kill her. Now, at this moment, she could move her fingers, she could blink her eyelids, she could breathe and feel and smell, and every beat of her heart sent living, hidden surges of blood flowing in her veins. How long would her heart be allowed to beat, how long her blood remain hidden? The simple act of continuing to live became inexpressibly dear to her as the sharp splinter of panic passed. Though her body felt weak and hollow, she was, thank God, once again the mistress of her mind. She got out of bed and groped her way to the window. Dawn was climbing the sky and the young day had a tenderness and a radiance that was past belief. It seemed to her that never before had she seen anything as beautiful as the rising of the sun.

*

That afternoon she had a visitor. For the first time Bleicher came into her cell. He said to her:

"Good afternoon, Lise."

"Good afternoon, Henri."

She sat on the bed. He walked slowly round her cell, looking with intense, preoccupied interest at the scratches on the walls. She could sense his embarrassment and she said nothing either to increase or dispel it. At last he sat down on her chair. As always he offered her a cigarette and she took it. He said after a long silence:

"You've been to the Gestapo?"

"Yes."

"Lise, I know what they did to you. Believe me when I say how sorry and how utterly ashamed I am. It had nothing to do with me and . . . and I couldn't stop it."

"That I believe."

"I'm glad. Is there anything, anything I can do for you?"

"Yes," she said, "there is. Have you seen Peter Churchill since I went to the Gestapo?"

"No."

"Are you going to see him?"

"Yes, this afternoon, when I leave you."

"Then there is something you can do. You can keep silence about"—she moved her feet—"about what they did to me. When we were arrested in Annecy, you know that Peter tried to escape and that he was beaten up by the Italians. They hit him with rifle butts and kicked him as he lay on the ground and he had a rib broken and two fingers."

"I knew he was hurt. I didn't know how badly."

"Well I don't want him to be hurt again, and I know that if you told him what the Gestapo did, he'd be . . . very angry and do something violent and foolish. Then he would be hurt again. So don't tell him—and also don't tell him that I've been sentenced to death."

"I won't. Lise, do you ever think of yourself?"

"Far too much. I am a very selfish woman."

He blinked behind his spectacles. He said weakly, after a long pause: "I hate to see you here—in this place among these vile and sordid people."

"The people here are not specially vile or sordid. Being in prison

" ARNAUD "

Captain A. Rabinovitch, Croix de Guerre
(Executed by Gestapo 1944)

doesn't change people. All it does is to underline and to accentuate their predominant characteristics; all it does is to make a strong person stronger and a weak one weaker. If you go to the window and look out, you'll just be able to see the little yard outside the punishment cells. Look, Henri."

He went to the window and peered out, he could see the airless, oblong space, surrounded by high walls. He came back. He said, "Well, what about it?"

"There is a prisoner here, an Englishman. I don't know his real name but we call him Johnny. He is a man of middle age, the sort of person we in England are apt to laugh at because he very likely wears an old school tie. He is, I think, of the social class that led Ribbentrop to call the English 'decadent'. Do you know who I mean?"

"Yes. I have met Johnny."

"We get to hear things in prison and I know that Johnny has been a prisoner for a very long time—for two years I think. For six months he has been in a punishment cell. The first Saturday I was here, Johnny had been defiant or something, God knows what, and he was ordered to march round that yard barefoot and only wearing a pair of trousers for twenty-four hours on end. It began at ten o'clock in the morning. I watched him from my window, walking round and round and round. It was raining and his bare feet slid in the mud. Sometimes I went away from the window because it was not pretty to watch a man being treated like a beast, but I kept on being drawn back to look. The guards smoked and leaned against the wall to watch him and make sure he didn't stop. They were changed every hour. You will understand that the task of watching a weak middle-aged man on the treadmill is a strenuous one so that is why the guards were changed. At about four o'clock in the afternoon, Johnny stumbled and fell on his knees in the mud. He had been walking that shameful circle for five hours and he could do it no more. I saw him trying to move forward on his knees while the guard shouted at him to get up and march. I called out to him, 'Courage, Johnny', because when you are deeply moved, you use words like that. The word went round the women's cells that Johnny had fallen down. One of them began to sing 'God save the King' to Johnny and the other women took it up. I don't think any of them knew the words except me and some of them didn't even know the tune, but something that was recognizable to Johnny came pouring out of every window in Fresnes. It was like an anthem. Johnny got to his feet and waved to our windows and saluted us. He was laughing. Then he took up his march again, with his back as straight as a guardsman. I am proud to be under the same roof as a man like that."

He stood up. His face was strained.

"To use your favourite expression, Lise, I have nothing to say."

"Give my love to Peter Churchill. And not a word about . . . anything else."

"Not a word." He hesitated. "Lise, may I come to see you again?"

"Isn't that rather odd, for a member of the all powerful *Abwehr* to ask a condemned prisoner for permission to pay a call?"

"No. I don't think it's odd. I will come again. *Au revoir*, Lise."

"*Adieu*, Henri."

                                    ★

The next afternoon a trivial incident occurred which was to have an incalculable effect on Odette's subsequent treatment in Fresnes. Two French prisoners of the *Droit Commun*, under the officious eye of an S.S. guard called Kirchstein, shuffled into her cell to mend the window she had broken. Kirchstein, was an ugly little coxcomb with boils, an ex-doorman from a cheap "Bazar" in Berlin, whose perverted delight it was to slam cell doors on women who sprang from a social environment other than his own. When the window was finished, he secured it unnecessarily with half a dozen four inch nails. Odette watched him with quiet disdain. She congratulated him on his contribution to the German war effort. "It must be a matter of satisfaction to you, Kirchstein, to know that you have shut out the sight of the sky from a woman in solitary confinement."

"My name is *Herr* Kirchstein," he said loudly.

"We have another name for you along the landing, a nickname."

"Oh." He preened himself and smirked. "And what nickname have the ladies of Fresnes given me?"

"We used to call you '*Noyau de cerises*', 'cherry stone'. Now we only call you '*Noyau*' or 'stone'."

He flung out of her cell. When he had gone, she went on with the fashioning of the last of four implements she proposed to put to a certain purpose. By the time she had finished, her cell was nearly dark. She hid her improvised tools under the mattress and lay down under the blanket. Stimulated by her brief skirmish with Kirchstein, she was conscious of a new sense of recklessness. For some extraordinary reason of their own the Germans had gone through the formality of condemning her to death. It was rare that they took the trouble to legalize their killings. She knew that there was no possible hope of a reprieve and that if the war lasted for ten years, she would either be dead or still in a cell ten years hence. The future held nothing and there was, therefore, nothing for her to lose. Rather than to weep or to surrender to that most insidious enemy, self-pity, she determined to squeeze every drop out of the present. It should not be difficult, for the opponents against whom she would pit her living wits were of poor quality. Men of the intellectual calibre of Kirchstein; middle-aged bullies who had entered the prison service to avoid the front; the blousy harridans in grey. She half-smiled. "*Quand j'étais petite, je gardais les vaches; maintenant ce sont elles qui me gardent. . . .*" She would very much like to find the woman who had written those words and take her by the hand and thank her. Now her cell was dark. She shut her eyes and prepared to set out joyfully on one of her nightly journeys to a place she loved. She chose Kew Gardens and, of the months, she chose April. With infinite joy, she crossed Kew Bridge, sitting on the front seat of an imaginary number 27 bus. She looked backwards to see the lovely Georgian façade of Strand-on-the-Green . . . and was just telling Marianne to take the bus tickets out of her mouth when her cell door was flung open, her electric light blazed and she was back in Fresnes.

Two S.S. women strode into her cell, followed by two men. Odette's heart gave a leap. She sat up in bed and took a deep breath. One of the women pointed to her and shouted: "You Frau Chambrun, you have been talking out of the window."

"I have not."

"Liar. You have been talking. Get up."

She seized Odette's blanket and flung it on the floor. Odette scrambled to her feet. Her palliasse followed and there, laid bare, was the evidence of another crime. She had torn her cloth into thin strips and knotted them together to make a line. Out of the end of one of her rusty bed slats, she had made a flexible strip, the length of a pencil. She had picked a small lump of concrete from her lavatory surround and twisted the handle of her spoon into a hook. The S.S. woman seized on them with triumph.

"Ho ho. These too will be of interest to the Commandant. You will be reported for talking out of the window and for having in your possession means of communicating with other prisoners."

"I have not been talking out of the window. You can see for yourself that the window is not only sealed but nailed—by no less a person than Herr Kirchstein himself."

The S.S. woman picked up Odette's scrubbing brush and aimed a furious blow. It struck Odette on the forearm. She shouted, "You will be reported," and slammed the door. Before the light was switched off, Odette had had time to note with satisfaction that the flesh of her forearm was slightly contused.

*

She woke early and dressed with as much care as she could. Then she took her scrubbing brush and hammered loudly on the panels of her door. She kept on hammering until the door was unlocked and an S.S. woman, the early morning watch, said sourly:

"Make less noise, Frau Chambrun. What do you want?"

"I wish to see the Commandant of the prison. Please inform him that Mrs. Churchill wishes to see him."

"Who?"

"Mrs. Churchill."

"But you are Frau Chambrun, not Frau Churchill."

"I am Mrs. Churchill and I demand to see the Commandant. You will please send him to me. That is all I have to say."

The S.S. woman gaped at her in astonishment and shut the door slowly. Odette sat down. So far so good.

A few minutes after eight, she heard the hurried steps of a

procession approach her cell and stop. A key rattled in the lock and the door was opened. Outside stood a German officer, a middle-aged Army Captain, in uniform. He saluted her punctiliously. With him was the S.S. woman who had entered her cell last night and the truculent Kirchstein, obsequious in the presence of his superior, blinked and fawned in the background. Spread out neatly for the Captain's inspection were the four objects that constituted Odette's crime. The display looked so ludicrous and so pathetic that Odette had difficulty in suppressing a smile.

She acknowledged his salute. She said:

"Good morning. Are you the Commandant of the prison?"

"No. I am the Captain in charge of the Women's Division."

"Good. I wish to make a complaint. Last night, I was falsely and unjustly accused of talking out of my window. You can yourself see that my windows are sealed and that your subordinate Kirchstein has even taken the trouble to use unnecessary nails. By the way, he accidentally left one nail in my cell. This I return to you—as a gesture of good faith. You will yourself realize the very good use to which a woman in my position could put a nail." She handed the Captain a solitary nail with the air of a woman giving a tip to a concierge. He took it in frowning silence. Odette went on. "Naturally, I denied the accusation. The S.S. woman behind you then struck me on the forearm with a brush. I would like you to examine the bruise." She displayed her forearm. "And I would now like to ask you, sir, if it is in order that a political prisoner in her right mind should be the victim of violence on the part of your subordinates?"

The Captain frowned. "No," he said, "it is not in order. Definitely not in order." He was obviously ill at ease. "But ... but I was informed that Mrs. Churchill wished to see me. Your name is not Churchill, but Chambrun."

"That is a matter I do not propose to discuss with you in the presence of your subordinates."

He spoke sharply to Kirchstein and the S.S. woman and they sidled away. Still standing at the door, he said:

"Now perhaps you will explain your change of name."

"The matter is a simple one. The name 'Chambrun' is a false one—as your friends in the Gestapo will be pleased to confirm. My name is Churchill and I am the wife of Captain

Peter Churchill, now in cell number 220 in the Second Division. It was under my true name of Churchill that I was condemned to death by a military court on the day before yesterday. If you require further proof, apply at number 84 Avenue Foch. May we now get back to the matter of the savage and unprovoked attack made on me last night?"

He touched the neat little array of implements she had made with his foot.

"There is also the question of these to be discussed."

"Oh those." She smiled disarmingly. "May I ask you, Monsieur, if you had any special training in penal matters before being appointed to your position in Fresnes?"

"I am a soldier," he said stiffly, "and a soldier's duty is to go where he is ordered. I am an officer in the German Army whose misfortune it was to find himself here. I have had no training as a prison official, nor indeed is it my *métier*."

"It is my theory that every prison official should himself serve a term in a cell before being made responsible for the confinement of others. If you were yourself in my position, would you not use all your ingenuity to get into touch with your fellow prisoners?"

"That is no excuse. These articles will be confiscated."

"I realize it is your duty to confiscate them. It is very sad for they took a long time to make. Now, Monsieur, this bruise on my forearm. . . ."

"That I regret—but I do not see what I can do."

She looked at him shrewdly, her head on one side. She sensed immediately that she had found, not an ally, for that was too strong a word, but a man to whom she could appeal, a man in whom the well of decency was not dry. This was no S.S. thug, but a soldier doing an unpleasant job with what grace he could. She was also aware with pride of the quite astonishing prestige of the name "Churchill" and, as a corollary, of the surprising fact that this officer wished to stand well in the sight of one who bore that hated, respected name. It was a pretty paradox—that of the gaoler seeking the good opinion of the condemned because she claimed to share the name of his bitterest enemy. She said tentatively:

"One could make a bargain. I would be inclined to exchange my bruised forearm against the retention of those...instruments."

A glimmer of a smile skimmed across his eyes, was instantly gone.

"No, Frau Churchill, that I cannot do. Two wrongs do not make a right."

"You wish me to go to all the trouble of re-making my tools?"

"If you do so and they are found, they will be confiscated and you will be punished."

"They will not be found, Monsieur."

"That is as it may be, Frau Churchill. I will find a means of compensating you for the injury that you have received at the hands of my staff." Involuntarily, he glanced at her feet and a shadow passed over his face. He said with difficulty. "I am, of course, responsible for the actions of my prison subordinates. I am not responsible for . . . for what may happen outside the walls of the prison. I would like you to understand that."

"I understand more than your words. I believe you to be a just man, surrounded by injustice which you cannot know about. To know Fresnes, it is necessary to live in a cell. If I, who do live in a cell, see unnecessary wrong or unnecessary suffering, I would like to know that I can bring the matter to your personal attention. That knowledge would be ample compensation for my bruised forearm."

"Within the limits of my duty, I will seek to rectify what you can prove to be wrong. You do not yourself ask for special treatment or consideration?"

"No Monsieur."

"Very well. The interview is over."

He saluted her and shut the door as if he were taking leave of his hostess in a drawing-room in the Avenue Kléber.

That evening a small parcel was sourly delivered to her cell by one of the S.S. women. In it were twenty-three ginger biscuits.

*

By the following afternoon, she had managed to remake her improvised tools. She was agog to see if they would work, and with some excitement, she called down the *bouche de chaleur*.

"*Michèle. Allo, Michèle.*"

"*Oui, Céline.*"

"Are you hungry?"

"Hungry! My God. . . ."

"Stand by for a ginger biscuit. And send me back a book, any book, I don't care what."

Odette put a biscuit and a tiny lump of concrete into the toe of a stocking. Then she slid the hooked spoon handle into the soft silk and attached it to her line. Using a strip of steel from her bed slat, she managed to slide the stocking through the grating of the *bouche de chaleur*. Very carefully, she paid out the line, inch by inch, and the weighted stocking sank slowly down the hollow shaft. . . .

"*Céline.*"

"*Oui, Michèle.*"

"I've got it. It's wonderful. Pull up again, very slowly. It's a book that interests me not at all but you may like it. *Doucement, ma chère, doucement.*"

Ten minutes later, Odette was sitting on her bed holding in her hands the first book she had seen since the 16th of April. It was *L'imitation de Jésus Christ.*

*

In the intervals between her reiterated visits to the Gestapo, Odette extended the field of her operations. She spent many days in the Avenue Foch and had, in all, thirteen interrogations. At one of them she was suddenly confronted with a photograph of a man, a British officer, whom she knew well. She was asked sharply if she had ever seen him before. It was difficult not to reveal by a flicker that she was looking at the features of a friend but she shook her head and shrugged and said that she had never seen him in her life. "He was, like you, trained in your school in the New Forest," said the Gestapo man easily. "That must have been a very interesting place—almost as interesting as Baker Street. . . . Now here is another photograph. . . ." One after another, they brought the moth-eaten rabbits of interrogation out of the top-hat and dangled them before her. Like a bored child to whom the secrets of the conjurer had long ago been revealed, Odette showed silent, polite interest. When she was asked a direct question, she replied in her time-honoured formula: "I have nothing to ay." The more subtle approach was met by regretted lapses in her memory. It was galling for the expert young gentlemen from Himmler's Number One Training School to have to confess themselves beaten by a slip of a Frenchwoman with no toe-nails, but there was nothing they could do about it.

Meanwhile in Fresnes itself, cell number one hundred and eight became a sort of secret telephone exchange from which she could not only communicate with her immediate neighbours but eventually with other divisions of the prison. She could talk through the *bouche de chaleur* to Michèle below and to the occupants of the cells above her on both the second and third floors. By whispering into the hole through which ran the lavatory chain, she could have conversations with the prisoner on her left, a young Communist girl who had been caught transmitting to the Russian Armies. She started a system of tapping, one tap for A, two for B, and so on, whereby she could talk to the woman in the cell on her right. This system was lengthy and laborious and was soon shortened to an easy code. As the grapevine developed, she found that she could soon transmit a message in a matter of minutes either to the whole landing or to any particular cell—always remembering the possible presence of an *agent provocateur*, a Gestapo spy, *un mouton*, among the genuine prisoners. The more timorous of the women were apt to take fright and refuse to pass on messages. But the prison population was constantly changing and these hold-ups were temporary. As fresh prisoners were brought in, news perpetually reached Odette of the ebb and flow of the war. She knew within a day of the Italian surrender and of Germany's swift reaction by the occupation of Rome; later in the month, the news ran round the landing like lighted petrol that French Commandos and patriots held half Corsica. Odette's problem was now to find a method of extending the filaments of her grapevine to the second division where Peter Churchill wearily paced the few square feet of cell 220. To jump this chasm she required accomplices and these Odette found, one of them emerging surprisingly from the ranks of the S.S.

The priest, Father Paul Heinerz, was the first to carry a message to Peter. It was a simple, straightforward message and he consented to report that he had seen her, that she was in good health and sent her love. To Odette he brought back a similar message—and one filament was established. The next exchange was made with the help of the official interpreter, a young German of twenty-three named Boucher. . He was a cheerful man, over six feet in height, with a passion for soccer. He had lived in Holland before the war, spoke fluent Dutch, reasonably good French and a little English. It was his practice to spend occasional half hours with Peter Churchill, and Odette, knowing this, asked him point blank one day if he would take a message to her husband in cell 220. He said guardedly that he would, but that it mustn't become a practice. She smiled. The second link was fixed.

Partly because she was now known to have access to the impartial ear of the Captain of the Division, but mostly because she claimed to bear the name Churchill, the S.S. women gave Odette a wide berth. She had the subtle art of robbing them of their sense of power and it was no pleasure to enter a cell whose occupant made them feel like scullery maids. As well, one would think twice about maltreating a woman of that name, detested as it was. Victory for Germany was, of course, certain but—it was as well to leave any relation of the British Prime Minister's alone. In the ridiculous event of victory not working out according to plan, one would be glad to have a lady of the name of Frau Churchill to speak up for one after the war. Among these lick-spittle bullies was one Trude S., a forty-year-old S.S. woman who was feared and hated even by those women whom she was pleased to make her favourites. To Odette's cell she came fawning—and left with a handful of ginger biscuits for delivery to Peter. Having once broken the rules at the instigation of a prisoner, she was clay in Odette's hands, and was thereafter forced to become a sort of degraded Hermes, shuffling on wingless feet on the errands of her imprisoned gods.

In late July, Michèle was suddenly released. To her bewilderment, her door was opened one early morning and she was told that she was free. Through the *bouche de chaleur* she told Odette the staggering news. "Is there anything I can do for you, Céline, anything?" Odette thought swiftly. She rejoiced at Michèle's good fortune but she knew that she would miss her sadly. She had been a good friend and over the months, she had shown herself to be hard and honest and trustworthy. Odette had never seen her and now she never would. It was strange to think that she could become so attached to a disembodied voice whose political sentiments she detested that she could repose trust in its owner. She came to an immediate decision.

"Yes, Michèle, there is something that you can do for me. Listen very carefully!" Odette gave her a name and an address in Paris. "Go to these people and say you have come from Lise. They will understand. Give them this message. . . ."

It took a long time for Odette's message to reach London. Arnaud had immediately reported by radio that Raoul and Lise had been captured, but since April, there had been no news. Now, months afterwards, the indomitable Lise had found a labyrinthine way to announce to Baker Street from Fresnes that she and Raoul were carrying on the war as far as was humanly possible from their respective tombs in the *Maison de Correction*.

*

To speculate deeply on human motives is an unprofitable undertaking; it is impossible to calculate what blend of the masochist and sadist prompted the persistent Bleicher to suggest to Odette that he could arrange to conduct a simultaneous interrogation, bringing Peter Churchill over to her landing. She had not seen Peter since the day they entered Fresnes together and the possibility of a meeting—even under Henri's sardonic eye—delighted her. She gave the answer of a true Frenchwoman. She would, she said, welcome a meeting with Peter. Naturally, on the other hand, she was conscious that she was far from looking her best. She knew Peter well enough to realize that it would greatly add to his distress if he were to see her in dirty, untidy or dishevelled clothes. The prison laundry—though no doubt admirable for washing the lice out of blankets—was hardly equipped to deal with the sort of clothes she was accustomed to wear. . . .

Half an hour later Henri left Fresnes with Odette's one spare blouse in his pocket. He hastened to hand it over to Suzanne L. for her immediate attention. The patient Suzanne's position as mistress of a German counter-espionage agent had already involved her in some curious tasks. It is doubtful if she had ever undertaken anything quite so bizarre as the washing and ironing of a condemned British Agent's blouse in order that she might look cool, fresh and *soignée* during a bogus interrogation with the man with whom she had been captured.

This meeting was the first of three to be held under Henri's auspices. By the use of a little guile, Odette found a means of exploiting another occasion where she and Peter could talk even more freely. One morning in September she was warned that she should be prepared to attend *la Rue des Saussaies* the following day where she would be photographed and her fingerprints would be taken. She at once sent for the Captain of the Division and asked if Peter Churchill was subject to the same indignity. Yes, he would undoubtedly be sent for in the course of the next few days but his name did not appear on to-morrow's list. "Then why not put it on?" said Odette blandly. "Surely it is all one to you whether he attends to-morrow or next week."

The Captain stroked his chin. He said after a pause:

"Frau Churchill, is it your wish that I should be dismissed from my post?"

"Far from it, Monsieur. It is unlikely that your successor could be as just and as understanding as you are."

He looked at her half-smiling. "Eventually you will get me hanged, Frau Churchill," he said. "I will see what I can do—but it means approaching the Commandant."

There were some sixty or seventy prisoners marshalled in the main hall next morning. Scanning the men's ranks, Odette saw Peter Churchill. He gave her an enormous wink as he was marched out to the Black Maria. She followed him almost immediately and, arrived at *la Rue des Saussaies*, stationed herself beside him among the Fresnes contingent. Alone in the crowd, they had nearly three hours uninterrupted conversation and even succeeded in sharing the same Black Maria back to Fresnes.

*

Bleicher came to see her for the last time on the 19th of August. He stayed about an hour, talking with a geniality which she sensed to be slightly forced, on a multitude of subjects. He spoke disparagingly of the Italians and with reluctant admiration of the British. He ranged from Mozart to Shakespeare and, suddenly, he began to talk about her children. She listened to him in silence and, after a glance at her, he changed the subject. He was ill at ease. He said once: "I would be very distressed, Lise, if you were to be sent to Germany," and she asked him, with a cool flutter about her heart, if that had been arranged. "No, no," he said, "there is no talk of it—yet. But against the Gestapo, one is helpless." As if taking refuge, he plunged back into music and drew a rather disjointed comparison between Haydn and Bach. She wondered what he had come really to say. At last, he said it, stammering a little.

"Lise, I would very much like you to leave this prison with me—if only for a day. I have much to say to you, and it is impossible to speak inside these walls. I would take you out in the morning and give you lunch and that sort of thing."

There was a long silence. She said at last:

"You asked me that before, when I first came in. I told you then that there can be no compromise for the members of the French Section. That is still true. Being here has made no difference to me at all. Thank you for asking me, but I prefer to stay here."

"Is that final, Lise?"

"That is final."

He stood up. He half put out his hand and then withdrew it. He said philosophically:

"This has been my last visit. I shall not come to see you again."

"That is as you wish. Good-bye, Henri."

"Good-bye."

*

In the summer, Odette had been able to hear the distant sounds of children playing outside the prison walls. These were the children of the French prison staff who had remained to look after the normal criminal element and it was with pain and nostalgia that she had heard their laughter. Now as the first winds of autumn began to chill the walls of her cell, she heard the children less and less. Her health was beginning to reflect the privation of her daily life and a cough hung persistently about her throat. A gland on the right side of her neck

K

swelled and caused her much discomfort. She was always hungry and was less able to resist the tantalizing thoughts of food that haunted her between the miserable meals that gave her brief satiety. *Ersatz* coffee at 6.30 a.m., 175 grammes of black bread at 10, soup at midday, more *ersatz* coffee at 3 in the afternoon—that was her gastronomic day. As the autumn deepened, the soup, always thin, got steadily worse. One day, she found a long splinter of wood among the rotting, unpeeled vegetables, another day a button. It had been easy enough to be brave and buoyant when her stomach had been full and her blood running strongly. But it was a different matter when her throat was raw from coughing and her stomach drawn with hunger, when the few steps to her window became a journey, finite and terrible, only to be undertaken after deep thought and with iron resolve. The Captain of the Division, increasingly perturbed at her condition, came to see her several times. He said at last that he had decided, in spite of direct orders from the Gestapo to the contrary, to move her to a warmer cell on the third floor where she would be more comfortable and where she would have companionship. To his astonishment, Odette said that she would prefer to stay where she was. He asked her why. She said that she knew by instinct that it was right that she should stay. "There is a reason," she said, "much greater than I am."

He went away shaking his head.

Lying shivering on her bed, Odette asked herself whence came this strong certainty that she belonged to cell one hundred and eight. There were practical reasons, to be sure, but compared with the inner knowledge of the rightness of her decision, they were unimportant. What were those practical reasons? She had established a system of communication with Peter which might not work from another cell. She would be able to talk less freely with the Captain in the presence of others and would thus lose a most useful contact with authority. God only knew who her new companions might be—and far better solitude than the perpetual society of uncongenial persons. These considerations, all of them, were as thistle-down. The real reason burned so strongly that she was blinded by its light.

By electing to stay in her cell and by continuing without bitterness to withstand loneliness, cold, hunger and pain, she was, she believed, helping in a most humble way to take away from mankind a tiny particle of the vast necessary burden of human suffering. She had come to believe that there was a fixed and bitter price to be paid by humanity for humanity and to her, Odette, had been give the glory of contributing in minute measure to that sum. By living as she lived, by accepting her lot without hope of reward, she had mysteriously acquired a reward. Tranquillity had come to her and, on its heels, a knowledge of power over evil that was infinitely precious. It was a power that ranged far beyond the narrow walls of Fresnes; more potent than the trumpet blast of Joshua, her silence crumbled the stone. It was right that she should stay.

By the end of October, she was seriously ill. The Captain took the decision out of her hands. "I am not prepared, Frau Churchill," he said curtly, "to let you die. To-morrow you will go to cell 337. It is an order."

That night, Odette said good-bye to her solitary cell. In a very extraordinary way, it had become her home. She read slowly the scratched sentence on the wall. "*Quand j'étais petite, je gardais les vaches; maintenant ce sont elles qui me gardent.*" She was beyond all that now and it amused her no longer. It might possibly give pleasure to the next occupant. Carefully she drew a line through the last day of her mural calendar. She lay down under her blanket and said good night to her children. Three times during the night, her light was switched on from outside and the guards looked through the peep-hole to make sure that she was alive. Odette hardly noticed the change from darkness into light. She was far away from Fresnes, walking in a realm where light was perpetual.

★

The Captain had chosen her companions with care.

Before being moved to her new cell, she was allowed the very great favour of a shower bath. In order that no other prisoner should be contaminated by the sight of so desperate a criminal, those who normally worked in the hall were locked into their cells, while Odette was marched to the showers. It was the first bath she had had since her capture in April, and though she had always managed somehow to achieve a cat-like cleanliness, it was a delight to her. Her bath was followed by ten minutes exercise—which meant trudging round a small dusty confine with iron bars at either end. Though it was a joy to breathe fresh air at long last the indignity of her prescribed circle oppressed her spirit. Thus had she seen elephants trundle round the circus ring, ponderously obedient to the crack of the trainer's whip, and she had looked away, saddened by the humiliation of any organic thing.

Next day Odette was received into Cell 337 by Mademoiselle Simone Hérail. "Received" is the exact word, for Simone and she sprang from the same *milieu* and they greeted each other with dignity and grace. Simone came from Provence where she had been arrested for underground activities. She had been in Fresnes for many months and had managed to retain all the gentleness and the decorum in which she had always moved. In the cell also were two Parisians, a mother and daughter, both of them witty and charming women. The daughter had been caught acting as courier for an underground group and, as her mother was suspected as well, both had been arrested and taken to Fresnes. In the society of these three women, Odette soon settled down and, as her physical health began to improve, started in again to re-establish her lines of communication.

It was, of course, too good to last. The Gestapo soon found out that the mother had been completely unaware of her daughter's activities and she was told that she was free. A request that she should be allowed to stay and share her daughter's imprisonment was met with loud guffaws of laughter —and she was replaced almost immediately by a bouncing, cynical back-street prostitute whose Rabelaisian abuse of the S.S. echoed daily down the landings. After that there was constant change. All sorts and conditions of women were flung into Cell 337, resentful, dirty, frightened, obscene and brave. A nymphomaniac was followed by a Black Marketeer, a pickpocket by a Communist. The cough came back to Odette's throat and her glands swelled alarmingly. The Captain of the Division put in a request that Odette should be sent—under guard—to a Paris hospital for treatment. This the Gestapo refused flatly. He asked her if she would consent to go daily to the Sewing Room where the uniforms of the German prison staff were mended by the internees. It would be a change from

the eternal confines of her cell and, again, it was warm. Odette
considered the question. As a political prisoner, *condamnée à mort*,
it was her right to refuse to do any work whatsoever and she
certainly had no intention of assisting the German war effort
directly or indirectly. On the other hand, to be in the Sewing
Room would give her freedom of movement—and more contacts. She put up a proposal to the Captain. She explained
that it was, of course, out of the question to ask her to patch
the pants of the Germans. She would, however, be glad to sit
in the Sewing Room and make dolls out of any old odds and
ends of material.

"Frau Churchill. I must remind you that this is a prison,
not a toy factory."

She shrugged. "I'm sorry. Dolls or nothing, Monsieur."

Next morning, she was marched to the Sewing Room. As
the Captain had promised, it was warm and it was a joy to her
fingers again to have something to do. With many a thought
of her own children in her mind, she fashioned little rag dolls
out of discarded scraps of uniform cloth. At first her dolls were
not very gay because the material at her disposal was drab and
colourless but it gave her subtle satisfaction, to transform what
had been woven to be strictly utilitarian into a thing that was
inconsequent and frivolous. Later she cut up old ammunition
bags from the 1914-1918 war. They were brightly coloured,
greens and reds and blues, and from them she made enchanting
peasant figures with tiny waists and full, flowing skirts. The
other women looked with longing at her dolls and with awe at
her. They would dearly have loved to busy their fingers with
such engaging trivialities because they were links with the
normal currency of life which they had lost. Their fingers
itched to make such things and to hold them.

On the 11th of November, she was summoned again to 84
Avenue Foch. It was a long, weary day with strong electric
lamps shining in her face and relays of Gestapo men asking
questions, this time about Peter Churchill. When had he come
to France? Where had he dropped by parachute? Who were
his contacts and in what criminal acts of sabotage had he taken
part? She sighed and repeated the story she had already told
ad nauseam. She was, she said, a Frenchwoman and, as such,
she had induced him to take up this work. He had been sent to

France and she, not only a patriot but a dutiful wife, had followed. In fact, the part he had played in the Resistance was a minor one. If the Gestapo wished to waste their time by asking him questions about subjects of which he knew nothing, that was their affair. The portrait of Peter left in their minds was exactly the one she wanted to create; that he was a muscular extrovert with the remnants of an undergraduate taste for policemen's helmets; that he had been largely influenced by a wilful and determined wife; that from him there was little of value to be obtained.

By the time the Gestapo had finished with her, it was after ten o'clock and the Black Maria had long ago left for Fresnes. A special staff car was ordered. In it were three S.S. men in uniform and one civilian. Odette glanced at him casually—and stiffened. Though she had only seen him once before in her life the very pores of his skin were known to her with a fearful familiarity. This and none other was the creature who, his pincers in his hand, had knelt at her feet, not in homage, but the better to perform his filthy surgery. She looked at him with a curiosity that was utterly remote. Under her gaze, he blinked his brown eyes and drooped his lids. She said at last, shaking her head as if trying to convince herself of a fact that was beyond the bounds of belief:

"To think that you are French. . . ."

"Be quiet."

The car moved through the darkened streets, swung into the Champs Elysées. In the masked lights of the car, Odette saw little groups of German soldiers and French women and, sometimes under the trees, solitary couples strolling, field boots and high heeled shoes in step. A whimper of music surged from a shrouded café, was lost as the car moved on. One of the S.S. men was in philosophical mood. He waved a hand towards the shadows under the trees.

"You see, Frau Churchill. . . . Feminine Paris in the arms of masculine Berlin. Do you think these people care for you as you appear to care for them? If you were shot in the courtyard of Fresnes to-morrow, do you think your death would sour the kisses of a single midinette when she met her handsome sergeant in the *Leibstandarte Adolf Hitler*? If you think that, you are a fool, Frau Churchill. The war is over but the dead won't lie down. The sooner you and the English realize that, the better for you and for them."

The car slowed down as they approached the Arc de Triomphe, gigantically black against a tapestry of bright stars. At little more than walking pace, they circled the monument. Under the lofty arch, the perpetual flame of the Unknown Soldier of France flared in the night wind, fitfully illuminating the rigid figure of the German infantryman who stood on guard. The car stopped.

"Well, Frau Churchill, look your fill. You know what day it is?"

"No."

"It is the 11th of November, Armistice Day, the day when Germany was once shamed. Look well, Frau Churchill, because I don't suppose you will ever see this again."

"I shall see the Arc de Triomphe again, Monsieur, but without a German soldier. And when I see it, I shall be in uniform, in British uniform."

He looked at her blankly. Then he said a dirty word and gave a sharp order to the driver. The car jerked forward and snarled its way back to Fresnes.

*

Christmas Day, 1943.

For some days Odette had been secretly making a special thing out of scraps and it was finished on Christmas Eve. She set it up on a ledge inside the door for her companions to see and to adore. It was a tiny crib in which the Infant Jesus lay sleeping. One of the girls had received a Belgian Red Cross parcel and in it was a little Christmas tree about four inches high. With intense, loving excitement, the green emblem was set up and the Infant slept in its shadow.

No work was allowed that day and Odette was glad when dusk came to the cell. Somewhere along the landing a woman began to sing and the S.S. for once did not shout for silence. *"Il est né, le divin Enfant,"* sang the woman with great tenderness and it was difficult for Odette to keep tears from her eyes as she remembered past Christmasses when she had been able to fill her children's stockings for them and when she had sung to them that very song.

*

It was bitterly cold in February, and the cough deepened in her throat.

In the Sewing Room one of the girls gave her a little *papier-mâché* pot of jam from a Red Cross parcel and—wealth indeed! —a scrap of lead from the top of a pencil. She prized off the lid and, with infinite care, split it. On a purloined piece of tissue paper, she wrote a note to Peter Churchill in minute calligraphy. In it she asked him to send her a book, any book, via the now obsequious S.S. woman, Trude S. Starting at page 50, he should make a tiny pinprick under various letters to form a reply. Odette then slid the tissue paper between the split *papier-mâché* and stuck it together again with an improvised paste of whitewash and water and sat on it until it was firm. She replaced the cover and inveigled Trude into delivering it to Cell 220 in the Second Division. The obedient Trude sidled away.

Two days later, on the 14th of February, she beckoned Odette into an empty cell. Her face was serious and she looked like a woman who was about to have the pleasure of breaking some bad news. She said, frowning: "Frau Churchill, I have something to tell you concerning your husband."

Odette sat down and her hand flew to her mouth. She swallowed and said:

"Tell me."

"He has been taken away yesterday."

"Has he been shot? I want to know. I am strong enough to know the truth."

"No. He has been taken to Berlin, to Gestapo headquarters in the *Prinz Albrechtstrasse,* for interrogation. That is as much as I can tell you."

Odette smiled. Though there was an even greater loneliness ahead for her in Fresnes, she knew now with certainty that Peter would survive the war.

★

Easter Sunday, 1944.

One of the panes in the window of the Sewing Room was open and, clearly in the sunshine, she could hear the voice of a boy calling piteously from the punishment cells below. He was very young, only seventeen, and already the Gestapo had been at him. Now he was condemned to death and was to be shot next morning. His mother was in the prison, on the far side of the landing, and again and again, he cried his message to her. The sound of his voice darkened the spring sunshine and Odette, filled with pity and horror, could bear it no more. She went to the German Guards and, in the name of humanity, begged them to transmit the boy's words on this, his last Easter Day. Even the guards, tough and unyielding as they had become, were moved by the urgency of her plea and one of them consented to break the rules. The boy's message was delivered to his mother and her answer came back. Through the open window, Odette called it out into the sunshine. The boy heard it and there was a long silence. Then his voice rose again, strong steady and resilient now:

"*Merci, camarade. Merci, merci, merci. . . .*"

*

12th of May, 1944.

At about 11 in the morning, the door of Cell 337 was unlocked and an S.S. woman came in. She gave Odette a long, oblique look. She said slowly:

"Frau Churchill, you are to pack everything you have got and be ready to leave in an hour. You are to go to Germany."

So this was it . . . Odette said calmly:

"Is Father Paul in the prison?"

"Yes."

"May I see him?"

"Yes. I will send him to you."

"Thank you."

She put together her pathetic store of odds and ends and waited. The priest came into her cell. She smiled at him. She said, "I wanted to say 'good-bye' to you, Father because you have been more than a good friend to me. I am being sent to Germany."

After a long pause he said to her with great sorrow:

"There is little I can say. You will yourself know that I am not very beloved by the Gestapo and I don't know if I will still be alive at the end of the war. I doubt it very much. But there is a thing I would hope to do for you. If you write a letter to your children now and give it to me, I will, if I live, see that they get it after the war. That I would like to do."

K*

Odette wrote a letter and handed it to him. One of her cell companions gave her a nightdress, another a bunch of lilies-of-the-valley that had reached her in a parcel from home. One of the S.S. women, a surly uncommunicative harridan, furtively wiped her eyes as Odette walked for the last time a'ong the landing, her head high. In the prison yard, the Black Maria was waiting. The Captain of the Division stood by the door and saluted her. He did it not perfunctorily, but with meaning. He said to her: "Frau Churchill, I have brought you some flowers. Please accept them." They were more lilies-of-the-valley, but she kept the two bunches separate. She thanked him. He saluted her again and looked as if he wanted to say something. She smiled and held out her hand and he took it silently. Then she climbed into the Black Maria and the door of her compartment was locked.

She had been in Fresnes Prison for a year and four days and the day she left, something died in the Third Division.

CHAPTER XXVII

PILGRIMAGE TO PURGATORY

A T half past one the Black Maria arrived at 84 Avenue Foch. The compartments were unlocked and, for the first time, Odette saw her travelling companions as they were hustled upstairs into one of the Commissars rooms. They made a party of seven women in all and they looked at each other with guarded curiosity. Suddenly the realization that they were, every one of them, members of the French Section of the War War Office, flashed round the room like lightning. Though strangers to each other, they were at once fused in comradeship and they spoke with freedom. The need for silence was long past for they knew in their inmost hearts that this was the first halt on a journey from which there would be no return. They made a vivacious and a gallant company. Their handbags had been returned to them and lipstick and powder at once became common property. Reminiscences were exchanged, of London, of the New Forest, of the field, of Fresnes—for all of them had parachuted down the same sky and travelled the same road. They told each other their real names as well as the names by which they had been known in their dangerous undertakings, feeling immense pleasure in their long-awaited return to truth. Death was not far distant for six out of seven women who met that sunny May morning in the Avenue Foch. Miss Andrée Borrel ("Denise"—courier and co-organizer), Miss Vera Leigh ("Simone"—courier), Miss Diana Rowden ("Juliette"— courier) were to die together in Natsweiler on the 6th of July. Mrs. Yolande Beekman ("Yvonne"—radio operator), Miss Madeleine Damerment ("Martine"—courier) and Miss Eliane Plewman ("Gaby"—courier), were to live a little longer and to die side by side in the hell of Dachau on the 13th of September. All of them were murdered insofar as they were executed without trial, and all of them met death with a cold courage which even shamed their gaolers. The last of the company, Mrs.

Odette Sansom ("Lise"—courier), was the only one who had officially been condemned to death and, by a sardonic twist, she was the only one to live.

In the middle of the afternoon, the Commandant of the Gestapo came in to inspect his victims. He announced what they already knew, that they were *en route* for Germany. The train would leave from the *Gare de l'Est* at 6.30 p.m. That was all. Had any of the ladies a request? Odette spoke up. She said that they had been confined in this room for some hours and that nothing would be more welcome than a cup of tea. "Not as it is made in France or in Germany," she said, "but in the English manner. One spoonful for each person and one for the pot. With milk and sugar, please."

He gave her a long, perplexed glance and left the room. A few minutes later, a woman came in with a tray on which was a teapot and seven cups of beautiful Sèvres china. When Odette had poured out, she despatched the woman to fetch more hot water. Spirits, already high, rose under the tonic effect of tea and cosmetics and the sombre journey to Germany became, to these gallant women, an adventure into which they were ready to step with calmness and with fortitude.

At 6 o'clock, an officer of the S.S. came into the room with half a dozen men in uniform. He made a short announcement. The time had come to leave for Germany. The women would be handcuffed in pairs. If there was any trouble or any attempt to escape, he and his men would not hesitate to shoot on the spot. "You will be taken to the station in an ordinary coach with windows," he said, "and you are forbidden to raise your hands or to indicate to passers by that you are anything other than ordinary travellers. Now we will begin."

Odette was handcuffed to Yolande Beekman. They smiled at each other with humorous resignation. The whole *mise-en-scène* was ridiculous and absurd. There were so many pompous Germans carrying so many revolvers and so few handcuffed, helpless women. As they filed down the stairs, one of the women began to sing and the others took up the chorus until roughly told to shut up. As they crossed the pavement to the coach, they walked between files of S.S. with machine guns. Odette laughed out loud. This was a perfect example of the ponderous Teutonic sense of fitness to summon a heavily-armed platoon of men to guard a handful of women. One of the Commissars who had many times interrogated her was standing on a balcony of the fourth floor. He had come out to witness the departure of the croco- dile and he looked down patronizingly with the air of a sophis- ticated vicar at a Sunday School treat. To his embarrassment and dismay, Odette saw him. She raised her handcuffed wrist and waved gaily.

"Good-bye," she called out laughing. "Good-bye, good-bye, good-bye."

He stepped back angrily and watched from behind the cur- tains until the coach had turned the corner.

It was a most beautiful evening and all Paris seemed to have come out to glory in the sunshine. The pavements were crowded and though talk and laughter rose from the cafés, the presence of the conqueror brooded over the roof-tops and curled in wisps under the coloured umbrellas and among the bay trees. To the casual observer, this was once again the Paris of the chestnut flowers, the Paris of folly and sentimental ballad. Away from the boulevards and out of the sunshine, the real citizens of this most resentful city fingered their Sten guns, sliding oiled cartridge clips into the butt, squinting along the sights, waiting for their summons to a new *jour de gloire*.

At the *Gare de l'Est*, two second-class compartments had been reserved and the prisoners were separated into four and three. An S.S. man sat on one side of the door, an S.S. woman on the other. The windows were similarly guarded and some eight to ten S.S. filled the corridor. Yolande Beekman and Odette faced Andrée Borrel and Vera Leigh. The train started. Soon the suburbs of Paris were left behind and open countryside was reached. They passed through a station, the marshalling yard of which had been crunched into irregular polygons. The S.S. man pointed to the rubble. He said to Odette, his face flushed:

"That is the work of the R.A.F. They have also destroyed my mother's house in Dortmund. I only wish that an accident could happen to the train for, if it did, it would give me great pleasure to crush your skull under my heel and save the German hangman a job."

Odette considered this statement with some care. She said judiciously:

"That is not true. You are a man under orders and it is your duty to deliver all of us, alive and well, to Germany. If an accident were to happen, your first care should be the safety of your prisoners. I frankly do not think you are very clever."

He called her by a dirty name. She said calmly:

"You are neither clever—nor even efficient." She held up her two hands, the wrist of one of them showing a red weal. "For example, it has only taken me thirty minutes to slip my handcuffs. I tell you that to show you how clumsy you are."

He started up and went into the corridor and came back with the officer who held the handcuff key. This time the steel band was snapped so tight that the bone of her wrist was bruised. Though painful, it had been worth it. Anything that deflated and humiliated these smug creatures was worth doing. She settled her head as comfortably as she could on Yolande's shoulder and, as dusk came over the fields of France, closed her eyes. The train jolted on through the night. Sometimes Odette slept for a few minutes, but the circle of steel hurt her wrist and she woke continually. The summer dawn came early and she watched the morning mists smoking off orchard and field as the sun rose. It was queer to think that the same sun was shining on Culmstock Beacon and the birds were flying gladly over English pasture and English plough. They passed over a broad river and the S.S. man grunted proudly that that was the Rhine, the dear German Rhine. A coldness settled momentarily on Odette's heart as the wheels of the train echoed hollowly over the bridge. There was something terribly final about crossing the Rhine. Until this moment, absurdly but comfortingly, she had felt that she was still in France and that the voices of the free people around her would be French. This was Germany. It was not the Germany of Goethe or the Germany of the poor charcoal-burner who had three enchanted flaxen-haired, blue-eyed sons. It was Hitler's bloody and perverted Reich, the dark fastness of the whip, the rack and the rope. Odette said to the S.S. man.

"Where are we going?"

"You are going to Karlsruhe," he said genially, "where you will be killed." His blue eyes softened. "You can well imagine how pleased I am that it was decided to kill you in Germany and not in France! It means that I get forty-eight hours unexpected leave and I can go and see *meine liebste Mutti*, my dearest mother."

Karlsruhe. . . .

The people on the platform looked plump and richly dressed. Though the women carried on their bodies the sartorial harvest of Europe, they succeeded in grafting on to their plunder a native bad taste which had to be seen to be believed. A hat stolen from the *rue de la Paix* was perched on a tight bun of tow coloured hair; sheer silk stockings from the *place Vendôme* vanished into brown, flat-heeled boots; a mink cape from *Rostov* covered a knitted artificial silk jumper; rings from the ghetto of Warsaw were worn over doeskin gloves from Brussels. Among men, uniforms abounded but there was everywhere a sense of heaviness. Faces were drawn and anxious and there was many a glance at the sky.

Odette and her companions were locked into an office on the station platform. A request that the handcuffs be unlocked so that the women could go privately to the lavatory was refused. In about an hour, they were taken out and, guarded now by a new relay of Gestapo, were put in pairs into taxis and driven to Karlsruhe Criminal Prison. The handcuffs were unlocked at last and the exhausted women separated. After the degrading formality of search by brutish wardresses, the seven members of the French Section were allotted cells as far away from each other as possible.

Eight weeks passed. It was Odette's misfortune to have, as one of her three German cell companions, a cadaverous, strap-breasted woman who called herself by a masculine name and who pestered her unceasingly with obscene and overt attentions. She folded Odette's blankets for her, she offered her scraps of food, she called her "*meine kleine Französin*", she leered and grimaced and tried to paw. It was a facet of the German female character of which Odette had already heard ugly whispers in Fresnes and to be forced to share a cell with one of this sinister sisterhood nauseated her. Almost healthy and welcome by comparison was a spotty drab of forty, sentenced under Hitler's racial laws to a year's imprisonment for having had sexual relations with a French forced labourer. This was a type well known in France, dismissed contemptuously by their paramours under the name of *les vaches amoureuses*, the cows in perpetual season who herded round the forced labour camps, mooning their sordid desire to the pent bulls inside the barbed wire.

Once a week, the women of the French Section were allowed
separate exercise. From her window, Odette could see her
comrades walking alone in the dingy yard and she would call
to them and wave with great spirit.

"Hullo, Denise. How goes it, Yolande? Hullo, Gaby.
Martine, good morning to you. . . ."

One afternoon in early July, she was marched to the office of
the Commandant. In it was a civilian, a little red-eyed man
with a notebook and a shifty look. This, said the Commandant,
was a reporter from the *Völkischer Beobachter*. He had come all
the way from Berlin to interview Frau Churchill. It was a
great honour for her.

The reporter balanced his notebook on his knee and gave her
a sidelong smirk.

"Well, Frau Churchill," he said, "you will be pleased to
know that we already have three Churchills in our German
prisons. We look forward to the arrival of yet another—of
Mister Winston Churchill."

"You will not have to wait long," said Odette, "but when
Winston Churchill comes to Berlin, it will not be as you think.
He will drive through the rubble of your city in triumph."

The Commandant snapped:

"Back to your cell. The interview is over. *H'raus, h'raus.
Schnell, schnell.* . . ."

Again she marvelled at the astonishing prestige of Winston
Churchill. The German women in her cell asked her continually
about him, about his character, about how he lived. How many
cigars did he smoke? Was he a friend of the English King and
was it true that he aspired to the English throne? Did he eat
raw steak for breakfast with blood running down his jowl?
Even the S.S. guards were curious about this extraordinary
man. What Odette didn't know, she made up. It was easy to do
for the people to whom she spoke were credulous and avid for
information.

One week none of her comrades appeared in the exercise
yard. She looked for one of them each day from her window.
She was never to see any of them again.

In mid-July she was told one early morning to pack. Instructions had come from Berlin that she was to take the next step
towards the execution of her sentence. In a Black Maria, she

left Karlsruhe prison and was driven to the station. It was a very hot day and, for her sustenance during the journey, she was given one slice of bread. She had no idea where she was going or how long her journey would last.

The train crawled out of Karlsruhe at about eight in the morning. She was forced to stand in the narrow passage outside a compartment which had been rebuilt into the shape of a prison cell. Inside were packed some half-hundred men and they shouted continually. A few miles along the line, the train stopped and waited for nearly an hour. The R.A.F. had been along the line and the permanent way was littered with bomb craters. Another train, a troop train, passed them slowly and Odette saw the faces of the soldiers, hopeless, sullen, past caring whither they went. There was much shunting as the troop train was switched on to the only intact line and, after an infinity of time, Odette's train moved on. She saw severed metals, bombed into twisted fingers of steel, and ruined stations and drunken signal gantries. Scraps of news were shouted to her from the locked cell compartment. The British and the Americans had landed and flung the German Armies from the Normandy shore. The sky was black with their aircraft and they were advancing deeply and inexorably into France. Now they were attacking at Caen and soon they would be storming the Rhine. "*Encore un peu de patience, camarade*," they shouted, "and Hitler's day is over". Again the train shuddered to a halt with a screaming of brakes. The torn metals pointed derisively to the summer sky like a gigantic, surrealist rake. "It's a long way to Tipperary", sang the prisoners and the German guards stared morosely at the desolation around them and fingered their Lügers.

As darkness came over the land, Odette saw the pallid geometry of searchlights and, from somewhere far away, the grumbling of gunfire. They waited for hour after hour, hungry, sweating, burning with thirst. The train crawled back the way it had come, stopped again, moved forward. At some time after midnight, they rolled under a shattered roof and stopped finally in the shambles of Frankfurt.

The administration—under pressure, no doubt, of the R.A.F.—had broken down and the advent of over fifty prisoners from Karlsruhe was completely unexpected. Guarded by heavily armed S.S. and police dogs, the miserable group waited in the sultry street outside the station and eventually, Odette was taken in a prison van to police headquarters. She was questioned, searched and roughly flung into a barred cage in which two verminous women were already sleeping. She lay on the stone floor and, shading her eyes from the naked electric light, waited tight-lipped for the dawn.

For six terrible days and nights she was locked in her cage like a beast. There was no rest and no privacy for the light blazed continually and the trellis of the bars was wide meshed for all to see. Her cage-mates were German *vaches amoureuses*, dirty, lascivious women who cringed before the guards. Compared with this, Fresnes had been a paradise and even Karlsruhe tolerable. To be on show, waking and sleeping, was a torture of the spirit and, for the first time since her capture, Odette longed to die. She heard the high jungle-snarl of British bombers overhead and, with all her strength, she prayed that one thrice-blessed bomb might blast her into oblivion for ever. And then the sap came back to her spine. A bucket of raw potatoes was put into the cage and the two women began furiously to peel, telling Odette that it was her task to help. Odette peeled three potatoes and then stopped. One of the women screamed for the guard and, pointing a quivering finger at Odette, said that this swine of a Frenchwoman refused to work.

"I have peeled three potatoes," said Odette calmly, "because that is the amount you give me to eat every day. I am a political prisoner and that is all I propose to do, to peel enough for myself to eat."

"You will be taken before the Chief of Police and punished."

She shrugged. "I have nothing to say."

She was roused at 3 o'clock in the morning and taken to the office of the Chief of Police. There she was handed over to the Gestapo. More orders had come in the nick of time and she was to proceed at once to Halle where she would join a convoy whose destination was *l'enfer des femmes*, the living hell of Ravensbrück Concentration Camp for women.

★

Halle. . . .

Odette was taken to the prison in the evening and searched.

She wondered wearily how many S.S. fingers had groped in her hair by now, and how many S.S. eyes had peered suspiciously at her thinning body. She was ordered upstairs and climbed innumerable steps to the attic of the cell block. A door was unlocked and she was pushed into a long windowless room under the tiles. It was dim and sultry and a choking cloud of fine sand rose as she stepped inside. The door slammed. When her eyes got used to the gloom she saw with growing horror that she was far from being alone. In the abandoned attitudes of the breathing dead and in conditions of indescribable filth, some forty Ukrainian women lay or squatted or sat in the thick sand, moaning, coughing, silent, spitting, weeping or rocking in an ecstasy of melancholy. Sanitation was non-existent and the smell of sweat, dirt, menstrual blood and human excreta was such as to turn her stomach in sickness. The women were patient in a timeless, animal misery, waiting for they knew not what. If the building were set mysteriously on fire from the sky, they should put sand on the flames. That was what the sand was for. That was as much as they knew or understood.

Odette spoke timidly to a woman. She was answered in a meaningless gabble of mouthed sounds. Odette shook her head as if banishing an evil thing and took the woman's arm and led her to the middle of the floor under the skylight. She pointed upwards and then indicated to the woman that she should crouch down on the floor. Odette took off her shoe and stood shakily on the woman's back and, with the heel, smashed the glass of the skylight into a thousand pieces. She could hear the jagged glass sliding down the tiles and falling into the yard below. A warm, clean breath of summer filtered into the fœtid room and Odette drew it deeply into her lungs. She got on to the floor again and lay down in a corner, her body involuntarily pressed against another woman's. The night was a furnace and the cool hour before the dawn a benediction.

When a bucket of soup was set down in the sand, the women fought for it, cupping their hands in the thin fluid and snarling like wolves. Rather than join in this ghoulish scramble, Odette stood under the broken skylight, breathing deeply. Even ravenous hunger was preferable to participation in the debased feast and, once the bucket had been licked clean by the starving women, she went back to her corner. Over the long burning hours of the day, she lay in a sort of dazed coma, hearing nothing seeing nothing. Evening came and bread was flung into the room. The hideous debauch started again. Odette did not stir. Sometime between the dusk and the darkness, when the light was *entre chien et loup*, the door was opened and a voice shouted harshly:

"*Frau Churchill. Ist Frau Churchill hier?*"

Odette swayed to her feet. If this cell meant her death, then death was a sweet and a welcome thing. She found her way to the door, stumbling over the stretched out bodies of the Ukrainians. A man stood there, a burly silhouette against the lit landing. She said weakly:

"*Oui. Je suis Madame Churchill.*"

"*Sie sind Frau Churchill?*"

"*Oui, Monsieur.*"

"*So.*"

The smashing blow of a clenched fist hit her in the mouth. She reeled back and fell over the prostrate body of a woman. As she spat fresh blood from her lips, the man at the door shouted:

"I give you that for Winston Churchill—with my compliments."

The door slammed with a crash that seemed to shake the walls.

*

Fürstenburg—the mountain of the Princes. All change for Ravensbrück, the bridge of the ravens.

Weeping, limping, bleeding, moaning their interminable dolorous songs, the Ukrainian women set out on the three mile trek from the station to the Camp. The well-worn path lay through the summer woods where shadows were long and cool and beside the shore of a lake on whose tranquil bosom were all the shimmering jewels of the evening sun. By the water's edge were villas, chalets with overhanging roofs and trailing flowers, and in their pleasant gardens men and women of the Camp S.S., murderers off duty, lay semi-naked to bronze their Nordic bodies in the last rays and to listen to the gramophone and to gaze lazily into the clear spaces of the sky. They did not bother to look up as the Ukrainian women shuffled past—and why should they indeed for over the years nearly a hundred thousand similar caricatures had already trailed by their miniature Lido and it was a spectacle that would be repeated to-morrow and the day after to-morrow and the day after that.

Submerged among the Ukrainians, Odette Sansom walked slowly because she was weak and sick and burning with thirst and because it was painful to put her mutilated feet to the ground. As the bedraggled cavalcade wound past the end of the lake, the high walls of the camp came into view. A machine-gun post; a grey wall; a black door, twenty feet high. Then, silencing the tuneless song of the Ukrainians, another song came to the ears of the women as a parallel column of female creatures in striped sacking marched briskly past. Their heads were shaven, their eyes were dead and the skin was drawn tightly back from the bones of their faces so that they were rows of skulls marching. They stepped out in time to the crack of an S.S. woman's whip, and, by order, they sang a merry song, opening and shutting the caverns of their mouths in macabre melody. The black door of the camp swung open at their approach and on the heels of these scarecrow travesties of womanhood, the new entry shuffled into Ravensbrück. The door swung to and the bolts were shot.

Odette looked around her. This was nothing new. The wheel had spun full circle and she knew that here and nowhere else was the tomb that lay beyond the cliffs of Normandy where she used to walk when she was a young girl in the spring of her days.

CHAPTER XXVIII

L'ENFER DES FEMMES

IT was in the evening of the 18th of July, 1944, when Odette limped through the black door of Ravensbrück.

With the Ukrainians, she crossed a square and followed the main street of the camp that ran between lines of oblong huts to the washroom which was to be their quarter for the night. Standing at the doors of their huts, the old inmates, long ago unsexed by privation and by the barber, gibbered at the newcomers and pointed with bony fingers, cackling. An S.S. woman, plump, confident and scornful, rode a bicycle down the street. She held a long-lashed whip in one hand and a huge dog trotted by her wheels. At her approach, the striped scarecrows scattered, sidling out of sight, cringing away, fearful lest the eye of Dorothea Binz,[1] Chief Wardress and terror of the Camp, should light on them.

There were rows of showers in the washroom, the nozzles set in pipes that ran along the ceiling. Odette turned one tap and a trickle of water spilled on the concrete floor. She drank greedily and sat down and undid the bundle she had doggedly clung to all the way from Fresnes. She had one blouse other than that which she wore, the red blouse in which she had visited the Avenue Foch to meet Himmler's expert young men. She had a pair of silk stockings, a pair of high-heeled shoes, the nightdress her cell companion in Fresnes had given her and one partial change of underclothes. With a tiny piece of soap, she washed herself and her meagre wardrobe. It was dark by the time she had finished and she spread out her things and lay down on the concrete floor. So utterly exhausted was she that she slept at once, oblivious of the reiterated vocal misery of the Ukrainians.

She woke to the first light of the morning sun and to the stentorian shouting of voices. This was "*Appel*", the daily roll-

---

[1] Sentenced at a British Military Court to death by hanging, February 1946, executed March 1946.

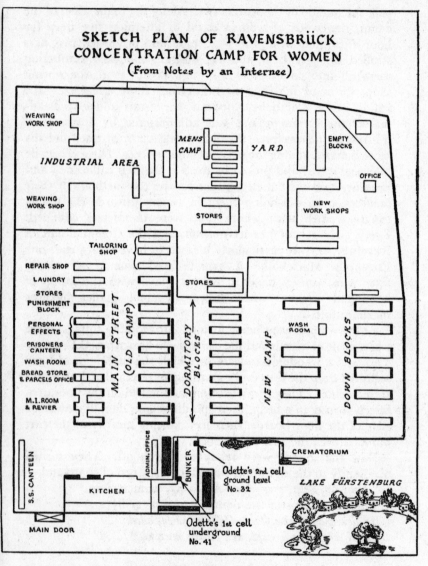

SKETCH PLAN OF RAVENSBRÜCK
CONCENTRATION CAMP FOR WOMEN
(From Notes by an Internee)

WEAVING WORK SHOP

INDUSTRIAL AREA

WEAVING WORK SHOP

MENS CAMP

YARD

EMPTY BLOCKS

OFFICE

STORES

NEW WORK SHOPS

TAILORING SHOP

REPAIR SHOP
LAUNDRY
STORES
PUNISHMENT BLOCK
PERSONAL EFFECTS
PRISONERS CANTEEN
WASH ROOM
BREAD STORE & PARCELS OFFICE
M.I. ROOM & REVIER

MAIN STREET (OLD CAMP)

STORES

DORMITORY BLOCKS

WASH ROOM

NEW CAMP

DOWN BLOCKS

S.S. CANTEEN

KITCHEN

ADMIN. OFFICE

BUNKER

CREMATORIUM

Odette's 2nd cell ground level No. 32

LAKE FÜRSTENBURG

MAIN DOOR

Odette's 1st cell underground No. 41

L'ENFER DES FEMMES

call, the parade of the scarecrows. Along the main street of the
camp, thousands of women stood at attention five deep for
hour after hour while the wardresses and privileged prisoners
strolled amongst them, abusing, pushing, shouting, numbering
them off into commandos for the weaving shop, the sewing
shop, for road making, coal heaving, stone breaking, tree
felling. Like a diabolic Roedean, the camp under its head-
master the Commandant, was administered by a system of
mistresses and prefects, the S.S. being the mistresses and the
more debased among the prisoners the prefects. These renegade
internees were hand-picked by the S.S. for their callousness and
brutality and were well content to ape the methods of their
mentors, even out-doing them in venom towards the unfortunate women with whom they were themselves confined.
Every girls' school has its matron, and the Commandant of
Ravensbrück was particularly pleased to have on his staff one
Elizabeth Marschall,[1] a granite-faced woman of nearly
sixty who worked hand in rubber glove with the group of
homicidal surgeons whose supply of female guinea-pigs was
inexhaustible.

As the women were being formed into working squads, there
was a rattle of wheels and the *charrette* was drawn past their ranks.
This was a wooden handcart in which the night's dead were
collected from the huts every morning for removal to the Camp's
crematorium. They sprawled limp and naked on the floor, ten,
fifteen corpses in a heap, their spindle shanks dangling over the
edge of the floor boards, their feet dancing merrily as the cart
bumped over the ruts in the road.

Now the squads were ready to march off. They turned
obediently to the right and waited for the word of command.

"*Also, ein, zwei, drei—los!* And sing, women, sing."

The gay chorus of the damned rose raggedly.

"*Adieu, mein kleine Garde-Offizier, adieu, adieu*
Und vergiss mich nicht, und vergiss mich nicht. . . ."

*

At about 10 o'clock, the washroom was unlocked and a

---

[1] Sentenced at a British Military Court to death by hanging, February 1946,
executed March 1946.

Gestapo man, as always in civilian clothes, called out Frau Churchill for interview with the Commandant. Carrying her bundle, she walked along the main street beside him. At the door of the Commandant's office, she kept the Gestapo man waiting while she changed into her high-heeled shoes and brushed her coat and skirt with her hands and tidied her hair. The name "Churchill", false or true, carried with it a responsibility which she was proud to share. While she did these things leisurely, he looked at her frowning. There was a calmness about her, a total absence of apprehension, a well-bred deliberation that astonished him. She might have been in her own house preparing to interview the butler. He said sourly at last:

"Are you quite ready now?"

"Yes. I am quite ready."

He knocked deferentially on the door, was answered by a curt *"Herein"* and Odette walked in to the presence of *Obersturmbannführer*, Fritz Sühren, Commandant of Ravensbrück and lord of life and death for a hundred thousand women.

He sat at a table, dressed in the green and silver uniform of the S.S. Penal Section. On his peaked cap the miniature death's-head gleamed ..i the sunshine; at his belt, a polished leather holster was undone to show the butt of an automatic pistol; his field boots shone like glass. He was young, in his middle thirties, fair-haired and blue-eyed. His skin was good and he looked as if he were in the pink of condition. Quick to observe, Odette noticed his hands. They were beautifully shaped and beautifully kept, with tapering fingers and flawless nails. He gazed at her for a long time without speaking. He saw a slim young woman in a grey coat and skirt and a red blouse. In a flickering glance he took in with surprise her silk stockings and high-heeled shoes, looked at her face again. Her brown eyes met his blue eyes with a steadiness which equalled his own. Speaking in a slightly bored, monotonous voice, he said:

"Sprechen Sie Deutsch?"

"Non, Monsieur."

He frowned and said in halting, stumbling English:

"You are a relation to Mr. Winston Churchill?"

"My husband is a distant connection of his."

"So." He lifted one of his beautiful hands and pointed to the window. "Here, in this camp, you are Frau Churchill no longer. Here your name will be 'Frau Schurer'."

"I have had many names in my life, Monsieur. One more or less makes no difference to me, no difference to me at all."

She saw that he did not understand. She didn't care. He said: "You will be put in the Bunker, the prison of the camp."

"Very well. As you wish."

The Gestapo man spoke in German. Odette was able to pick out the gist of his words.

"*Herr Kommandant*, would be so kind as to decide the conditions of imprisonment. Firstly, as regards food. . ."

"She will have the normal ration of the punishment cells, no more, no less."

"Exercise, *Herr Kommandant?*"

"None."

"Books, *Herr Kommandant?*"

"None."

"Baths, *Herr Kommandant?*"

"None. She will have nothing, take her away."

"*Jawohl, Herr Kommandant.*"

She walked out of the office with the Gestapo man and into the summer sunshine. They crossed a dusty compound and came to a long, low L-shaped building. The Gestapo man stopped. He said: "This is the prison, the Bunker. Here you will stay."

Odette looked upwards at the sky. It was a beautiful day— the sort of day when sun and wind and water and leaf and tree all combine to shout aloud the glory of God. The door of the Bunker was opened by a woman in S.S. uniform, Margarete Mewes,[1] a peevish, mean little harlot with a bovine face and a receding chin. She and the Gestapo man spoke together and he beckoned to Odette. She took one last look around the blue depths of the sky as if she were trying to absorb all its clarity and all its light into her very self. Then she stepped into the Bunker.

                                    *

There was a short passage with a barred gate at its end, its

[1] Sentenced at a British Military Court to ten years penal servitude, February 1946.

Obersturmbannführer FRITZ SÜHREN

Commandant : Ravensbrück Concentration Camp for Women.

(Found among his private papers captured by Odette, May 5th 1945)

spikes touching the floor and the ceiling. On one side of the passage were the cheerful rooms occupied by the S.S. The wardress unlocked the gate with the key at her waist and Odette walked through to the inner Bunker. The gate swung to on the spring lock. Before her was a flight of stairs, leading downwards. She descended them and walked along an underground passage, white with electric light. The wardress unlocked a door and Odette stepped into a cell whose darkness was opaque. She had to feel her way with her foot and she stretched out her hands before her like the sightless so as not to walk into the far wall. The cell door shut with a crash and she heard the sound of retreating steps. For three months and eleven days, for two thousand four hundred and seventy-two hours, she was to live in a darkness only broken and made more intense by the brief and blinding visits of her gaoler.

*

Night and day followed in one sombre stream.

At some hour in the darkness, a hatch in the door was opened and a mug of thin coffee and a slice of black bread were thrust inside; later, two or possibly three hours later, a bowl of thin soup followed; after a pause of some hours, another mug of coffee was given her. Then, presumably, it was night for she was left alone for some sixteen hours. With the unwinding of this black ribbon of time, Odette began slowly to acquire a knowledge not only of the man-made divisions of eternity but also of the unseen colour of the sky. The knowledge came on her unawares and she found, without surprise, that she could open her eyes and gaze into the darkness and know with certainty, that it was morning and that there was a south wind and that the sky was grey-blue with high, scurrying clouds. She knew too that the evening was the time when the women were flogged. She would hear the clang of the iron gate upstairs and the sound of steps descending, marching and shuffling, as the victims were dragged to the cell beside hers. She heard the thick sound of each stroke and the demented screams of the beaten and, in time with the ghoulish overseer, she would count the strokes, learning her German numerals by way of this macabre dictation. When the screaming stopped, it

usually meant that the victim had fainted. Then she would hear
the rattle of a bucket and the splashing of water and, after a
pause for consciousness to return, the tale would be taken up
again.

"*Elf . . . zwölf . . . dreizehn . . . vierzehn. . . .*"

Twenty-five was the usual number. *Vingt-cinq. Fün fund
zwanzig. . . .* One terrible night a woman was given forty
strokes. *Quarante. Vierzig.*

These mighty beatings were not only criminal acts against the
individual. They were the minor tactics of a larger strategy, a
strategy so inhuman and so cynical that its contemplation
chilled the blood. The conception of Ravensbrück—and that
of all its sister hells—was difficult to grasp because it was a crime
directed against humanity as a whole. She had herself been
cruelly tortured. For what the Gestapo had done to her spine
and to her feet, there was at least an explanation if not an
excuse. She was a British agent, there was a war and she alone
had possessed information vital to her enemies. They had sought
by foul and not by fair means to loosen her tongue and they
had failed. Her personal pain was unimportant and trivial.
There was even a glimmer of justification for its infliction. For
Ravensbrück, there was none. These women who were flogged
and starved and maltreated until grim death seemed as
unattainable as paradise, were not British agents with the secrets
of war behind their eyes. They were women, and their only
crime lay in the fact of their womanhood for, by the humiliation
of their loved bodies, those who loved them could be brought to
heel. Ravensbrück, camp of women, existed for the intimidation of men.

For Odette, what had been designed to be the torture of
loneliness became the gift of liberty. She could leave her body
in its dark cell and stop her human eardrums to the rhythm of
Ravensbrück. In a dream untroubled by hope, she had the
freedom of the universe. In the early days of her imprisonment,
when her body was still strong and resentful of her cell walls,
fantasy had piled on wilder fantasy. She had looked at her cell
door in Fresnes and visualized with all her strength that it was
bursting open before her eyes, that she could see a smiling
British soldier in battledress on the landing and he would say,
"Lady, you're free," and she would walk out of her cell and

along the landing and out into the yard and see khaki everywhere and hear kindly voices and have a cup of tea and be
taken to an airfield and ride the clouds back to the England of
the hedges and the buttercups and the foaming blossom. . . .
Most inappropriately, Baudelaire was mixed up in this ridiculous dream of England

> . . . *Emporte-moi, wagon, enlève-moi, frégate*
> *Ici la terre est faite de nos pleurs.* . . .

and the "*wagon*" of Baudelaire was the rusty reaper and binder
in Mrs. Marshall's yard and, in her dream, it was drawn
through the corn under Culmstock Beacon by a sweating Shire
horse and on its back, laughing, rode Françoise and Lily and
Marianne.

She was long past all that beguiling wish-fulfilment now.
Escapism, real or imagined, belonged to the days before she
limped through the black door of Ravensbrück.

Hovering over the thin figure of Lise, condemned British
agent, Odette had time to consider, with a sense of wonder,
the extraordinary facts of life. Whence sprang the bodies that
the Gestapo could beat, the feet that danced their German jig
over the tail of the handcart, *la charrette?* She was herself the
mother of three children—at least the thin, aching figure on the
floorboards was. It became a most extraordinary thing, forgotten and unrealized in the turmoil of living, of being a
mother, of feeding, washing, loving and fearing, to realize that
new human beings, never before known, or aware, should grow
from eighteen inches long to six feet high; that these miraculous
beings should transform portions of other living things, animals,
vegetables and inanimate minerals, into their own bodies and
thus grow; even more extraordinary was the fact that they
should fall in love with each other and become exclusively
desirous of one other being, that they should unite to produce
yet another self, grow old, wear out senses, muscles and
memories and die—or be beaten to death by the prison staff of
Ravensbrück.

Three of these new beings—her own mysterious creation—
had had to be fed and, sustained by the miraculous chemistry of
her body, they had become strong. She considered the whole
surprising sequence of occurrences and their significance until

she was lost in the dizzy spiral of personal identity and sought for refuge from the frightening austerity of thought in the contemplation of practical things. Her children's bodies had to be clothed. She would clothe them from the dark cell of Ravensbrück, stitch by stitch and garment by garment.

For fourteen months, she had been the victim of a system designed deliberately to deteriorate her physical and mental condition and consecutive thought was no longer as swift and as agile as it had been before her capture. But it was more detailed and more profound. First of all, she planned the materials and their colours. This vastly important matter occupied the dark fusion of many nights and days for there were interruptions and it would be callous indeed to go on comparing piqué and gingham while women were being flogged in the next cell and their screams piercing her walls. On the last day of the month, she had another unexpected interruption. Fritz Sühren came to her cell. The door was flung open and the light switched on. She stood up, shading her eyes from the painful dazzle while bursting circles of light swam and dissolved into blinding stars. He stood at the door in uniform, Margarete Mewes, the chief wardress of the Bunker, beside him. He said to her in his guttural, practised English:

"Is everything all right?"

"Yes thank you."

"Do you wish anything?"

"No thank you."

He gave a brief perfunctory salute. The door was shut and the light switched off. She was glad when he had gone for it meant that she, too could go back to the absorbing comparison between printed cottons for Marianne and more sophisticated crêpe-de-chine for Françoise.

On the 15th of August, a considerable airborne Army of British Commandos, French and American troops stormed into the south coast of France. This military operation was to have a direct repercussion in the Bunker of Ravensbrück in a display of vicarious spite which would have been ludicrous were it not so bestial. The central heating, controlled from outside her cell, was turned on at full strength so that the room, normally cold, became an inferno. In desperation, Odette soaked her blankets in cold water and wrapped herself in them, alternately burning and shivering. No food of any sort was brought to the hatch that day, and already weak, she lay on her floorboards, her stomach a twisting lens of pain and her brow an anvil. Four days and nights crawled by before she sank into a sort of dazed coma. Two more days and nights passed . . . and she emerged from her black sleep to feel the stab of a hypodermic syringe in her arm and to see bending over her, the face of Elizabeth Marschall, Matron of Ravensbrück. There was anxiety in her pale blue eyes, anxiety not for a woman who was gravely ill, but for a precious prisoner lest she should cheat her future executioners.

This week of starvation was the final blow to Odette's physical health. The cough racked her throat again and scurvy spread over her skin. Recurrent dysentery tore at her entrails and the dark hours, once thronged with thoughts of home and cleanness and normality, were peopled now with nightmares. Only the brightness of her spirit was undimmed.

On the last day of August, Fritz Sühren came again to stand at her door.

"Have you any complaints?"

She said, keeping her voice even, almost matter-of-fact:

"Yes, I have. For no reason that I know, the central heating was turned on in my cell, and for a week I was left without food."

"There was a reason. The British and the Americans landed in the South of France where you worked as a British spy. Because of that, you were punished by order of the Gestapo."

"You are aware that it is almost a year and a half ago since I was arrested?"

"Yes."

"And now the Gestapo orders the punishment of a woman in a dark cell—because the Allied Armies have the temerity to invade the coast where she worked—a year and a half ago?"

"Yes."

She laughed weakly: "Monsieur, I find the action of the Gestapo very droll."

He said curtly:

"Do you wish anything?"

"No thank you."

*

By the last days of September, Odette was so weak that she could only stand with difficulty. An S.S. man and a woman took her out of her cell and supported her as she stumbled up the stairs to the ground floor. At the door of the Bunker, she reeled back from the brightness of the sunshine. Like needles, the rays of the sun pierced her inflamed pupils and the fresh air, leaping into the starved cells of her lungs, sickened her like gulped ice-water. For some minutes she sprawled on the ground while her eyes and her lungs attuned themselves to the richness of light and air. When she could see, she saw women; debased and hideous though they were, Odette saw human beings walking and breathing in the sunshine and, wonder upon wonder, she saw a little gipsy girl, a child, a living child. The S.S. helped her roughly to her feet led her across the compound to the camp hospital.

It was a hut like the other huts, as dirty and as insect-ridden as the worst of them. She was told to wait, and while she leaned panting against the wall, she watched the daily sick parade. There were up to fifty women in the queue, their bodies stark naked, their heads shaved. Swollen bellies and dirty feet; shrivelled breasts and knees that bulged on the stalks of their legs. Spots, sores, blisters or suppurating wounds scarred their emaciated bodies and there was fear in their eyes. They knew only too well the meaning of a casual decision that they were unfit for work. It would mean that—to use the elegant phrase of Doctor Schidlausky,[1] Senior Medical Officer of the camp— they would leave Ravensbrück "through the chimney".

Odette's lungs were X-rayed and drops were put into her eyes. Her scurvy was treated and she was given a bottle of some liquid. The S.S. were waiting and she was led out of the hospital, into the sunshine, across the compound and into the Bunker. The iron gate swung and she went down the stairs and along the corridor. The door was opened and Odette stepped back into the darkness of Cell number 41.

*

Two things had happened in her brief, sunlit holiday.

---

[1] Sentenced at a British Military Court to death by hanging, February 1946, executed March 1946,

One of the nurses in the hospital had whispered to her in French that the British and the Americans, mighty with weapons, were smashing their way across France to the black frontiers of Germany. The other thing was to bring her joy and a new sensitiveness to the wonders of God. She had stooped and picked up a single leaf as it had blown across the dusty compound.

*

The monthly visits of Fritz Sühren were a nuisance to her, for they meant that she had to come down from where she was and slip into the fevered skin of Lise, of Mademoiselle Bedigis, of Madame Metayer, of Madame Chambrun, of Frau Churchill, of Frau Schurer. The fingers of these women fondled the leaf, stroking it, tracing its shape. The eyes of Odette saw it and the mind of Odette marvelled at the delicacy of its spine and its ribs and the pigment that coloured it. A seed had been blown by the wind or planted by hands in the earth and it had germinated and quickened and moved and from it a stem had struggled through the darkness of the earth into the light and grown and become strong and tall and thrust its arms out and burst into leaf, fed by the uprising spring sap. The wind that had blown the seed had now blown the leaf, and like a gift, it had come over the wall and through the electrified wire of Ravensbrück and into the compound at the very moment when she had passed. It was a miraculous and inspired chain of events that had brought the leaf to the fingers of the woman on the bed, and Odette was deeply grateful. She was alone no more.

30th of September 1944.
Fritz Sühren stood at the door of her cell.
"Is everything all right?"
"Yes thank you."
"Do you wish anything?"
"No thank you."
He hesitated. He said laboriously:
"We have received the result of the X-ray. All this is to be changed. You will be moved upstairs, to the light, as soon as a cell is free. You will have better food, exercise. If you are sick, you will go to the S.S. hospital. All this is to be changed."

L

"Thank you."

"That is all." Again that mechanical salute, that stony-eyed glance. The door shut. Lise shrugged in the darkness. Odette went back to consider the seed, the wind, the sapling, the tree, the branch and the leaf.

★

She remained in the darkness for another three weeks though her food improved at once. At the end of that time, she was taken upstairs and lodged in Cell Number 32, from the window of which she had an uninterrupted view of the entrance to the crematorium. Though it was light in her cell, it became bitterly cold with the advent of winter and the central heating, lavish in torrid July, was turned off to coincide with the first frosts. On the 30th of October, Fritz Sühren came on his monthly inspection. This time he did not stand at the door, but stepped into her cell and held out his hand. She ignored the gesture, looking at him steadily. His hand dropped to his side and he said:

"Is everything all right?"

"Yes thank you."

"Do you wish anything?"

"No thank you."

★

East, west, north and south of Ravensbrück, the war was mounting in pace and fury. Inside the electrified wire and the walls of the camp, the death rate rose steeply as more and more lines of communication and supply were severed by bombing and by the advancing Allied armies. The pitiful rations of the prisoners were halved—and halved again while new thousands of hungry women shuffled through the gates of the camp to die. They died from undernourishment, overwork, exposure, over-crowding and systematic ill-treatment by the staff. As the Allies closed in and the area of the war diminished, the sadistic frenzy of these S.S. seemed to increase. It was about this time that a plan was mooted for the evacuation of the camp in face of the Russian advance and Heinrich Himmler paid a visit to lay down policy. Those prisoners who were still capable of working and marching should be taken away, those who were ill or old or lame should be killed. To assist the Commandant in his picking and choosing, Johann Schwarzhuber,[1] and Adolf Winkelmann[2] arrived from evacuated Auschwitz and the mass slaughter began. Wholesale rather than retail was the way of doing business so the personal bullet was replaced by the totalitarian gas chamber. For some years, the medical staff of the camp had been conducting various experimental operations on the persons of the internees. Artificial gas gangrene had been induced, bones had been removed, new methods of sterilization tried out. Now all this fascinating surgical research had come to an end. It was a question of all medical hands to the pump and the sole task of the doctors was to issue pink tickets to the doomed. The recipients of the pink cards were humourously told that they were very lucky women because they were going to Mittelwerde, a convalescent home in Silesia. This alleged destination was one of the standing jokes of the S.S. Mittelwerde was at the time well behind the advancing lines of the Russians.

*

When Margarete Mewes remembered or was not too busy doing other things, Odette was given a few minutes exercise in the yard of the Bunker. On one of these occasions, two or three days before Christmas, a woman slipped Odette a tiny piece of chocolate, no bigger than her finger-tip. The fishy eye of Mewes lit on this precious contraband and she snatched it in triumph. She put it into her mouth and chewed luxuriously while she decided on Odette's punishment. Three days without exercise. *H'rein, h'rein. Schnell, schnell* . . . .

On Christmas Eve, the Bunker S.S. had a party and got very drunk. They bawled songs in their cups during the early hours of the evening and, as midnight approached, they seemed to sink into a maudlin tear-stained lethargy.

"*Stille Nacht, heilige Nacht,*" quavered Margarete Mewes, "*Krist, der Retter, ist da.* . . ."

[1] Sentenced at a British Military Court to death by hanging, February, 1946, executed March, 1946.
[2] Found dead in his cell during the last days of his trial by a British Military Court, February, 1946.

It was a clear night and the stars shone brightly over the camp.

★

January was a terrible month, echoing with the rattle of the execution squads. In February the woman who had given Odette the scrap of chocolate was shot in the yard under her window. It was a fearful sound. The next day, Odette was taken to the dentist, the bald Dr. Martin Hellinger[1], whose main function was to rifle the mouths of the murdered. He was attending to a little girl of seven or eight, the daughter of one of the S.S., and Odette was ordered to wait. She watched him at work. He talked gently to the little girl, taking the greatest care not to hurt, telling her the story of a golden-haired princess who lived in a palace all made of gold and precious stones. When he had finished, the little girl jumped off and said, "*Danke schön, Onkel Martin,*" and curtsied to him. As she left the room, she saw Odette. She stopped and smiled at her and said, "*Guten-tag,*" and curtsied again.

The Gestapo had failed to break Odette's spirit. The simple, decorous act of a child melted her and moved her nearly to tears. It was with difficulty that she retained her outward composure until she was back within the concealing walls of Cell Number 32.

★

"Is everything all right?"
"Yes thank you."
"Do you wish anything?"
"No thank you."
There was only one way for Odette to preserve her sanity in those black days of early spring when brittle, cold sunlight came into her cell and she knew that the earth outside the camp was stirring and quickening to the timeless reveillé of the sun. More and more she thought about the leaf and in its contemplation, she was linked to God. This was not the God of her childhood, the bearded Man on the awful throne. This was a nebulous knowledge that she was in harmony with a nebulous upstriving

[1] Sentenced at a British Military Court to fifteen years penal servitude, February 1946.

of the spirit of man, an upward surge that had been going on since man crawled out of the primaeval mud. In the long groping continuity of human conscience, she was an infinitesimal part and so she would remain for as long as she could continue to live without self-pity or complaint. At any moment of the day or of the night, she might die and her body be transmuted into the smoke that rolled unceasingly across the sunlight from the chimney of the Crematorium, sullying her cell.

March became April. The orchestra of death and destruction increased its tempo to a jangling *prestissimo* of horror. In speaking under solemn oath of those last nights and days, Odette was later to answer the shocked questions of learned Judge Advocate of the Forces in this way.

Q. Will you describe, as clearly as you can, any incident that you saw in which you say some human being was put alive into that crematorium.

A. The last few days of the war, I saw people being driven to the crematorium. I could hear them screaming and struggling and I could hear the doors being opened and shut.

Q. When they were dragged to the crematorium, what did you see then? How did it end when they were dragged there?

A. I didn't see them any more.

*

On the 16th of April, 1945, a direct order was received from Himmler that every living soul in the Bunker was to be killed. No witnesses were to be left to testify as to conditions in the inmost hell of Ravensbrück. The order was faithfully carried out —with seven exceptions. Only God knows what prompted Fritz Sühren to stay the hands of the executioners at seven arbitrary cell doors, but stay them he did. For the next twelve days, the flames of the crematorium shone into cells most of which were now empty. In one of the few that still held a living person, Odette sat on her bed boards, gazing at the leaf in the bright and baleful illumination that was so much more terrible than her first darkness.

The 28th of April was her birthday, the day when she would be thirty-three years of age.

At midnight on the 27th, Fritz Sühren came to her cell. He was alone. He stood at the door, staring at her with a fixed expressionless stare. He made no movement and spoke no word. Then he did a fiendish thing. He lifted one of his beautiful hands and stretched out one manicured finger and slowly drew the nail-tip across his throat and let it fall again to his side. Odette gazed at him. His mouth moved and he said:

"You will be leaving to-morrow morning at 6 o'clock."

*

All night long, she lay on her bed boards and listened dimly to the mounting turmoil of the camp. She was ready at 6 o'clock, in a sort of calm hopelessness, not knowing and past fearing what this, her birthday, would bring.

At 8 o'clock, Fritz Sühren strode into her cell. He was determined and energetic now, the man of action. He shouted for Margarete Mewes and she came running to his command. He told her to take Frau Churchill to the washroom and not to let her out of her sight. "*Schnell,*" he said, "time is short."

She went to the washroom, rinsed her hands. Fritz Sühren followed immediately and stood by her. He took her through the frantic mêlée of the compound to a huge Black Maria, told her to stand in the corridor between the compartments, slammed the door. Orders were shouted and the great door of Ravensbrück swung open. Bumping and rocking on the rutted road, the Black Maria swayed out of the Camp. As she looked back through the grill, Odette saw a sight which lifted her heart.

The S.S were running away. Stripped of their uniforms, the demi-gods of Himmler streamed out of the hell they had themselves created. Disguised in the clothes of the murdered, the murderers sought to identify themselves with their victims as they fled from the approaching menace of the Russian cannon. On bicycles, on foot, in horse-drawn carts the guilty convoy got under way. At a bend of the road, a weeping Margarete Mewes clutched the hands of her three illegitimate children and begged hopelessly for transport to anywhere in the shrinking Reich where she would be safe from the vengeance either of the living or of the dead. Above the camp wall, only a wisp of smoke came from the chimney of the crematorium as the unfed furnaces cooled at last.

CHAPTER XXIX

"THIS AYE NIGHTE . . ."

"This aye nighte, this aye nighte, every nighte an alle
Fire and sleet and candle lighte
And Christe receive thy saule . . ."

28th of April

ENCIRCLED by a loop of advancing steel, the remnants of Hitler's Reich were in chaos. Augsberg fell to the 7th Army and the victorious Americans pressed on to the Austrian frontier. While Heinrich Himmler, butcher on the dole, wandered about North-West Germany vainly offering his services to the Allies, Mussolini and his lady-love made a bid for Switzerland, were taken by partisans and died the death. Romance was obviously in the air, for it was on this night that Hitler, hitherto the alleged bridegroom of the German people, committed bigamy with Miss Eva Braun in the cellars under the doomed Chancellery garden.

*

At nightfall on Odette's momentous birthday, the Ravensbrück convoy rumbled through the barbed wire of the concentration camp at Neustadt and the occupants of the Black Maria were hustled into a hut and locked in. A Red Cross parcel—loot from Ravensbrück—was flung into the hut and shared. No food had reached the camp for days and the men and women were demented from hunger and the hourly hope of freedom. They ranged the electrified wire end to end, shouting and beseeching the tight-lipped S.S. guards to open the gates.

"*Zurück, zurück! Schnell, schnell. . . .*"

29th of April

British forces crossed the Elbe, the Russians entered Mecklenburg. Venice and Mestre fell to the 8th Army. Though the loop was being drawn tighter, the S.S. were still without orders, while their master Himmler went on tapping at the Allied door.

"Back from the wire, back from the wire. *Zurück, zurück. Schnell, schnell. . . .*"

30*th of April*
The 3rd Army stormed into Moosburg, liberating over a hundred thousand prisoners of war. Munich fell to the Americans, Friedrichshaven to the French. Still no word came to the camp at Neustadt and the S.S. stood firm. A dead and swollen horse lay inside the wire and, in the sunset, Odette saw a flock of starving women crouch by the carcase, tearing and gulping....

1*st of May*
In the morning, an order came that all the ex-occupants of the Ravensbrück Bunker were to be taken away immediately. Odette and her companions stumbled out into the seething compound to find the Black Maria waiting. They were flung into it and the convoy, diminished by now, crawled out of Neustadt and took again to the teeming roads. It was an interminable day of stopping and starting, instruction and counter-instruction, discord and rifle-fire. In the evening, the Black Maria screeched to a final halt and Odette, limping into the fresh air, found herself in yet another camp. Here the last shred of discipline had gone. Ragged scarecrows who had once been men marched round screaming and the flames of a gigantic bonfire licked up to the sky as the frantic internees tore doors and bed boards from the huts and hurled them into the furnace. Round the wire, as always, the S.S. waited silently, their machine-guns trained on the hysterical dancers. They did not have to wait long. . . .

2*nd of May*
Soon after dawn, a new convoy of male prisoners was spewed into the camp. These men, raving and gabbling, infected the already frenzied inmates with their own madness and, suddenly, there was a concerted rush for the gates. Odette saw the turmoil foam past her windows, heard the machine-guns of the

S.S. begin to stutter and bang as the guards raked their human targets. When she looked again, the compound was littered with dead and dying. They lay or jerked within a few feet of freedom, shabby bundles of striped rags fluttering in the wind.

At some hour in the morning, she left the shelter of the hut, and stepping over the bodies of the dead, made her way to the dishevelled offices of the camp. She demanded to see *Obersturmbannführer* Fritz Sühren. While she waited, she heard an unattended radio set blaring out the news. Berlin had fallen to the 1st White Russian and 1st Ukrainian Armies. The German Armies in Italy had surrendered and the British 2nd Army had reached Lübeck. and the Enchanted Baltic. . . .

Fritz Sühren came out of an inner office. She saw to her astonishment that he was crying. He mumbled, the tears streaming down his face:

"What do you want?"

"I want to know why you don't open the gates of the camp. The war is over. It is useless murder to keep people here."

"They would die on the roads."

"Better to die on the roads than to be killed here."

He said, his mouth working and twitching in ungovernable grief:

"Adolf Hitler, Führer of Germany, is dead. He died as a hero in the forefront of the battle."

"Really. Are you proposing to do the same thing, to die as a hero?"

"Go back to your hut. I have not finished with you yet."

"Will you open the gates? I have never asked a favour of you in my life. Now I do. For God's sake. . . ."

"No. The war is not over."

She returned to her hut, joined her companions. Their food was exhausted and they lay relaxed on the floor. She could tell them nothing. The day passed and, in the evening, a self-appointed working party made a pile of the dead in the compound. With the darkness, the bonfires started again and the night was filled with flame and eldritch singing.

3rd of May

In the early afternoon, an S.S. man kicked open the door of the hut. He looked around and shouted:

"*Ist Frau Churchill hier?*"

"I am she."

"You are to come with me at once. It will not be necessary for you to pack your things."

"Where am I going?"

"You will see."

Odette said good-bye calmly to her friends. The fact that she had been told not to bring her few belongings was to her a clear indication of the purpose of her summons. She wondered where they would do it, in the camp or outside. She would like to see the sky for the last time from the far side of the wire.

She walked beside the S.S. man to the gate of the camp. The guards opened it to his command and she walked out. Three large cars waited, the first and last full of uniformed S.S. At the running-board of the middle car she saw Fritz Sühren. His was a superb black Mercedes-Benz. There was a nondescript woman in the back seat and, crouching on the floor, Sühren's white dog "Lotti". Sühren said to her curtly:

"Get in front, beside the driver's seat."

She got into the car. He sat down beside her, pressed the starter and waved. The little convoy of three moved off down the road and then, as the streams of refugees increased to choke the way, the leading car crashed through a hedge and bumped over the fields. Sühren followed.

They drove like this, in silence, for over two hours. When they came to a wood, Sühren sounded the horn and the convoy stopped. He said to her:

"Get out."

So this was where they were going to do it. . . .

He opened the back of the car, took out an armful of official papers, walked to the fringe of the trees and made a pile. Two more armfuls followed and then he set fire to the whole heap. They were records of Ravensbrück and evidence of one of the darkest episodes of Germany's dark history. Merrily they crackled in the afternoon sunshine, burning as the women whose names they contained had burned. He stood by, watching the black ashes eddy in the wind. When the pile was consumed, he stirred the smouldery ashes with his foot, making sure that there was nothing left. He said to Odette:

"So. That's that. Are you hungry?"

"Yes."

"There are sandwiches in the car—and a bottle of wine. I will get them."

The sandwiches were wrapped in a snowy napkin and they were made of meat and lettuce leaves. He showed her the label on the wine bottle. It was a *Nuits St. Georges* and he said: "There you are. A real French Burgundy. It goes very well with these." He had also brought a jar of crystallized cherries and he ate them mincingly, holding them with his manicured little finger outstretched. Odette watched him in silence. The whole *mise-en-scène*—the wood, the bonfire, the napkin, the cherries and the guardian carloads of S.S. waiting in the crumbling Reich on their master's pleasure—belonged to the realms of Dr. Caligari. He finished his feast, smacking his lips over the wine, he said:

"Get back into the car."

The convoy started again. Most of the time, they drove across fields and once, for a short distance, they found a deserted road and made fast pace. Sühren drove with skill and care. In utter exhaustion Odette closed her eyes, bumping and swaying in a daze.

"You know where I am taking you to?"

She said wearily:

"No. I don't understand anything. I suppose we are going to another prison. I don't know. "

"Do you want to know?"

"Not particularly. I don't care."

He gazed straight ahead. He said:

"I am taking you to the Americans."

His words meant little to her. She had already had some knowledge of his sense of humour. This was the Commandant of Ravensbrück, the mass murderer who wept for Hitler, the man who had drawn his finger across his throat, the man who ate his cherries with the affectations of a suburban typist. To humour him in this, his last sadistic and perverted joke, she said:

"Don't you think it a little foolish to drive to the Americans with an escort of armed and uniformed S.S? The Americans will certainly open fire on the cars and we shall all be killed. Or is that the heroic death you seek—in emulation of Hitler?"

He said seriously:

"You are quite right. I had forgotten that the Americans are likely to fire." He sounded his horn and held up one hand. The convoy stopped. He went forward on foot to the leading car and gave orders that it should follow him at a distance of five hundred metres. He would now lead. He came back and passed the car. The S.S. looked at him curiously as he edged to the front, slipped into top gear and drove ahead. He did not speak again, but stared at the road, handling the huge car as if it were a sensitive horse.

Dusk dimmed the flat fields and shrouded the pine woods. The sun sank in a cohort of colour and the evening star hung like a diamond in the sky. At about 10 o'clock, the car slowed down to enter a village. At the point where the road narrowed, Odette saw a group of soldiers in strange and unfamiliar uniforms. One of them cuddled a Tommy-gun in the crook of his arm, stood in the middle of the road, and shouted for the car to stop. Fritz Sühren jerked the gear lever into neutral, put on the brake and switched off the engine. It was very quiet after the long, grumbling sound had stopped. He said in his laborious English:

"This is Frau Churchill. She has been a prisoner. She is a relation to Winston Churchill, the Prime Minister of England."

Odette got out of the car stiffly. Sühren followed her and stood in the street. He looked deeply into her eyes. It seemed to her that he was trying silently and with all his will-power to transmit a message to her, but she didn't know what it was, and she will never know. She said deliberately:

"And this is Fritz Sühren, Commandant of Ravensbrück Concentration Camp. Please make him your prisoner." To Sühren she said: "Give me your revolver."

He took it out of its holster, handed it to her. She said, "Thank you," and put it in her bag. Then she turned on her heel and walked into the village.

CHAPTER XXX

THE LEAF

THE American officer listened to her story with growing incredulity. He said at last:

"We'll have to check up on you with the British, honey. You know that?"

"Of course."

He wrote her out an authorization to move freely about the village. He said that he was sure that the first thing she wanted was a bed, a real bed. Odette shook her head. She would prefer to stay out all night under the sky. She had a reason. She would give her word of honour to remain within call. As well as her reason, there were still some documents in Sühren's car which might be of interest to her Government and it was her duty to look after them.

She found the car in a farmyard. Sühren and the non-descript woman had vanished but the dog "Lotti" crouched in the back. She stroked him and he licked her fingers. The other two cars, still full of uniformed S.S. were drawn up along the wall of a cowshed. She walked over and said:

"Do any of you speak English or French?"

One man said that he could understand a little English.

"Good. Tell your friends it is useless to run away. There is nowhere for you to go, nowhere in Germany or in the world. You are finished. To-morrow, when more Americans come, you will be arrested and looked after. I give you this as an order. Is it understood?"

"Yes. It is understood. *Gute-nacht, gnädige Frau.*"

Gnädige Frau! It was a strange courtesy on the lips of the S.S., given to a thin woman with a swollen neck, no toenails and unkempt hair halfway down her back. She said formally: "Good night."

She went back to Sühren's car, got into the front seat. She sat without moving a muscle, gazing into the darkness. She had no sense of triumph or of elation, but only one of infinite weariness. She was unable to attune her mind to the knowledge that she was free and she had no wish to move away from this place. To be allowed to be alone in the silence of the summer night was her only desire. A clock chimed the hours as the moon climbed the sky and, so profound was the silence that Odette could hear the slow, strong beat of her own heart. At some time after midnight, the silence was broken by the sound of footsteps tip-toeing across the yard. A tall S.S. man, the one who spoke English, said politely: "Excuse me, *gnädige Frau*, it will soon be cold so I have brought you my coat." He spread a sheepskin flying jacket over her knees, tip-toed away.

It only wanted that last attention from one of yesterday's tyrants to convince her that she was living in a dream from which she would wake within the walls of Ravensbrück. To conquer the bitterness of wakening, to be ready buoyantly to face the prison sunrise, she took the leaf in her fingers and, in unrealized freedom, began to trace the wonder of its spine and its ribs and to ponder again the seed, the wind, the sapling, the tree, the branch and the leaf. . . .

THE END

Lübeck, London, Paris, Annecy, Sark.   *July*, 1947-*June*, 1948.

ST. PAUL'S, KNIGHTSBRIDGE
May 7th, 1948.

In love and homage to :

MRS. YOLANDE E. M. BEEKMAN, Croix de Guerre
MISS DANIELLE BLOCH
MISS ANDRÉE M. BORREL
MISS MURIEL BYCK
MISS MADELEINE DAMERMENT
MISS NORA INYAT-KHAN, George Cross
MRS CECILY M. LEFORT
MISS VERA E. LEIGH
MRS ELIANE S. PLEWMAN, Croix de Guerre
MISS LILIAN V. ROLFE
MISS DIANA H. ROWDEN
MRS. YVONNE RUDELLAT
MRS. VIOLETTE R. E. SZABO, George Cross

Extract from Third Supplement to

THE LONDON GAZETTE

of Friday, the 16th of August, 1946

CENTRAL CHANCERY OF THE ORDERS OF KNIGHTHOOD,

St. James's Palace, S.W.1.

20th August, 1946.

The KING has been graciously pleased to award the GEORGE CROSS to:

Odette Marie Céline, Mrs. SANSOM, M.B.E.,

Women's Transport Service (First Aid Nursing Yeomanry.)

Mrs. Sansom was infiltrated into enemy-occupied France and worked with great courage and distinction until April, 1943, when she was arrested with her Commanding Officer. Between Marseilles and Paris on the way to the prison at Fresnes, she succeeded in speaking to her Commanding Officer and for mutual protection they agreed to maintain that they were married. She adhered to this story and even succeeded in convincing her captors in spite of considerable contrary evidence and through at least fourteen interrogations. She also drew Gestapo attention from her Commanding Officer on to herself saying that he had only come to France on her insistence. She took full responsibility and agreed that it should be herself and not her Commanding Officer who should be shot. By this action she caused the Gestapo to cease paying attention to her Commanding Officer after only two interrogations. In addition the Gestapo were most determined to discover the whereabouts of a wireless operator and of another British officer whose lives were of the greatest value to the Resistance Organization. Mrs. Sansom was the only person who knew of their whereabouts. The Gestapo tortured her most brutally to try to make her give away this information. They seared her back with a red hot iron and, when that failed, they pulled out all her toe-nails. Mrs. Sansom, however, continually refused to speak and by her bravery and determination, she not only saved the lives of the two officers but also enabled them to carry on their most valuable work.

During the period of over two years in which she was in enemy hands, she displayed courage, endurance and self-sacrifice of the highest possible order.

EPILOGUE

NEARLY four years have passed since I was flown home to England to drive from Croydon to London through streets hung with the flags of military victory. It was a bewildering hour.

Now I ask myself the extent of that victory. With great sadness, I believe that, for mankind, the choice between liberty and slavery has still to be made. In the camps, we used to believe that those of us who might survive would enter a more tolerant and tranquil world where the ancient virtues of truth, honour and gentleness would surely prevail. In the war, we fought a human enemy, one who had been infected with the germ of inhumanity. Though we defeated the host, we failed to defeat the parasite. Rendered the more virulent by its recent frolic, that same parasite is about the world to-day and, unless it is utterly destroyed, the Camp of Ravensbrück will merely be the shadow and the symbol of a greater darkness to come.

I am a very ordinary woman to whom a chance was given to see human beings at their best and at their worst. I knew kindness as well as cruelty, understanding as well as brutality. I completely believe in the potential nobility of the human spirit.

It is with a sense of deep humility that I allow my personal story to be told. My comrades, who did far more than I and suffered far more profoundly, are not here to speak. Because of this, I speak for them and I would like this book to be a window through which may be seen those very gallant women with whom I had the honour to serve.

ODETTE CHURCHILL.

"... PORT AFTER STORMIE SEAS"

Françoise, Lily, Odette, Marianne
(Summer 1945)